Praise for *Haunted Experiences*

"Though we're not related, Michelle Belanger and I do have more in common than just the same surname. We share a passion for the unexplained, the haunted, and the spiritual. *Haunting Experiences* will take you behind the scenes into Michelle's life and show you how one occult writer, researcher, and reluctant medium was made. Michelle takes her readers on an exciting and esoteric ride as she navigates you through her upbringing and the many haunts and experiences that have left a profound impact on her life and work."
—Jeff Belanger, author of *Our Haunted Lives*
and founder of Ghostvillage.com

"Enter a realm of lost souls and death angels, shadow people and 'mindless husks adrift on currents of energy.' Michelle Belanger's fascinating true account of her haunted life is spine-tingling and compelling."
—Annie Wilder, author of *House of Spirits and Whispers*

D1377506

About the Author

Michelle Belanger is an author, lecturer, and occult researcher who has appeared on a number of television and radio shows in the United States and abroad. Although she is best known for her expertise on vampires, Michelle studies a wide range of topics, including energy work, paranormal phenomena, shamanism, folklore, and the Gothic subculture. She is the founder of House Kheperu, a magickal society based in part upon the concept of death and rebirth. Together with the other members of House Kheperu, she teaches a unique style of energy work and ritual at private workshops as well as national conventions.

In addition to her esoteric studies, Michelle is also a talented vocalist and songwriter. She has performed with several musical groups, including the dark metal band URN and the Gothic duo of Nox Arcana. In the 1990s, she was the editor of *Shadowdance*, a magazine dedicated to dark and fringe culture that has since been reborn as a free online podcast.

To Write to the Author

If you wish to contact the author or would like more information about this book, please write to the author in care of Llewellyn Worldwide and we will forward your request. Both the author and publisher appreciate hearing from you and learning of your enjoyment of this book and how it has helped you. Llewellyn Worldwide cannot guarantee that every letter written to the author can be answered, but all will be forwarded. Please write to:

Michelle Belanger
℅ Llewellyn Worldwide
2143 Wooddale Drive, Dept. 978-0-7387-1437-0
Woodbury, MN 55125-2989, U.S.A.

Please enclose a self-addressed stamped envelope for reply,
or $1.00 to cover costs. If outside the U.S.A., enclose
an international postal reply coupon.

Many of Llewellyn's authors have websites with additional information and resources. For more information, please visit our website at http://www .llewellyn.com.

Haunting
experiences

encounters with the otherworldly

Michelle Belanger

Llewellyn Publications
Woodbury, Minnesota

First Edition
Second Printing, 2009

Book design by Steffani Sawyer
Editing by Brett Fechheimer
Cover design by Kevin R. Brown
Cover image of woods © 2009 Polka Dot / Punchstock
Cover image of raven © 2009 IT Stock
Interior artwork courtesy of the Llewellyn art department
Llewellyn is a registered trademark of Llewellyn Worldwide, Ltd.

Library of Congress Cataloging-in-Publication Data

Belanger, Michelle A.
  Haunting experiences : encounters with the otherworldly / Michelle Belanger. —1st ed.
      p. cm.
  ISBN 978-0-7387-1437-0
  1. Supernatural. 2. Ghosts—United States. I. Title.
  BF1434.U6B458 2009
  133.8092—dc22
  [B]
                                    2008050905

Llewellyn Worldwide does not participate in, endorse, or have any authority or responsibility concerning private business transactions between our authors and the public.
  All mail addressed to the author is forwarded but the publisher cannot, unless specifically instructed by the author, give out an address or phone number.
  Any Internet references contained in this work are current at publication time, but the publisher cannot guarantee that a specific location will continue to be maintained. Please refer to the publisher's website for links to authors' websites and other sources.

Llewellyn Publications
A Division of Llewellyn Worldwide, Ltd.
2143 Wooddale Drive, Dept. 978-0-7387-1437-0
Woodbury, Minnesota 55125-2989, U.S.A.
www.llewellyn.com

Printed in the United States of America

Contents

Tales from a Reluctant Medium

When I was a little girl, my mother and some of her sisters would tell me tales about growing up in a haunted house in Lakewood, Ohio. They lived in an old Victorian on Cohassett Avenue, and the most haunted place in the house was the attic, where most of them had their bedrooms. I remember hearing about a rocking chair that would rock itself, ghostly melodies whispered in the night, and even a playful spirit who seemed to engage in games of tag with a chilly, spectral touch. Certainly some of the stories may have been exaggerated for the benefit of my young ears, but as I grew older, my mother and at least one of her sisters stuck by their tales. By that time, I had experienced several ghostly encounters of my own, so swapping tales of haunting experiences became something of a Belanger family tradition.

From this bit of information, it would be easy to paint an idealistic image of my childhood, as one in which psychic abilities and paranormal phenomena were embraced openly and without reservation. But reality is never that simple, nor that ideal. Although many of my relatives had ghostly encounters as well as psychic experiences, several of them were also devout Catholics, and they were never entirely certain how to interpret these experiences within the context of their faith. Others were hesitant to talk about their encounters with the otherworldly anywhere except behind closed doors. They then had the option of denying their words should anything get back to someone they didn't feel so open around. No one was guiltier of this behavior than my maternal grandmother, who also happened to be the woman who raised me from the age of five.

My grandmother was a complicated woman. If I had to reduce her often contradictory personality to just one phrase, it would be "What would people think?" While she actively avoided dealing with anyone outside of her own family, she nevertheless seemed obsessed with the opinions of these outside people. They formed a nebulous but potent power in her world—the prejudicial masses from whose prying eyes all quirks and eccentricities must be hidden. One big quirk that she felt must be hidden at all costs was psychic ability.

My grandmother had some very strong opinions about psychic abilities, and not all of these opinions were exactly logical. On one hand, she believed in extrasensory powers. She even offered the opinion on more than one occasion that individuals gifted with such powers are the next logical step in the evolution of humanity. Despite this, however, she often resented those selfsame powers. She herself was psychic, but she had prayed fervently as a child to have her abilities taken away. She felt that they were both frightening and burdensome. Considering that some of her most striking early experiences involved dreams that accurately foretold death and disaster, it is easy to see why these abilities scared her. Her fear was never powerful enough to drive her completely away from the otherworldly, however. She retained an active interest in the paranormal throughout her adult life. She seemed reluctant to read nonfiction books on psychic phenomena (somehow, studying them officially was a bad thing in her eyes), but nearly all of the fiction works that she devoured contained some psychic or ghostly element. Whenever there was a television special on ghosts or psychic phenomena, she was riveted to the screen, and, when we sat together late at night, gazing at the stars from her bedroom window, our talk often turned to the subject of psychic experiences.

I treasured these late-night talks, but they left me with an ambivalent legacy. While my grandmother would open up about her own experiences when we talked one-on-one, she also made it very clear that she reserved the right to deny anything she said during these talks should I be so indiscreet as to repeat them. Most of this came down to that endlessly reiterated phrase: *What would people think?* I don't think my grandmother ever doubted her own sanity, but she was well aware that others would doubt it for her, should tales of her experiences be shared too widely. Her sister, who lived with us, worked in a psychiatric institute, and this helped reaffirm my grandmother's fears. People who saw things or heard voices in their heads got locked up and put away where they couldn't be a danger to themselves or others. My grandmother didn't want that happening to her, and she didn't want it to happen to me, either. Thus, she taught me that silence, and not honesty, is the best policy.

During the process of writing this book, I came to realize that my grandmother's conflicting attitudes had indelibly colored many of my early paranormal experiences. I had been raised on a diet of secrecy and shame, yet the object of that secrecy was still frequently acknowledged as something valid and real. These mixed messages ultimately nourished in me an overwhelming sense of mistrust. On one hand, I was afraid to trust my own perceptions, because doing so might open the door to that looming specter of insanity.

As a result, I would check, double-check, and triple-check my own experiences, struggling to determine whether an impression was legitimately psychic, or if it could be explained away through mere psychology. Sometimes I clung to doubt in the face of all other evidence, just because it felt saner than committing myself to belief.

On the other hand, I was afraid to trust others with the truth of my experiences. Like my grandmother, I did not want to be judged, and because of my grandmother I was certain I already knew the tenor of those judgments. As a result, I ended up compartmentalizing my life in an attempt to shield myself from prejudice. If I let anyone in, it was only on an individual basis and then only in stages. Whenever I got involved in a larger social group, I would hover on the fringes for the first few weeks, studying the others before I became actively engaged. This was kind of my trial period, during which I took stock of their beliefs, trying to determine how much or how little of the paranormal they were willing to accept. Once I had a firm idea of what was acceptable, whenever I dealt with that group of people I would present only the portion of my life that I thought they would be comfortable with. This led me to present myself as nothing more than a widely read researcher to one paranormal group, while a few others knew more about my background with ghosts or with energy work.

That probably sounds duplicitous, but consider that everyone does it to a certain extent. If you're really into a hobby, like stamp collecting, and you have to hang out after work with your friends from the office, you're probably not going to talk about stamps all evening. In fact, if you started talking shop about stamps, in all likelihood you would end up with some very bored friends. Stamps are just not a huge focus in most people's lives. Once you get into any specialized area of interest, there are whole realms of experience, including slang and jargon, that do not translate easily from one group to the next. This is why we end up with fan clubs and genre-specific conventions. We all exist in many different groups, and it is common for us to adapt our language and even our manner of dress to accommodate the specific nature and function of each group.

The same goes for beliefs. You don't generally talk about ghosts with your buddies at the office. Ghosts are not a part of that world, and forcing the topic may even be seen as intrusive. Going from my grandmother's point of view, however, you also do not give your office buddies any reason to think that you might *want* to eventually turn the conversation to ghosts. You simply hide that part of your life away where it cannot be used to hurt you. Anyone who's had to live their life "in the closet" understands her point of view.

Oddly, when I first started working on this book, I had not even thought about these things. Initially, all I wanted to do with this work was to tell a few good ghost stories. I wanted them to be chilling and fun to read, and the twist was, of course, that they were all true. But in order to remain truthful in these tales, I often had to put myself back in the mindset I had when I was experiencing them. Considering that this volume includes stories that span literally thirty years of my life, that was a tall order all by itself. But I approached it, at least at first, more for the benefit of the tales themselves. I wanted to find the voice of the person I was when I experienced these things so the experiences would feel more real and immediate to the reader. In several cases, I had journal entries or field notes to go on, which made it easier than struggling to take an accurate trip down memory lane fifteen years after the fact.

What I saw in the journals was enlightening, and it changed the overall shape of this work. Instead of simply being a collection of entertaining ghost stories, *Haunting Experiences* became a chronicle of the lessons that I learned from direct and repeated interaction with the world of spirits.

The Undiscovered Country

The realm of spirits is the ultimate unknown. Its very mystery has both frustrated and fascinated humanity for thousands of years. Whole religions have been founded in an attempt to answer that ubiquitous question: *What happens to us after we die?* Of course, the dead know, but how certain can we be of their communication? Many people are not even thoroughly convinced that they continue to exist once their physical bodies expire.

My earliest experiences were not the result of some attempt to understand these earth-shattering mysteries. Like most people who undergo spontaneous psychic experiences, I didn't even know what to make of my experiences at first. It is significant that I encountered at least two spirits before the age of five, and it was only after the fact that I even realized that these were ghosts. One of these spirits turned out to be a friend of my mother's, deceased before I was even born. Despite this, I remembered that she played with me sometimes when my mother visited other friends, and I was able to describe the deceased friend perfectly. I had never seen photos of this woman. My encounter with the other spirit that I mistook for a person occurred at the library in my hometown. The experience is recounted here in the chapter "The Lady in Blue." With these two early experiences, the spirits were completely indistinguishable from living people. I seemed to see them with my physical eyes, even though, once I got older, I rarely perceived spirits in such a deceptively physical fashion again.

Since I grew out of that very visual level of perception, I never really thought of myself as a spirit medium. Spirit mediums are people like my friends Jackie Williams and Sarah Valade, who still occasionally mistake the dead for the living. Jackie is an artist, and spirits appear to her with all the clarity and apparent physicality of flesh-and-blood people, to the extent that she has used some of them as models for her artwork. Sarah has been able to see and speak with the dead since she was a little girl, and, like Jackie, they appear to her with all the visual clarity of living people. Sarah's gifts were so obvious when she was little that her mother, who had no personal interest in the paranormal, nevertheless sought out a respected local medium to help teach her daughter how to fully harness her gifts.

Compared to Sarah's ability to converse with spirits and Jackie's ability to paint them, my own perceptions of the otherworldly seemed nebulous at best. Aside from those two early childhood experiences, I almost never mistake spirits for living people. I may know when a spirit has entered a room, but not because I've perceived its entrance with my physical eyes. All of the visual information I receive now seems to come from an inner eye, and even then it feels as if visual detail is the closest thing into which my brain is able to translate its perceptions. When I communicate with spirits, I don't have a complete conversation like Sarah seems to do. I hear the voices of the dead as whispers, not with my physical ears but with some internal faculty. As a result, it can be very difficult for me to be absolutely certain that the voice in my head is actually a spirit, rather than one of the many voices of my admittedly creative imagination. This, of course, brings us right back to the influences of my early childhood and that specter of insanity.

Yet in discussing these perceptions with Jackie as I worked on this book, I learned something very interesting. Just as I had never thought of myself as a spirit medium because I could no longer physically see spirits, Jackie had never thought of herself as psychic because she often has trouble *hearing* spirits. Both of us tended to think of our abilities as different from (and lesser than) Sarah's because Sarah could hear, see, and sometimes even feel spirits as if they were living people. And yet all three of us had accurate impressions of spirits. We were simply each born with slightly different faculties of perception.

This was something of a revelation, and it taught me how uncertain our understanding of the spirit world really is. When someone is born with a certain capacity that other people don't tend to have, that person is often perceived as being special or gifted. I think it's natural to assume that such gifted people automatically understand their gifts, but at least in the case of otherworldly perceptions, this could not be further from the truth. As my talks with Sarah and Jackie confirmed, not one of the three of us started out with a complete grasp of our gifts. All three of us struggled with different degrees of doubt and acceptance, and all three of us had to work to understand the rules that governed our perceptions. And as if this were not complicated enough, it would seem that those rules differed for each of the three of us because the very nature of our perceptive abilities is different.

The Quest for Understanding

Being born psychic is not the equivalent of being born with all of the answers. If there was an instruction manual that was supposed to come with some of these gifts, it got lost along the way. I have stood peering into the same mysterious world that has confounded humanity for generations, and the only thing that separates me from anyone else is the fact that sometimes I can see vague shapes moving in the gloom. Seeing these vague shapes might lead to understanding, but it's not a guarantee.

Although I was born with some instincts regarding the use and meaning of my gifts, the circumstances of my childhood led me to seriously question those instincts. Instead, as the stories in this volume will help to demonstrate, I had to learn like everyone else: through repeated experience and experimentation. It was comforting to learn that everyone, regardless of how amazing their psychic abilities may seem, had to undergo the exact same learning process. I know that my grandmother successfully crippled my ability to trust my own impressions, so I just happened to experiment more fervently than most. I did not always do this wisely or with the best intentions, but in the end I learned as much from the failures as from the successes.

The location of most of those experiments is important, and within the scope of this collection, that location almost becomes a character unto itself. It represents my starting point, and it often lends context to my own attitudes and the attitudes of the people around me. The stories in this collection would have been radically different had I grown up in China or even California. Each region of the world has a different culture and differing attitudes toward the paranormal. The West Coast tends to be more open-minded than the stolid American Midwest. As a result, the tranquil forests and old-fashioned small towns of northeastern Ohio helped to shape my internal landscape as much as any of my experiences with my grandmother. The history and the attitudes of the place I call home inevitably influenced my own attitudes and beliefs.

I grew up in small Ohio town called Hinckley. It's a quiet, rural village nestled among parks and lakes and trees. Downtown Hinckley is nothing more than the intersection of two roads with a few churches, shops, and a town hall clustered around that intersection. Even though a number of new housing developments have gone up in the town since I moved away, when I pass through Hinckley, it still feels like a throwback to a simpler, earlier age. And, like most small towns throughout the country, Hinckley has its quirks. The township fêtes the return of turkey vultures every year around the ides of March, and none of the folks who live there find that the least bit strange. For nearly thirty years, the town's library was located in a building virtually everyone knew to be haunted. No one really gave the haunting a second thought. It was just one of those things native to Hinckley, much like the ugly carrion birds whose return we celebrated on Buzzard Day. Hinckley was where I started my formal experiments into the realm of the otherworldly, reading voraciously about ghosts and spirits from the time I was six or seven, trying to understand the rules that governed that unseen realm. The fact that I started so young is probably also revealing.

When I moved beyond books and into the realm of hands-on investigation, I started close to home. Most of my referrals came from friends, and there were ample locations in northeastern Ohio that had a reputation for being haunted. It's not like Ohio is an exceptionally haunted state, although I have heard several people claim that it's more haunted than most. It's simply that this is where I started out, and one can only start where one begins.

My quest for understanding, which started in Hinckley, eventually led me to other locations: big-shouldered Chicago, metropolitan New York, sultry New Orleans. In all the years and all the places that I have sought out experiences or had them spontaneously happen to me, I have learned important lessons: My understanding, however experienced, will forever be incomplete. For every rule I thought I knew about the nature of ghosts and the supernatural, there is an experience that turns that rule on its ear. And for every experience I think I understand, there remain five others that completely baffle me.

Even now, I have no idea what to make of the mysterious shadow people that appeared to a number of my friends in 1996 and 1997. I can't even know if the dates are significant. There are too many variables and not enough solid information. In addition to the mystery of the shadow people, there is the extended enigma of a place in Geauga County that I call Whitethorn Woods. Two years in a row I stood in the midst of so many experiences in such a short amount of time that my mind boggles about it even now. And although I have some theories, I will probably never find a satisfactory answer as to what nature of being or beings walk those haunted woods.

An Enduring Mystery

In all likelihood, the rules that govern interactions between our world and the world of spirits will remain forever mysterious. That's not to say that the realm of the paranormal lies completely beyond the bounds of any laws, nor that we are utterly incapable of understanding the laws that govern it. What I mean is that we only ever seem to get incomplete glimpses of the world that moves within and beyond our own. Consider how even people naturally gifted with an ability to perceive spirits have those perceptions manifest in different ways. Our picture of the realm of spirits seems to remain forever shifting and incomplete.

Some hauntings are very predictable and understandable. Someone dies in a house and, for whatever reason, their spirit lingers to restlessly walk its halls each night. This is perhaps everyone's most classic idea of a haunting, and it is so ubiquitous that somewhere in my very early childhood, I had already picked it up. When all we know about hauntings is that ghosts often linger in the places where they died, however, our image of the realm of spirits is woefully incomplete. The very first story in this collection involves a spirit of a young boy who essentially wandered into my childhood home. While the house was apparently *somewhat* close to where he had died, the real reason he had manifested there had more to do with people (namely me) who could perceive him. He was lonely.

That emotional aspect of spirits is something that is often overlooked. Ghosts aren't static objects that stay anchored in just one place. Some things in the spirit world are dependent upon a specific location, but they are not what most people define as ghosts. If we are going to accept the idea that at least some ghosts are the lingering spirits of human beings, it only makes sense to assume that those spirits are going to behave like human beings. People are by definition fickle, emotional, and mutable. They move from place to place. They get bored with one group of people and then move on to the next, seeking new connections and new experiences. While I agree with the notion that a lingering human spirit tends to remain as a ghost because of unresolved earthly attachments, those attachments do not universally result in the spirit remaining tied to one specific place. The place may be a factor, but there are spirits that are definitely not bound to remain in a single place. They can move around like the living do and, unlike the living, they are unlikely to put in an official change of address.

This brings us to another complex and confusing aspect of the spirit world. When I first started consciously interacting with spirits, I knew that there were ghosts. Ghosts were the spirits of people, and they often haunted the things that were important to them in life. That was nice, neat, simple, and tidy. And then I ran into something that was obviously not physical. I perceived it like a ghost, yet it clearly had nothing at all to do with humanity. Having been raised Catholic, the only other nonphysical entities I had any context for were demons or angels, but it certainly didn't seem like either of these. So the question remained, what on earth was it?

In the case of "The Thing in the Crawlspace," the spirit was a residue, which is essentially a pile of psychic debris that collects in a big mass, kind of like a dust bunny. Some residues are like crystal-clear images of one intense or traumatic emotional event burned upon the fabric of reality. Others are amorphous blobs of built-up emotion that just sort of hang in the atmosphere of a place, emitting more of that same emotion. And a few seem to take on a life of their own, but they're mostly just mindless husks adrift on currents of energy.

At the time that I encountered my very first residue, I was sure that, somewhere in the world, there must be a book that outlined each and every species of spirit a person is likely to encounter on the Otherside. Since that time, I have studied the folklore, myths, and religions of a dozen different cultures spanning most of known history. In my studies, I have learned that many books attempt to categorize spirits, yet none of them are complete. People from many different times and cultures have tried to write that book, cataloguing the names and species of spirits that one may encounter from across the Veil. Here and there, despite the different languages and names, a few of the things are strikingly similar. And then there are a score of other entities that seem utterly fanciful and simply incorrect.

The medieval Christian response was to classify all the spirits as demons and to quote Mark 5:9 by saying that their names are *legion*. But from my experience, this interpretation is also only partially correct. If demons are defined as anything that is not an angel or a human spirit that has ascended to heaven, then the medieval classification holds on a technicality. But if by demons we mean wholly evil entities whose very existence is focused upon the corruption of humanity, then there are some holes in the theory. There are evil spirits. There are good spirits. There are spirits that fall somewhere in the gray areas in between. I think the only thing we can say with absolute certainty about spirits is that we cannot know everything.

It's the most frustrating of answers, but again and again I have been reminded that it is the answer that applies most frequently to our haunting experiences.

Every rule has its exception, and nearly every assumption that I started out with has been proven wrong—or incomplete. And yet, as frustratingly vast as this field of experience can be, every new encounter means that I learn something I didn't know before. And this, if nothing else, keeps me coming back to the subject of spirits. I don't know if it is possible to know everything about how things work on the Otherside. I don't know if we're meant for that kind of understanding even once we get there. But its appeal lies in its very mystery. We may have run out of places to explore in our physical world, but the realm of spirits presents an endless wilderness that we can return to again and again, each time bringing back another facet of experience.

I can't write the book that catalogues all the different types of spirits, their names, and the realms in which they dwell. I would not even attempt the endeavor. But I can offer you the map of my own journey. It is a journey that reveals as much about me as it reveals about the realm of the otherworldly. It shows how much I don't know, how much I've learned, and how many misconceptions I've had to abandon along the way. It reveals the scars of my childhood in the way that I sometimes swing between doubt and belief, even when I'm immersed in experiences that would make anyone else believe. More than anything, it demonstrates how integral experiences of the spirit realm have been to my experience of our living world. And, I think, it reveals significant truths about each.

Playing with
Dead Things

Spirit boards, Ouija boards, Oracle boards . . . again and again we are cautioned not to play with these dangerous things. We are told by many in the field of the paranormal that they are doorways to an evil realm, that they can lead to demonic possession and worse. Do Ouija boards attract evil spirits? Certainly the opening scenes of *The Exorcist* seem to attest to this fact. And yet, how many of us, especially as teens, have been tempted to call up a dead relative through the use of one of these boards? Or maybe we had a friend pull one out at a slumber party, and then we all gathered round after a spine-tingling game of "Light as a Feather" to ask the board when one of us might die—or, if we were in a merrier mood, we'd ask which one of us would find true love before all the rest.

I played with my share of Ouija boards, and I'll admit that they probably shouldn't be approached as toys, but not for the dire reasons that others in the paranormal community might suggest. As I laid my finger on the pointer with my friends, I did not discover some tenebrous door to hell. However, I did notice that the majority of spirits who responded to our giggling call were easily as whimsical as we were. Through lighthearted sessions with the Ouija, I learned early on that like attracts like when you're dealing with the spirit world. When the callers on the board are just out for a cheap thrill to keep them awake all night long, they are highly likely to attract mischievous trickster spirits that are only too willing to oblige. And when the callers are practically children themselves, curiously reaching out to the Otherside, the voice that answers may also in be that of a child.

I was in sixth grade when I started playing with such occult toys as Ouija boards. I had learned just the year before about a variety of methods for contacting the dead, and I'd made the board myself. Carefully and artfully, I scribed out the two rows of letters, just like an illustration I'd seen. I added *yes, no, hello,* and *goodbye* to the corners, placing *maybe* in the middle just above the first row of the alphabet. For a pointer, I employed a large slice of a geode, polished to a high gleam. I'd acquired this treasure at the natural history museum years before. This choice might seem strange, but it was the result of a whole afternoon of experimentation. In the end, the slice of geode was the only item I owned that glided effortlessly across the smooth poster board that I used to create my Ouija. It even had a slightly heart-shaped form, so it could discernibly point to the letters. The geode was also just big enough for up to three sets of young fingers to balance carefully along its edges, allowing the stone to glide wheresoever it would.

In sixth grade I was twelve, which might seem like a ridiculously young age to begin experimenting with contacting the dead. And yet I started life as a precocious child, and I seemed drawn to the paranormal from the very start. Born with a grave heart defect, I died and was revived at least once before the age of five. Perhaps it was this experience that left me with an affinity for spirits. At such a tender age, I had myself crossed over—and even though the doctors brought me back, it was easy to imagine that something of the spirit realm still clung to me. Perhaps death never surrendered me up entirely, and my sensitivities were born from some in-between state where I always walked with one foot in this world and one in the next.

I personally believe that much more than just a chance near-death experience went into making me what I am, but from the many studies done on NDEs, we know that the experience itself is enough to change a person. Such a brush with death leaves an indelible stamp that, rather than ruining a person, appears to open up some hidden door within. Although I did not always understand its nature and meaning, I often seemed to be peering through that door, even when I was a very little child.

At twelve, I wasn't just peering through the door. I had learned a few things about that otherworldly aperture upon whose threshold I seemed destined to stand. Through books, television, and even one amazingly open-minded teacher, I'd gleaned enough to know that I wanted—needed—to know more. I yearned to be able to control my sensitivities, but before that could happen I knew it was imperative that I truly believe in those abilities. At twelve, I often still struggled with this belief. Things happened around me with an alarming regularity—in my childhood home, doors would often open and close of their own volition. The kitchen cupboards would come open despite the latches that should have held them shut. My dog, Laddie, often barked at a mysterious point about eight feet up in the air in the middle of the living room that was apparently inhabited by an intruder only he could see.

And then there was the chandelier. That summer it started, every once in a while, to describe a lazy circle in the air just above the dining room table. Old and stained yellow with nicotine from my great-uncle's endless smoking, the chandelier had no business moving on its own, and yet it did. My grandmother, who took the slamming doors and moving cabinetry in stride without so much as a comment, maintained the same unflappable demeanor when the chandelier began its curious behavior. On the occasions that I bothered to point out the strange motion of the chandelier, my grandmother's response was always the same. Utterly blasé at this point in her life to the paranormal activity that surrounded her, my grandmother's answer was to blame the chandelier on a passing truck, since our house was situated on a main road. Growing up, I'd learned to keep well clear of that road, which had claimed countless neighborhood pets. Huge eighteen-wheelers plummeted down the road, clipping along at a smooth fifty-five miles an hour and more. Their passage would make our windows rattle so completely that when a small earthquake hit northeastern Ohio in 1986, we found it hard to tell the difference.

Of course, the chandelier's activity was a recent development, one of many little weird things that had been building since I was a child and that I now suspect might have been tied to my approaching adolescence. I'm not ignorant of the research that places young prepubescents at the center of most poltergeist activity. I cannot deny that at twelve, I fit the bill. To my grandmother, I maintained that the chandelier did not ordinarily swing in a lazy three-sixty whenever a big truck rattled past the house, nor did it make any kind of sense that the chandelier would then pause in its circular motion, *reverse itself*, and continue along on a slow, merry swing. But my grandmother told me to quit making a big deal about it. Eventually, I did, and the circumnavigating chandelier became just another bit of the scenery in our strange household, no more remarkable than the spot that only the dog seemed able to see.

I wanted to believe. You would think, surrounded by so many curious phenomena, that belief would come easily. And yet the opposite was true. The incidents in my childhood home were so commonplace that they hardly seemed strange at all. Reinforcing this impression was the fact that my grandmother, who witnessed the vast majority of the strangeness, was utterly unfazed by anything she might see. Her brother, who also lived with us, glibly attributed each and every single instance of self-propelled cabinetry and doors to the wind. A hard-drinking early retiree of a steel mill, he simply ignored the chandelier whenever it started swinging over his head. In his narrow intellectual world, such anomalies should not exist, and thus they did not, even when they happened to be existing right in front of his nose. Their older sister, who also shared the house with us, had a similar approach, although admittedly she put in such long hours at work that she was rarely home and awake enough to witness much of anything, save the insides of her eyelids as she dozed in front of the television.

Because the adults did not make a big deal about things and because nothing ever grew so intense as to seem threatening, none of the incidents that I bore witness to as a child really sank through my intellectual armor. If my great-uncle could shrug off the circling chandelier with such stoic ease, who was I to assume that such apparently impossible activity was not, in fact, mind-numbingly commonplace? I was probably just making a big deal about things because I wanted to believe.

In many ways, this is what led to the Ouija board. If I could make contact and discover an intelligent spirit that laid claim to the mysterious activities, perhaps that would be enough proof to convince everyone that something peculiar was going on. Of course, I would need a witness to such a revelation—and who better than my best friend in all the world, Katie?

Ordinarily, I was not allowed to have sleepovers. In fact, only very rarely did my grandmother allow my friends to visit me in my home. Gram was reclusive; she really didn't like visitors of any sort, and hyperactive, giggling girls least of all. But Katie and I pleaded and wheedled, begged and cajoled, until her parents and my grand-mother finally relented. We were going to have a sleepover at my house.

We watched TV. We ate enough candy to practically throw ourselves into a weeklong fit of sugar shock. And we waited—not entirely patiently—for all the adults to go to bed. Finally, the house was quiet, and so we sneaked down from my room. I pulled out the Ouija board I'd made, proudly displaying its workmanship to my friend. We set things up on the dining room table, not because I was expecting the chandelier to spook Katie by suddenly describing lazy circles in the air, but because the chandelier was equipped with a dimmer switch. Dialing the light down to a glow dim enough to resemble the glow of candles, I gleefully explained to Katie what we were going to do. She was as excited as I was by the prospect of talking to ghosts, and so, suppressing giddy giggles, we set out to make contact with the great Beyond.

The first few minutes were disappointing, and if we hadn't worked ourselves up over the expectation of talking with the dead, we might have grown bored and just put the Ouija away. But then, just as I was beginning to doubt the efficacy of a homemade Ouija board, the little slice of pink and clear geode twitched toward the word *hello*.

"You're pushing it!" Katie declared.

"No, you are," I responded.

We locked eyes over the board, each trying to discern the true intentions of the other. Neither of us removed our fingers from the pointer, however. As we stared each other down, the pointer moved again, this time with much more confidence. We both gasped and looked down at the board. The slice of geode now clearly lay over *hello*. The air in the dining room felt suddenly taut, and the shadows that lurked at the edges of the dim lights seemed to coalesce with a life of their own.

"Tell me you did that," Katie pleaded.

I shushed her. The game had begun.

Over the next hour or so, we carried on an extended conversation with a spirit who claimed his name was Mikey. He was nine, or at least that's how old he was when he said he died. When we asked what he had died of at such an early age, he laboriously spelled out C-O-N-S-U-M-T-U-N. We were confused, and we asked him to spell the word again. He came up with a slightly different spelling, but I thought I knew what he was talking about. I watched *Little*

House on the Prairie with my great-aunt now and again. Remembering something from the show, I asked, "Consumption? Did you die of consumption?"

The pointer swung rapidly over to *yes*. Katie was nonplussed, having no idea what the disease was. Further inquiries led Mikey to reveal that he had died at least a hundred years before, although he did not give us an exact date. He said that he was haunting my house.

Katie was a bit suspicious. She knew as well as I did that my house hadn't been around for a hundred years. The postwar construction suggested that it had been around only a little more than three decades at the time. Both of us believed (mistakenly) that a person had to die in a house in order to haunt it, and so we questioned Mikey on this point. He explained, slowly, and with a number of misspellings, that the house he had lived in wasn't around anymore. It was not directly situated on my grandmother's property but had stood nearby. He didn't specify how near. According to Mikey, he had wandered over to my house to play, mostly because there were people living in the house who could perceive him. He was especially interested in me. He made it clear that he was both lonely and bored, and he kept asking if we would play with him.

Throughout this whole exchange, Katie and I stopped giggling, stopped even accusing one another of pushing the pointer. We just sat there, intently watching the pointer slide around the board, reading with one voice the letters it selected each time it stopped.

The entire house seemed eerily quiet, and a tension hung on the air, as if waiting for something more spectacular to happen than the rapid sliding of the pointer from letter to letter. The heater switched on with a *click* and a *whoosh*; unused to the sounds of the house, Katie nearly jumped out of her skin. As I calmed and reassured her that it was a completely rational noise, we both heard a subtle creaking from the kitchen. I recognized it as the sound of a cabinet door slowly easing open upon its hinges. Katie whipped around, peering into the kitchen. One of the doors of the cupboards stood partly open.

"Don't worry about that," I said. "Those doors don't fit tight."

Katie did not seem calmed by this assertion, but eventually she turned away from the shadowed kitchen. Cautious now, she placed her fingers lightly upon the pointer. The polished slice of geode sprang almost immediately to life, and Mikey told us again that he wanted to play. As he finished spelling this message out, something slammed shut in the kitchen. Once again Katie jumped. When she pulled my attention to the kitchen, all of the cabinet doors were closed again.

"They shut themselves, too?" she demanded in a panicked hiss.

"Come on, let's talk some more," I urged. "Poor little Mikey!"

We focused on the Ouija board. Mikey just told us, over and over, that he wanted to play. Each time he spelled the message out, the pointer seemed to move faster, as if imbued with Mikey's impatient insistence. Katie was getting more and more jittery. From the look on her face, the game had stopped being fun.

"What if he needs us to die to play with him?" she asked. "Maybe he'll kill us in our sleep!"

"Come on," I said. "Ghosts can't kill people. Besides, why would he want us dead? He's just lonely."

I started trying to explain the finer points of ghostly abilities and motivations, at least as far as I understood them at the tender age of twelve, when the shadows in the room seemed to shift strangely. It was like the darkness had taken on a life of its own and had begun subtly moving. At about the same time this caught my attention, Katie froze her fingers on the pointer, abruptly stopping its motion. She was making this weird strangled noise in the back of her throat. I looked away from the dancing shadows long enough to glance at her. Her eyes were fixed on the chandelier. Very slowly, teardrop crystals swinging, it had started moving in a clockwise circle above our heads. Katie stared at it, transfixed. I was about to offer the same explanations for its behavior that my grandmother always offered me when, from the kitchen, two or more cabinet doors creaked open and slammed rapidly shut again. At least, that's what it sounded like. That was enough for Katie. She bolted from the table, knocking over the dining room chair. She was out of the room and pelting up the stairs to my bedroom before I could offer any further explanations as to why cabinets and chandeliers in my home often moved on their own.

I felt kind of sorry for little Mikey, but Katie's panic was contagious. I slipped the makeshift Ouija board underneath the tablecloth, where my grandmother wouldn't be likely to find it the next morning. Then, pocketing the polished slice of stone that had served as our pointer, I rushed after Katie up the stairs. I didn't bother turning off the lights. Even as I glanced down from the landing, the chandelier continued to swing.

In my bedroom, Katie had sought refuge under the covers. My grandmother and I shared a room, and she had graciously given Katie her bed for this little sleepover. Katie was already in bed when I came into the room, the blankets pulled up to her chin.

"You okay?" I asked.

Speechless with fright, Katie just shook her head.

"You want to just go to bed, then?"

She nodded, still not trusting herself to talk.

"That's too bad. I think Mikey really wanted to play."

Katie just glared at me.

My bed was against the opposite wall, although it faced away from my grandmother's bed. Leaving Katie brooding beneath the covers, I kicked my slippers off and prepared to turn in. The one lamp that lit the room was next to my grandmother's bed. It was this old-fashioned-looking thing built kind of like a hurricane lamp, only fitted with a light bulb. One of my aunts had given it to Gram for her birthday several years before, and my grandmother treasured it. It had frosted glass with a design of pink flowers, and instead of a standard switch it had this ornate bronze key. In order to turn the lamp on or off, you had to turn the key one hundred and eighty degrees. It turned stiffly, and always made a clear, audible *click* when it finally moved into the on or off position. I had just propped myself up on my elbow and was about to ask Katie to turn off the light when I heard the key turn in the lamp. With a click, the room went dark.

"Thanks, Katie," I said, then started to roll over.

From Katie's direction, I heard that strangled sound again. She was so full of fear that words were lost to her. That weird pressure that I'd felt downstairs was in the room now, and Katie continued to whimper. I sat up, straining to see her across the room in the dark.

"Katie? You okay?"

The light clicked on. I turned to look at Katie. She was huddled against the wall, as far away from the bedside lamp as she could possibly get. With hands that trembled, she held the blankets up to her nose. She stared in terror at the lamp.

"You didn't turn the light off, did you?" I asked.

Silently, never once taking her eyes from the lamp, Katie shook her head.

"Mikey!" I cried. "Is that you? Cut it out! We want to go to bed!"

Even before the last few words were out of my mouth, I heard the soft grinding of the key. I looked up in time to see two astounding things. First, Katie's eyes got wider than I ever thought human eyes could possibly get. Second, I *visibly* saw the key turn in the lamp. The key clicked home and the light went out.

It took Katie approximately two seconds to break through her paralytic terror, untangle herself from my grandmother's blankets, and dive into bed next to me.

For his part, Mikey was quiet for the rest of the night, but it was a very long time before Katie could be convinced to sleep over at my house again.

The Lady in Blue

People have often asked me, "When was the first time you saw a ghost?"

You would think the answer would be easy. One's first ghostly encounter should be a memorable experience, something that really stands out. But it's not as simple as that. The truth is, I'm not really sure what constitutes my first ghostly encounter, mainly because I didn't always realize that I was seeing ghosts!

If this sounds like a strange excuse, let me tell you about an experience I had at the library in my hometown. The old Hinckley library stands at the corner of Ridge Road and Route 303, the very heart of the little Western Reserve township where I grew up. The library is a converted residence, a quaint little white house with black shutters and trim. It was once home to Vernon Stouffer, king of frozen foods, whose name lingers still in every grocer's freezer case. Prior to Stouffer's residence, which was built in 1845, a log cabin occupied the same site. It's about as picturesque and small-town as you can get, and I spent a lot of time there when I was a kid.

The experience in question happened in the early summer of 1977. I was only four years old. My mother had taken me to get some books for the summer (I was an early reader), but she had also stopped in to meet up with a friend who worked at the library. I remember the library being under construction at the time. Parts of it were cordoned off, and some rooms were completely bare. I know now that the library had only very recently been opened to the public. Four years earlier, in 1973, the Friends of the Hinckley Library had purchased the derelict Stouffer home and began the extensive repairs needed to convert it into the town's library. It opened its doors as a library in 1975, but some renovations were still ongoing even then.

When I was there with my mother, the entire upstairs was off-limits. My mother made it very clear to me that I was not to go up there. I've been a chronically curious person since a very early age, and so this admonition only inspired me to wonder fiercely about what was up there—and to plot over how to get a peek. Eventually we got my books, and my mom went to check them out for me. As she did, she got wrapped up in conversation with her friend, the librarian. I used this as my opportunity to steal away and explore the forbidden zone beyond the bare wooden staircase.

Someone had strung a sign across the bottom of the stairs. It was neatly hand-lettered, and I could read *Do Not*. I didn't bother with the rest of it—I just ducked under the sign and started sneaking up the stairs. I could still hear my mother's voice and that of her friend, talking and laughing. As long as she was occupied, I was safe to explore.

Upstairs there was a hallway but all the doors were closed. I tried the nearest door, and I remember thinking that it had a funny knob. The knob was hard to turn, and I had to use both hands. Then I had to press all of my weight against the door to get it to open. Beyond the door was a white room with a bare wooden floor. I remember seeing a sawhorse and a drop cloth off to one side, and near these was a can of paint. White paint was spattered on the drop cloth. But what really caught my attention was the woman standing at the window.

I was a little startled to find her there. Aside from a workman in coveralls, who I had seen disappearing through a door downstairs, I thought my mother and the librarian were the only other people there. But I was four, so I just accepted the presence of this new person without reservation. She was fascinating because she was dressed so differently from the people I was used to seeing. She had dark hair, lots of it, and it was all piled up on top of her head. I'd never seen a hairstyle like it, just as I'd never quite seen anything like her dress. The dress was a very pale blue, almost white, and it had all these little blue flowers on it. There were about a million tiny buttons that ran up the back to a high, delicately laced collar. I remembering wondering how much work it would be to have to fasten all of those buttons. The skirt of the dress was button-free, and it swept all the way down to the floor. I don't remember ever seeing her feet.

The one detail that failed to register at the time was the way the sunlight streamed through the window. I had no direct sense that it was shining through her in any kind of obvious way, but her presence at the window did nothing to diminish the sunlight that brightened the room. Thinking back to where she was standing, especially since she stood between the window and me, she should have cast a shadow. One of the things that struck me about the room was how bright everything was, with the sunlight streaming in through the window. I don't remember her casting a shadow at all.

The woman didn't turn and look at me right away, and I just stood in silence, gaping at her. Then she looked away from the window, and I saw that she had a pretty face but her eyes seemed very sad. She never said anything, and I have no idea if she was going to, because that was when my mother noticed I was missing. I heard her calling my name, not far from the bottom of the stairs.

Panic-stricken in the way of all four-year-olds who are caught doing something they're not supposed to do, I whirled around and glanced down the hall. I expected to see my mother charging up the stairs. Apparently, she hadn't thought to look up there yet, so I was safe, for the moment. I turned back to say something to the lady.

Only now, she was gone.

With a child's logic, I decided that the lady wasn't supposed to be up here any more than I was. Quite obviously, she didn't want to get caught being in an off-limits room either, only she was more clever than me: she had found a hiding place while my back was turned. It made perfect sense at the time. I didn't waste much time debating it, since hiding, at least for me, would only delay the inevitable with my mother. I gave the room one more look and scurried back down the stairs. When she finally found me, Mom was more relieved than angry. I never really got punished much at that age. Of course, this might have had something to do with the fact that I was scheduled for a dangerous, life-saving surgery later that summer.

Thirty years after it initially opened its doors to the public, the Hinckley library was moved from the Stouffer house. The library's collection had grown too big for the quaint little house, and the nineteenth-century timbers were literally collapsing under its weight. As a kind of memorial, I decided to write an article on the Hinckley library ghost for *FATE* magazine. The librarians were very helpful in my research. They had an entire box of clippings from newspaper stories that had featured the library and its haunted history over the years.

I learned from the articles that the library was reputed to be home to not one but two ghosts.

One was the distinguished Dr. Orlando Wilcox. Wilcox had come to Hinckley in 1831. He was the owner of the log cabin that had originally stood on the Stouffer house site. Wilcox was described as a craggy-faced, whiskered man who was never seen without his old plug hat. A learned doctor, he soon became known as the town's "walking encyclopedia." He served as a Sunday school teacher in addition to working as the township clerk for nearly fifty years.

The ghost of Dr. Wilcox was rumored to hang out most often at the bottom of the staircase I had crept up so long ago. But what really caught my attention was the description of the second ghost. This was the spirit of Wilcox's eldest daughter, Rebecca. She is remembered in Judge A. R. Webber's *History of Hinckley* as "handsome in form and feature, beautiful in character, artistic in taste, and skilled with her needle." Tragically, she died young and unmarried. The death notices from the day tell us that she passed away of "congestion of the lungs" on February 3, 1869.

In all of the articles about her ghostly appearances at the Hinckley library, Rebecca is most commonly known as the "Lady in Blue." She earned this title because she was always seen wearing the same blue dress. One of the families who had owned the Stouffer house prior to its renovation as a library reported experiences with the ghosts. Mainly, the activity was focused on the staircase. At one point, they had placed a rack for winter coats along the bottom of the staircase. After waking each morning to find all of the coats and boots thrown about in the night, the family eventually got the hint and moved the rack to a location more acceptable to the spirits.

By the 1970s, when the building was purchased by the Friends of the Hinckley Library, the house had stood empty and derelict for many years. If Rebecca or her father had made any appearances, no one was around to make note of them. But once the renovations got under way, there was a spike of activity. One of the librarians that my mother knew remembered passing by the library while it was being worked on, only to see a light in one of the windows.

Through the window, she could see a young woman in blue, sitting on the stairs. She had her elbows on her knees and held her chin in her hands. It was night, but with the renovations there were a lot of people coming and going from the library at all hours, so she didn't think much of it at the time. Sometimes when you see a ghost, the spirit looks so completely like a living being that you will never realize that you saw anything otherworldly until much later. You may not ever realize it at all.

That was certainly the case with my encounter with Rebecca Wilcox. I probably would never have known that my four-year-old self ran into a ghost if not for the research that I did on the library's haunting. But now there is no doubt in my mind that I spent at least a few moments in the same room as Hinckley's ghostly Lady in Blue.

From Cradle to Grave

My grandmother may have often downplayed their significance, but I'm not the only person in my family with psychic abilities, and I'm certainly not the only person who has experienced ghostly encounters. This worked to my benefit in sixth grade when I was invited to take part in a writing contest. The contest was called the Young Authors Program, and students were encouraged to write, illustrate, and bind their own books, then present them for display throughout the school district. Over that summer I had read several collections of real ghost stories, and I decided that, for the contest, I would write a collection of ghost stories of my own. (I would later revisit the idea, in the form of this current book!)

I titled the work *The Clock Struck Thirteen*, and I intended to include thirteen tales of ghostly encounters in the book. Since I was in the sixth grade, I felt quite clever about the title matching the number of stories in the book. Some things make more sense when you're twelve, I suppose. By that age, I already had a couple encounters of my own to relate, but I was a long way off from my goal of thirteen. Having heard various family members talk about ghostly experiences, I started asking them to share their tales so I could put them in the book.

One of the most interesting stories came from a relative whom I'll call Patricia. Patricia told me that the house she was living in at that time was haunted. I was a little confused by this, since Patricia's house was brand new. I could remember walking with Patricia and my mother through the housing development as the house was being built. We would hunt for fossils in the newly upturned soil, and I had several prized brachiopods from these afternoon forays (though sadly I never found any trilobites, our state fossil).

Prior to the houses going in, the development had been nothing more than rolling fields and trees. No older houses stood anywhere near that area. Since most of the books I had been reading at the time implied that hauntings only occurred in places where people had died, I questioned Patricia's story. But she was very firm on the matter. Her brand-new house already had spirits—not just one, but several.

Patricia herself confessed to being a little surprised by the fact that a house that had just been built was already haunted. She was under an impression similar to my own—that hauntings typically occurred in places where people had died. I've since learned that ghosts are far more mobile than many people suspect, but at the time the idea of a brand-new house having ghosts seemed a little strange. Still, Patricia had no other explanation for the things she had experienced almost from the first night of moving in.

Patricia was married, but her husband often traveled because of his job. As a result, she spent several nights alone in their brand-new house. One of these nights, she woke up to the sound of children giggling. At first she thought it was coming from outside, even though it seemed strange that children would be out playing at three in the morning. The voices she heard were those of little children—the sort who would certainly be in bed before such a late hour.

The sound died away and she almost decided that she'd imagined it. And then, there it was again. Children giggling.

Now, the house was not only new, but it was also quite a bit bigger than the house that Patricia was accustomed to. Although her husband's job often meant that he was away, it also came with a salary that allowed them to move up in the world. With a much bigger house, Patricia had not yet learned the different sounds that it made or the way it felt at night. There was so much space, and she was the only person in all those empty rooms. Compounding these problems was the fact that not all of the furniture had been moved in, so most of the rooms had odd echoes anyway. It was entirely possible that she was hearing something ordinary and simply misinterpreting the sound.

Patricia tried to think of a logical source for the sound. Maybe it was a neighbor's television. This would have made more sense in her old house, however, where the neighbors were much closer together. This new house stood on half an acre of land, and a television would have to be blaring at an ear-shredding volume to be heard all the way from one house to the next.

Patricia lay motionless in her bed, all of her muscles taut as she just concentrated on listening. The new housing development was situated not too far away from a major highway, so she could hear cars and the occasional truck rumbling in the distance. There was a distinctly muffled quality to the sounds that were coming to her ears from beyond the closed windows. The sounds of the children started up again, and there was no denying it this time. The sounds had to be coming from somewhere *inside* the house.

At this point, Patricia became grateful that her door was partially closed. The way her bed was situated, she would have been looking right down the upstairs hallway to where she thought the sounds were coming from. She didn't want to see what was in the darkness there. She wasn't sure why she should be frightened by children, but there was an unearthly quality to the sound of the laughter.

As frightening as an unexplained sound can be, the kind of tension that gripped Patricia as she lay in bed listening can only last so long without a release. When nothing further happened, Patricia found herself starting to relax. Eventually, she dropped back off to sleep. The next morning, the sun seemed to chase the phantoms of the night away. Patricia decided that she had probably imagined the sounds in the night, or else the stress of the move coupled with having her husband away had led her to misinterpret something perfectly ordinary, making it seem sinister in the darkness.

Over the next few days Patricia busied herself with unpacking boxes and organizing the furniture in her new home. The creepy laughter was forgotten as she lost herself in the process of making her new house a home. And then, late one night, she found herself once again dragged out of sleep by strange sounds. She heard the laughter again, but this time it was accompanied by another sound. She could distinctly hear several pairs of little feet running up and down the hall. She said it sounded almost as if they were racing one another or playing tag. The voices would whisper as well. They definitely sounded like children's whispers, but she could never make out any of the words.

As with the last time, Patricia listened carefully as she lay motionless in her bed, trying to identify some logical source for the sounds. The ghostly children continued to play tag in the hall, and the sound of their giggles came to her ears is if the hall were hundreds of feet long. Despite the strange echoing quality to the sounds, they still sounded closer than any of the highway sounds coming from outside the house.

As she listened, it seemed to Patricia that the children were coming closer and closer to her bedroom door with each pass they made down the hall. At any moment, she told herself, one of them was going to slam into the door. She shut her eyes, afraid of what she might see should the door suddenly swing open.

As with the other night, however, nothing else happened except for the sounds. Eventually, the game of tag seemed to come to an end, and Patricia relaxed enough to go back to sleep.

She spoke with her husband about the ghostly children, but he was reluctant to believe her. He wasn't your typical skeptic, however. He believed in UFOs, and his worldview certainly allowed for psychic sensitivities. But he insisted that he had felt nothing out of the ordinary in the house on any of the occasions that he had been there. He suggested that it was just her imagination playing tricks on her, mostly because she was in a much bigger house and sleeping alone. But if the children were just playing and giggling, he allowed, they probably didn't mean any harm. Half joking, he suggested that the next time she heard them, she should go out in the hall and join them in their game. She wanted children of her own, after all.

If their games were harmless, why did they leave her feeling so unnerved? Maybe it was just the fact that she was hearing something so impossible. Patricia wasn't certain what to think. As time passed, she began to grow accustomed to the sounds of the children playing in the night. She didn't hear them every night, but she heard them often enough that the intermittent giggles and whispers, and the sound of tiny, running feet, grew to be as ordinary as the ticking of the furnace in the basement or the sound of air whispering through the vents. The most unsettling event was yet to come, however.

Months after the initial appearance of the ghostly sounds, Patricia had settled very comfortably into her new house. Her husband had been home for several weeks at a stretch, and the unearthly sounds tended to manifest less often whenever he was around. This should have prepared Patricia for a spate of activity when his company sent him on yet another lengthy business trip. Still, nothing had prepared her for what happened next.

Patricia lay on one side of the roomy queen-sized bed, habit causing her to leave her husband's side vacant. She was deeply asleep, but she awakened with a jolt when she felt the unmistakable sensation of a tiny hand patting the side of her face. Her eyes flew open, and the sensation was so real that she fully expected to see a flesh-and-blood child standing beside her bed. Instead, there was nothing there.

Staring into empty darkness, she could still feel the tiny hand upon her cheek.

Patricia sat up in bed with a yelp, her own hand flying to the spot where those phantom fingers had lingered. As she reached for the light, she swore that she heard tiny footsteps retreating down the hall.

For most other people, being touched by a ghost crosses a certain line. If Patricia had been someone different, she might very well have demanded that her husband sell the house so they could move to a less spirited residence. But once the initial shock wore off, Patricia realized that there had been nothing malevolent in that ghostly touch. Instead, it had been gentle and even affectionate. She suddenly felt much less fearful of her little ghosts. Patricia suspected that they were just lonely, and they were reaching out to someone they perceived as a motherly figure. Although Patricia and her husband as yet had no children, they had bought the new house with the intention of having room to grow. Perhaps the little spirits had sensed this, Patricia reasoned, and they had been drawn to her home.

After this, she came to welcome the nightly games of the ghostly children. On the nights that her husband was away, and she could hear them running in the hallway or giggling, she felt less alone. She still had no solid explanation for where the ghostly children had come from, or what they were doing in her newly built house. She asked around among friends in the development only to learn that theirs were the first houses that had stood on that section of land for many years. No disaster involving children had occurred anywhere near the location, at least nothing that anyone was aware of. Eventually, she decided that the house had been built near an old Indian burial ground, and that was the source of the ghosts.

This explanation sounded dubious to me even when I was in sixth grade, so I left it out of the original version of this story. I had no satisfactory explanation for the source or identity of the little lost ghosts, however; I just had to let it hang. At the time, I accepted that such was the nature of real-life ghost stories. Sometimes there is no satisfactory explanation for what is going on. It seemed a shame to have such an initially chilling tale just sort of deflate into nothing, however.

In this case, it seems I didn't have all the information. Years later I learned some details about Patricia's life that made me rethink the nature and origin of the dead children who played at night outside her room.

Patricia and her husband had bought their nice new house with the intent of filling it with children. They weren't a new couple, however. They had been married for a number of years, and they had been trying for a long time to have children. When I learned this, I started to wonder if Patricia hadn't imagined the sounds of children playing, since she so desperately wanted to hear those sounds from flesh-and-blood children in her house. And then another detail came to light that made the identity of the ghostly children seem chilling all over again.

Patricia had endured no fewer than nine miscarriages by the time she and her husband moved into their new house. Nine children had died in her womb. It wasn't the house that was haunted. It was Patricia.

The ghostly children who giggled and played in the hallway at night may well have been the spirits of all the children she had lost. The only thing that's puzzling about this interpretation is the fact that they only manifested after the move to the new house. But perhaps what brought them out was the very fact that the new house was intended to be a home for future children. The old house hadn't had enough extra room, but the new house had not one but two rooms set aside in the hope that little ones would eventually grow up there. In setting these rooms aside and decorating them with baby things, perhaps Patricia unconsciously invited these ghosts to come to her new home.

Notably, the ghostly visitations ceased once Patricia successfully gave birth to a baby girl. Perhaps the little unborn lives that once stroked her face in her sleep felt that they no longer had to keep their mommy company, since a living sister could now be the focus of her love and attention.

Mr. Parson's
Last Sonata

Many of my psychic abilities come down to me from my mother's side. Both of her parents had psychic abilities, and her father very openly embraced them. It was his belief that the entire Belanger line had a penchant for three things: art, music, and the paranormal (ironically, this probably helped encourage my maternal grandmother to steer me away from my abilities, since she associated them so strongly with the husband she divorced). My mother was no exception to his rule. She painted, she sculpted, she sang, and she played the violin. The violin is a challenging instrument, but my mother could make the violin weep, laugh, and sing. Sounds of Vivaldi and Rossini filled my early childhood, and the scent of the rosin on the strings brings back memories even now. My mother had a number of paranormal experiences throughout her life, but by far the most poignant of these involves her sonorous violin.

My mother was one of five children growing up together in a house in Lakewood, Ohio. The family didn't have a lot of money, but my grandmother believed in cultivating the talents of her children. Thus, when my mother showed an interest in playing the violin, a teacher was sought out and lessons were procured. Mr. Parsons worked out of a music shop not far from where they lived, and he recognized my mother's great potential. She became one of his favorite students, and if her payments for lessons were sometimes late, he never complained.

Mr. Parsons had a huge impact on my mother. My grandmother had gotten divorced when my mother was seven or eight, and she took extreme measures to ensure that my grandfather stayed out of his children's lives. As a result, my mother grew up fatherless in an age when single-parent households were fairly uncommon. Mr. Parsons not only became one of my mother's role models but, from the way she grew attached to him, I suspect that he also became something of a surrogate father figure as well. He may or may not have been aware of this, but it seems that he went out of his way to look after my mother in whatever little ways he could.

One of the things my mother admired most about Mr. Parsons was his passion for his music. Like so many violinists, he didn't just play the instrument. He had a love affair with it. He would often stand and play for hours, just losing himself in the rhythm and the sound. All musical instruments evoke a certain amount of emotion in the people attuned to them, but there is a special magick to violins. Their sound is the closest to that of the human voice, and in their music we can often hear that voice laughing, sighing, weeping, or singing with joy. If you have never really connected to the sound of a violin, you won't know what I mean, but understand that it is so. For those who play the violin and for those who have a deep appreciation for its song, the music of this instrument can convey emotions more profoundly than the most eloquent words.

Mr. Parsons shared that level of communication with my mother. I think it was his way of bringing something positive and beautiful into the life of a middle sibling who lived in a financially struggling, broken home.

When Mr. Parsons taught at the music store, he rarely left his little music room. If he had a break between students, he would simply stand in the room and amuse himself with his own music, filling the back hall with the trilling notes of Vivaldi or the bittersweet tones of a Brahms concerto. My mother admitted that she would sometimes steal up to the music room ever so quietly and wait on one of the chairs outside, postponing the start of her own lesson for five or ten minutes just to allow him the chance to finish what he was playing. There was no window to the little music room, so he had no way to see that she was already there, just listening. When she finally got around to it, she would go up and knock on the door, then make up some excuse about being delayed. I suspect that he was well aware of her game and he played with the intent that she would listen. When it came time for my mother's final lesson with Mr. Parsons, events strongly suggested that this was the case.

Despite her willful tardiness, my mother was a dedicated student. Given her abilities with the violin, Mr. Parsons believed that she could one day earn a chair in the violin section of the illustrious Cleveland Orchestra. Week in and week out, he helped her work toward this dream. His gentle but persistent encouragement helped my mother to believe that she could one day accomplish anything she set her mind to do.

Of course, if she were going to play for the Cleveland Orchestra—or even try out, for that matter—she was going to have to have an instrument worthy of the task. Her family had done the best they could with what they had, but Mr. Parsons wanted to get his little Mary Jane something more suited to her skills. Violinists who are serious about their art often want an instrument that will grow as they grow, something they can play for years and years. Mr.

Parsons had already been planning a trip overseas to pick up some instruments. He decided that one of these would be a gift to my mother to help set her firmly on the path of becoming a great concert violinist.

And here is where we encounter the difficulty inherent in a secondhand tale. I only know what my mother told me about this experience, and what she said was that Mr. Parsons traveled to Poland to buy her a violin. But the violin that my mother left to me after she passed away in 2004 was made by the Roth workshop. The Roth workshop was located in Germany.

Roth violins are hardly inferior instruments. They were each made after Stradivarius originals, a name that even those uninitiated into the mysteries of violin-playing should recognize as the undisputed master of the instrument-maker's art. My mother's violin was crafted in 1966 after a Stradivarius violin that was created in Cremona, Italy, in 1722. What all of this esoteric information means is that Mr. Parsons bought my mother a top-quality violin, something crafted in the spirit and style of a long and honored tradition. It is a deep-throated violin, with a dark and sometimes brooding voice, and that voice is wholly unique to that specific instrument. If this was the instrument that he felt was worthy of the talents of his fourteen-year-old pupil, then Mr. Parsons had a very high opinion of my mother's gift.

While Mr. Parsons was overseas, my mother's lessons were on hiatus. She was to resume her lessons once he got back, at which point he would present her with the new violin. Obviously, my mother was looking forward to the new instrument, but she also missed her weekly hour with Mr. Parsons. She especially missed listening to him play. I don't know how long his overseas trip took, but I do know that he had given himself a week or so to recover once he returned before starting up his lessons again. Mr. Parsons was an older man, and he had expected the rigors of travel to weigh heavily upon him.

Finally, the day for her next lesson rolled around. Excited at the prospect of seeing her beloved teacher again, my mother rushed straight from school to the music shop. As was her custom, she stole quietly down to the back hall where his classroom lay and sat in one of the chairs outside the room. She could hear Mr. Parsons playing even as she strode down the hall, and so she sat for a while, just reveling in the sound of his music. She loved her teacher's style and the subtle way he had of evoking depths of emotion from the simplest bars of music. This afternoon, his playing seemed utterly inspired, better than she had ever heard him play. As a result, she lost track of time, and ended up sitting outside of the music room for nearly half an hour. Mr. Parsons seemed to be lost in the music as well, because he never opened the door to check to see if his student had arrived. He simply played song after song, filling the back hall with the bittersweet notes of his violin.

Then she heard footsteps coming down the hall, and the music stopped. When my mother looked up, she saw the owner of the music store walking toward her. He had a strange look on his face, a mixture of apology and sorrow and concern.

"You're Mary Jane, right?" he asked. "One of Mr. Parson's students?"

Just from his tone, my mother knew that something was amiss.

"You've been waiting here this whole time," he muttered. Then, he asked, "Didn't anyone tell you?"

"Tell me what?" fourteen-year-old Mary Jane asked, not really certain she wanted the answer.

The man from the music store was just as reluctant to give it. But it had to be said.

"The lesson was canceled today. They're going to be canceled for a while, at least until we can find a new violin instructor."

"But Mr. Parsons would never leave!" my mother objected.

"I'm sorry that nobody told you before today," the owner apologized. "But Mr. Parsons passed away very suddenly last week, right after he got back from Europe. It surprised all of us."

My mother sat, stunned.

"But," she managed, "I was just listening to him play."

"You must have imagined it," the owner insisted. "Nobody's in there."

He held open the door to prove it. There was only one door in or out of the little room, and there was no way anyone could have walked in or out without passing right in front of my mother. The music stand was there, just as he had left it, but there was no Mr. Parsons. There was, however, a package on his desk.

"What's that? Has he been here?"

The store owner nodded.

"He stopped over right after he got back to drop off some packages. Instruments for some of his students. Did you order something with him?"

My mother was already walking into the silent little room. On her teacher's desk was a package. Taped to the top was a little note, torn off from a sheet of yellow legal paper. The note bore two words in Mr. Parson's handwriting: *Mary Jane.*

"This is mine," she said.

The shop owner let her take it. Then he said, as gently as possible, "You go on home, Mary Jane. We'll give your mother a call when your lessons can start up again."

After he left, she still looked around, half-expecting to see Mr. Parsons hiding in a corner somewhere. But he was gone. She started crying then, angry that she hadn't had a chance to say goodbye. But then she remembered the songs. That had been Mr. Parsons playing. She was sure of it. There was no mistaking his style.

He had come to say goodbye after all.

My mother took the new violin home, but the death of her beloved teacher left a serious hole in her life. She never lost her passion for the instrument, but she did lose some of her drive to become a concert violinist. The music had become too personal, too tied up with the echo of loss. Perhaps appropriately, the voice of the violin that Mr. Parsons had brought back for her was perfectly tuned for this emotional spectrum. Every time she stroked its strings with her bow, there was a note of mourning to its tone. Even the bright, cascading notes of Vivaldi's *Four Seasons* took a somber turn when played on that violin. I can hear that touch of ineffable sadness on the instrument even now, every time I try to evoke the memory of my mother's music with my inexpert hands. I think it was haunted when she got it, and of all the possessions that she left me, her violin haunts me the most.

The Thing in
the Crawlspace

It's a universal childhood fear. The thing the closet. The monster under the bed. All the hungry, malevolent things that lurk just beyond our sight in the dark and forgotten places of our homes. Our parents always assured us that the sense of looming darkness emanating from that dusty old attic or the crawlspace just beneath the basement stairs was only our imagination. But what if it wasn't? Ghosts are just our imagination, too—at least, that's what some would insist. So what do you do when the monster in the dark turns out to be something very real?

This was a question I had to answer many years ago, when I was in college. There was a fellow a year ahead of me whom I'll call Evan. I met him my very first day at college, and he invited me to the university's gaming club. He was a quirky little guy who was heavily into anime back at a time when anime was still pretty exotic to most people. To this day, I swear his passion for anime arose from the fact that he bore such a striking resemblance to one of its stock character archetypes. If you have ever seen any anime you'll know who I mean: that young, crazy, girl-chasing guy who's perpetually hyper, socially awkward, and often used for comic relief. Think Tenchi, or Carrot from *Sorcerer Hunters*, and you'll have Evan to a tee.

Evan was a rich kid from suburbia, and unlike scholarship cases like me, he had an apartment off campus. His apartment was really just an older house renovated into a duplex. He lived downstairs. Another family lived upstairs. The house was at the end of a quiet street in a residential neighborhood in Cleveland Heights. And Evan was convinced that the place was haunted.

Now, Evan was one of the first practicing Pagans I ever met. This wasn't necessarily flattering to the Pagans. Much like he was a dead ringer for a certain stereotype in anime, Evan was also a dead ringer for a certain stereotype among modern Pagans. You'll probably recognize this one as well: young kid, just trying to figure his world out, quietly trying to rebel against Mom and Dad in a way that won't get him cut off from their financial support. Picks up a Wicca 101 book and decides that he's Pagan, then subsequently sees magick and witch wars everywhere.

I've seen a lot of Pagan teens start off this way, and then grow into a more mature expression of their faith. Evan eventually got better, but at the time it was hard to take his claims of a haunted house too seriously. He was a hyper little guy who was convinced he was seeing spirits at every turn. He claimed to have created a protective construct in one of his Robotech action figures. Considering that you can use just about anything as a focus for energy, maybe he did, but that didn't stop the claim from sounding ridiculous. Mostly, the other guys and I in the gaming group just let Evan blather, since he seemed harmless enough.

As strange and hyper as Evan could be, he was basically a good guy, and I ended up hanging out with him quite a bit. He never wavered on the fact that his apartment was haunted. Eventually, he had a couple of roommates move in. One was an older guy. (And by older, I mean older than all the rest of us, which meant he was somewhere in the neighborhood of twenty-eight. To a college freshman, this seemed ancient.) The other roommate was this guy's girlfriend. The couple was a little unusual, at least for our crew, in that they had some very traditional notions about the role of the male and the role of the female in a relationship. He worked, and he expected her to stay home, look pretty, and do the housework. I wasn't sure I approved of this arrangement, but she didn't seem to mind it, so who was I to judge?

Evan was always going on about the creepy portions of his house—from the back bedroom, where he was convinced some guy got shot and died, to the basement, which was shared between the downstairs and upstairs apartments. He went on so often about what he sensed in these places that eventually it just became background noise to any conversation a person had with him. But Amy, the female component of his roommate duo, was a pragmatic little thing. She hung around a lot of Pagans (her boyfriend was Pagan as well), but she herself had been raised Jewish. She still nominally adhered to that faith, and so she was far less inclined to see spirits at every turn. Most of the Reform Jews whom I met at that same time didn't seem to believe in much of anything supernatural. Their religion seemed to place most of its emphasis not on the otherworldly, but on practical values like tradition and community. That's why I found it so unusual when Amy mentioned the thing in the basement.

The apartment had a washer and dryer shared between the upstairs and downstairs residences. These appliances were stored in the basement, which was sort of a common no-man's land. The basement was unfinished and decidedly creepy, even on a good day. The walls were brick or cinderblock, covered over with sad, flaking white paint. The paint was discolored in spots where water had seeped in over the years, and there were cobwebs all over the place. The few ground-level windows intended to let light into the place were thick with cobwebs and dust, so even the sunlight that occasionally slanted into the basement seemed washed-out and gray. The one vaguely clean and dust-free location in that uninviting hole in the ground was the area immediately around the washer-and-dryer set. That was thanks to the upstairs neighbor—you can't really expect a college-aged bachelor to keep much of anything clean unless you hold a gun to his head.

I think I had poked my head down into this dim and dusty cellar a grand total of once, when Evan had done something to break the washer and didn't know what to do about it (judging by the pile of laundry in his room, his solution was simply to never again do laundry). Otherwise, I avoided the place, largely because it was not my apartment, and I had no business being down there. But Amy did her boyfriend's laundry. She was a good little housekeeper, so she was down there quite a bit. And she claimed that there was something under the stairs, watching her.

She didn't say anything about it right away, logically assuming that she didn't like the basement for very ordinary reasons. It was dark and cobwebby. There was only one bare bulb for lighting. It took no imagination whatsoever to presume that entire colonies of spiders called the place home. In short, it wasn't haunted. It was just a nasty, neglected basement.

But the feeling persisted, even after she'd rationalized it away. And it always seemed centered on the same location: a cramped little crawlspace under the stairs. The crawlspace was packed with dilapidated boxes that may have belonged to the upstairs neighbor or may have been left behind by residents who'd moved out of the house thirty years before. They could have contained Christmas decorations, or they could have contained desiccated body parts. Underneath the thick layers of dust, it was impossible to tell, and no one ever felt inspired to make a closer investigation.

But every time she did the laundry, Amy felt she was being watched. It was a pervasive impression, something that made the hairs on the back of her neck stand up, especially when she had her back to the crawlspace. That was bad enough, but, over time, she started to feel that the presence was taking an active and malevolent interest in her. The shadows would seem deeper.

During her final encounter, Amy stood at the washer and dryer. She had just finished emptying a load of whites out of the dryer and was now moving the batch of dark clothes from the washer to the dryer. Whenever she moved something from one machine to the other, she had to turn her back to the space under the stairs. She was doing her best to ignore the presence that she sensed there, since she didn't know what else to do about it. And then she got the distinct impression that whatever was back there was starting, very slowly, to creep forward. She could not shake the impression that this thing—whatever it was—was exploring the space beyond its dank little realm of dusty boxes and moving closer to her. Doggedly trying to finish her work and ignore the chills running up and down her back, Amy kept thinking to herself, *It's just my imagination. It's just my imagination.*

And then the lone bulb that lit the cellar popped and went out, leaving her in darkness.

Understandably, Amy dropped her laundry and pelted up the stairs. There was a moment of panic when she realized that her route of escape would actually take her closer to the unseen, creeping thing, but her urge to flee overrode any other concerns. Imagination or not, she wanted the hell out of there.

She had been reluctant to tell anyone about her encounters with the thing for fear of sounding like a lunatic. However, she had no intention of going into the basement again—*ever*—and she had to explain to her boyfriend what happened to the laundry.

Throughout the weeks that Amy was silently enduring her encounters in the basement, something had been going on in the rest of the apartment as well. These events were not quite as obviously connected with something otherworldly, but they seemed strange nevertheless. Since Karl and Amy had moved in, the atmosphere in Evan's apartment had grown somehow heavier and more oppressive. It wasn't something anyone noticed all at once, but gradually the place seemed darker. A sense of threat hung in the air, like something was lurking just outside the apartment, waiting to get in. In this environment, Evan had gone from hyperactive to highly nervous, and some days he was so consumed with anxiety that he skipped out on school. Karl and Amy's relationship became strained as well. Despite their throwback-to-the-fifties attitudes on women's work, they had started off a happy and reasonably well-adjusted couple. Now they were fighting all the time, mostly over stupid things. All of these things individually might have been simple stress—the inevitable cost of living. But taken all together, there seemed to be some outside agency influencing how people felt when inside the apartment.

After Amy's panicked encounter, I decided to go poking my nose into whatever was lurking down in the basement. I still wasn't sure I believed in Amy's "monster under the stairs" claim. I had no doubt that she believed it, but the idea of some nameless thing lurking in the shadows of a dank cellar was so cliché that it was hard to accept without reservation. And at the time, despite the fact that I openly used my abilities to sense spirits and work with energy, I was still mostly a skeptic. It's hard, in retrospect, to adequately explain my attitudes at the time. I had abilities, and I frequently used them, but I still wasn't certain whether or not these abilities were all in my head. I accepted that I could be deluding myself about some or all of my abilities to sense and work with energy, and I tried to rely not on belief but on results. If someone told me there was a spirit in a certain location, I had to go and experience it for myself, and only if my perceptions were overwhelming would I believe in its existence without reservation. And when it came time to do energy work—whether to heal someone or to reach out and act upon a spirit—I also relied not on belief or assumptions, but results.

This was the mindset I was operating under when I went down into the basement. Given the cliché nature of the "thing in the crawlspace," I didn't expect to find much of anything down there.

I assumed that the basement was simply a basement, creepy for the sheer fact that most basements are creepy.

That was why I was so shocked when, about halfway down the basement stairs, I ran smack into a wall of . . . ick.

I paused, trying to be certain that I wasn't just reacting instinctively to the dark of the cellar. However, I've never been afraid of the dark, and where most people dislike basements, I've always preferred the underground portions of houses. Being surrounded on all sides by earth makes me feel safe and secure. I love caves for the very same reason. So, once I determined that what I was feeling had nothing to do with instincts or psychology or my reptile hindbrain, I tried to figure out what else it could be.

At this point, I should stop to point out that my understanding of spirits at that time was pretty rudimentary. Certainly, I had studied the topic more widely than the average person my age, and I'd had a number of experiences of my own. I had read about the Spiritualist movement, with its séances and ectoplasm and tabletipping. I'd played with pendulums and Ouija boards. But I still labored under the notion that all ghosts are dead people. In the books that had been available to me, I'd learned that hauntings were caused by death, almost universally. Spirits got tied to a house or other residence because that was where they died, and they had failed to move on. I had a basic notion that some ghosts were more like echoes or psychic video recordings, imprinted on the energy of a place, but I did not grasp the notion that spirits could have inhuman origins—well, aside from demons, which I flatly disbelieved even existed.

So it was with much surprise that I poked at the oppressive *something* hanging in the air before me and came back with no sense of a proper ghost at all. There wasn't even a sense of sentience. There was just this thick, heavy, twisting cloud of ick that felt for all the world like a big otherworldly slug slowly creeping up the stairs. I was too curious to be scared—a quality that I'm sure is going to lead me to a messy end some day—and so I just kept standing there, putting out psychic feelers and trying to take in every aspect of the thing.

As I peeled back the conceptual layers of my impressions, I started to realize that it wasn't just a bug clump of generalized ick. There were strata of emotions, mostly negative ones. People arguing. The upstairs neighbor worrying about money. Evan's fears about flunking out of college. Amy, secretly holding back a need for independence out of a desperate love for Karl. Images and feelings that seemed connected to other people, all of them worried or frightened or generally frustrated about life.

I didn't have a word for it at the time, but I had come face to face with my first psychic residue. A residue is a collection of energy, often negative energy. Residues can be generated all at once as the result of a highly traumatic event (such as a murder-suicide) or it can build up over time, with layer upon layer of (typically) negative emotions. Most residues are completely inert, seeming to just cling to the forgotten spaces in the homes where they were created. They settle most naturally into the disused portions of homes, like attics, closets, and basements. This is because the normal day-to-day activity in uncluttered and highly trafficked areas of a dwelling tends to keep energy in motion, breaking residues up before they form into something significant. Allowed to fester in the forgotten spaces, however, they can sometimes seem to take on lives of their own, although they never seem to achieve sentience. They are sometimes mistaken for ghostly hauntings because they tend to exude the same type of emotional energy that originally went into making them. In extreme cases, they can trap echoes of the events tied to these emotions, which can seem as if those events are replaying themselves on a spiritual level.

At the time, however, I knew none of this. I only knew that I poked at its energy and it tasted nasty. And it was no longer under the stairs but slowly making its way up them. I got the impression that it was following Amy. The thing wasn't exactly conscious about following her, but Amy was a strong source of pent-up negativity. I had no clue until that moment how her relationship with

Karl had been wearing on her. But she was generating a lot of what appeared to have made this thing in the first place. And even if it didn't seem sentient, it did seem to have some vague sense of self-preservation—or at least self-perpetuation. It was seeking the strongest source upon which to feed. I suspected that Amy had somehow galvanized the thing into action, that her many trips down to do laundry (probably grumbling silently to herself the whole while) had woken it up from the crawlspace where it had originally coagulated.

Well, those were my impressions, anyway. I had nothing at all to back them up, especially since none of the books I had read ever said anything about semi-sentient balls of negativity that grew like fungi in the dank corners of neglected basements.

It didn't seem *consciously* malevolent, which had been Amy's main worry. And it also seemed very slow. It was creeping up those stairs like molasses in January. So I deemed it a minor threat and went back to the others to report my findings.

The first thing I told Amy and the others was, "It's not evil, exactly." Whenever I've done a haunting investigation, that is almost universally the first thing that I'm asked: "Is it evil? Is it trying to hurt me?"

Well, the thing from the crawlspace didn't seem intent on causing any harm, but I got the impression that it naturally generated the same kind of emotions that had gone into creating it in the first place. Which could have explained the slow progression of fear, frustration, and anxiety that had been plaguing the occupants of the nearest apartment for several weeks now.

I told Amy, Evan, and Karl my impressions and theories, leaving out any conjecture about the state of Karl and Amy's relationship. Karl was skeptical. Amy was relieved to know that she wasn't going crazy. And Evan acted like Evan—which is to say he overreacted, rather dramatically. He had read a thing or two in some of his Pagan books about psychic self-defense, you see, which apparently involved carving runes into the scabbard of his broadsword, among other things.

While Evan ran around trying to put wards up on every door and window to the house, I wondered if there was a way to get rid of the thing. It was essentially just an overgrown clot of energy—a kind of psychic dust bunny grown so large that it had taken on a life of its own. I might not have known everything about ghosts and spirits at the time, but I had a really good handle on energy.

"Before you go all bell, book, and candle over there, let me try something," I offered.

Evan had torn through his wire-rack bookshelves in search of an Ed Fitch book and was busy reciting a hymn to Odin. Or Thor. I don't remember exactly. It might have been Tyr, since that was the main rune he kept using.

While he was running around, and Karl and Amy were trying to help him, I went back to the basement.

Energy work is something that has always come naturally to me. For as long as I can remember, I have been able not only to sense energy, but also to consciously shape it and harness it. It was something I believe I was born knowing. I know that's a tall claim, but it's the only way I can explain why it's as simple as breathing for me, and sometimes just as hard to explain. At the time, however, even though I knew how to do things, I didn't possess an unshakable faith in my methods. It was that skeptical streak in me. Even though the knowledge was there, I had not yet learned to trust it fully. Instead, I adopted a rather open-ended set of expectations. I figured that, if the energy work was all in my head, then it certainly wouldn't hurt to try to use it. Conversely, if the energy work was more than just my imagination, then I might just accomplish something. If I got results, then I could believe.

The thing in the crawlspace—now perhaps a foot closer to the top of the stairs—was nothing but energy. Really, it was a big ball of cast-off emotions, built up year after year after year. Einstein tells us that energy is neither created nor destroyed—but you can certainly change its state, and I had an instinctive ability to reach out, grab energy, and do things with it. Usually I worked with people's energy, but I realized that this big ball of negative emotions had originally come from people. It was nasty as hell, but if I truly believed that I could work with people's energy, there was no reason that I couldn't grab it and harness it the same way that I grabbed the energy of those around me.

So, I stood at the top of the stairs and concentrated on the thing. And then I imagined whips of my energy lashing out and striking it. I beat on it for a little while, suspending any stubborn sense of disbelief and giving myself over to instinct. Eventually, I wrapped my own energy completely around the thing, breaking it down until it was pulverized into manageable chunks.

Still holding on to the now-broken-down ball of ick, I backed up to the front door just beyond the top of the basement and swept everything out into the yard, just as I might sweep out the remnants of a killer dust bunny. Since hanging out with Evan, I had been doing some reading on the Pagan faith, and the one thing I totally grokked was the notion that Mother Earth eventually recycles everything. That was no excuse for us to tax her abilities with needless waste, but when it came to energy that you didn't know what else to do with, the best solution was what the Pagans called grounding. So, after beating the energetic nasty to a pulp, I let the remnants of it seep into the soil and added a silent request asking Mother Earth to clear it away for me.

The whole process took perhaps ten minutes. It felt a little silly, before and afterward, considering that all I did was stand at the top of the basement stairs, enter into an imaginary battle with some invisible thing, and then top it all off by talking to dirt. But when I stepped back into the basement, it certainly felt less oppressive, and that pervasive wall of ick was no longer there.

The real test was to see if any of the others noticed a difference.

Evan and Karl were still by the back door doing something with the sword and a bucket. The bucket was doing double duty as a cauldron, since no one in the apartment owned a proper iron cauldron. I didn't even know where one could get such a thing. I left them to it and got Amy.

"You can probably go get your laundry," I suggested.

"Did you get rid of it?" she asked.

I shrugged. "I tried something. Just go see."

She looked like she didn't really believe me, but I think Karl had chewed her out about the laundry. She headed toward the basement, flashlight in hand. After a little while, she came up with the basket of laundry.

"It's gone," Amy said, wonderingly. "How did you do that?"

I smiled and said, "I'm just that cool."

Or something equally ridiculous. I was, after all, barely nineteen.

The Haunting at
Whitethorn Woods

Something walks the woods at Whitethorn. To this day I cannot say for certain what it is. I have heard theories from others who shared my experiences in those woods and, while some of those theories seem plausible, they are nevertheless extraordinary. But the things we encountered on this deceptively tranquil property in Geauga County, Ohio, were themselves extraordinary. Even though I was there to bear witness to these events, I doubted my own perceptions for years. Some places just seem alive with spirits. Whatever else it may be, Whitethorn Woods is one of those places. That rural property is haunted not just with ghosts but with something born of the very land.

It was October 1992, and my college was sponsoring an event for inner-city youth. The event was being held at this gorgeous property in Geauga County, Ohio, and we had all of fall break to prepare that property for the event. Out of respect for the university's privacy, I am going to call the property Whitethorn Woods, because of the profusion of thorn bushes that grow throughout the acreage. Whitethorn consists mostly of extensive wooded acres with a pond, a large lake to the east, and several lochs that were at one time part of an old canal system. The only entrance to the property spans a very narrow, very old stone bridge that separates the lake from the lochs. The stonework of the bridge is old and weathered, dating back to the early part of the twentieth century, if not earlier. This was the oldest piece of human construction I encountered on the property. Everything else seemed to date to the fifties or sixties. Despite the relative youth of the structures on the property, stepping onto Whitethorn Woods felt like stepping somewhere out of time. There was a pervasive feeling of otherworldliness to the property. At first, I attributed this only to the beautiful setting of lakes and trees. After moving to the city to attend college, I had missed the wooded expanses that blanket much of northeastern Ohio. Later events would make this initial perception feel more like a presentiment.

The property has two summer houses, hardly more than cottages. They stand across from one another, divided by a steep gully. A little wooden footbridge spans the gully, connecting one house to the next. Both houses have the look of someone's vacation cottages. Deep in the woods behind the furthest cottage, an overgrown tennis court added to the sense that this property once belonged to some affluent family who used it as a summer retreat. Both cottages had been recently renovated, and they were outfitted with state-of-the-art security systems. The gray plastic numberpads with their softly glowing LED screens stood in stark contrast with the rather woodsy décor within each of the cottages, and they were almost invasive reminders of modernity.

The first thing that struck me as odd the first day I set foot on Whitethorn Woods was a peculiar habit the other students working there had developed regarding these two summer cottages. Both cottages were obviously built around the same time. Both are completely furnished and decorated in a very cozy, albeit woodsy, style. Both have clean, working facilities; heating and air conditioning; as well as working fireplaces. Additionally, both are equipped with identical security systems. However, the students avoided the house located on the far side of the gully. No matter how many of them were sleeping over at the property, they all crammed themselves into the closest cottage, choosing to sleep two to a bunk rather than spread out into the other little house.

At first, this seemed like a matter of convenience. With the gully that separates the two houses, the only way to really access the second cottage is to go across the wooden footbridge. There is no way to drive a car up to the side of the second cottage, so anyone wanting to bunk in that cottage would have a bit of a walk to make with their luggage. University students are notorious for doing as little work as humanly possible, so it made sense to me that they would naturally prefer the closer house. But then I heard the nicknames that the students had given to the two cottages in order to differentiate them. The closer house had been christened the "good house." In contrast, the house that was farther into the woods had earned the moniker of the "bad house." When I asked about the names, no one could precisely explain why they referred to the houses in this way, beyond mentioning that the "bad house" felt creepy.

It's my belief that everyone is psychic to one degree or another. Most people simply never become conscious of their psychic impressions. Despite this lack of conscious awareness, the average person will nevertheless respond to psychic impressions. People avoid certain rooms in a house because they just feel "bad." People make instant judgments of others sometimes based on nothing more than the fact that the person had a "bad vibe." Sometimes I think that psychic abilities are hard to accept not because they are rare, but because they are so commonplace that we have developed other names for them.

I suspected that unconscious psychic impressions were at work as soon as I heard the reasoning behind the names for the two cottages at Whitethorn Woods. The students were unconsciously reacting to their impressions of the second house by avoiding it and refusing to sleep in it. Their unconscious impressions were then clearly given voice in the apparently arbitrary designation of one house as "good" and the other house as "bad." This put me on the alert for something strange going on in that farther house. As it would later turn out, both houses had their surprises, but it was Whitethorn Woods itself that had the most in store for its visitors.

Of course, the fact that people naturally found the "bad house" creepy made our jobs much easier. When the kids from inner-city Cleveland were bussed back to town after a fun-filled afternoon in the country, we then had a few hours to ramp things up in the "bad house" to make it as spooky as any of us wanted. For the rest of the weekend, the property was open to students from our college as part of our own Halloween festivities. For these nights, there was a bonfire with the traditional roasted marshmallows and spiced cider, and we put every effort into making the "bad house" as genuinely scary as possible for those who chose to venture into it.

This didn't take much doing. While we were still in the planning stages of this grand Halloween weekend, most of us found that we did not like being left in the "bad house" alone. There was nothing overtly scary in the house at this time, unless you counted the taxidermied deer's head and the freakish number of spiders that had taken up residence in the corners. Our job initially was just to clean the place out, and from the layers of dust it really seemed like the house had been closed up and left empty all season. Again, beyond the fact that one cottage was located beyond a little footbridge, I never could figure out any rational reason behind this disuse. The so-called "good house" was obviously lived in, and the only part of that building that attracted spiders was the basement. The "bad house" just seemed different across the board.

Everyone, male and female alike, was more nervous and far less talkative when they were in the "bad house." And we were constantly having mishaps. On Friday afternoon, a relatively new tape player ate a brand-new tape of music we were considering using for atmosphere at the house at night. This was a tape of chants by the Gyuto monks, purchased by me the day before and played several times without incident on my stereo at home. Light bulbs, which worked fine the first time we turned them on, often blew out when we turned them back on later when it was starting to get dark.

And then there was that state-of-the-art security system. Identical units were installed by the university to protect both houses from trespassers. We had no troubles whatsoever from the unit in the "good house." The "bad house," however, was another story. On several occasions, the digipad refused to take the code, locking us all out of the house. More disturbing were the times when the security system malfunctioned and locked us in. This most often happened once it started to get dark outside and we were all eager to return to the cozier sanctuary of the "good house." I just couldn't shake the feeling that the "bad house" wanted to keep us in there all night.

The security system in the "bad house" also had a habit of making beeps we couldn't quite explain and going off even when no one had gone in or out of the doors to which it was attached. On one hand, I have to admit that none of us was completely familiar with the system, and some of our problems might have resulted from nothing more mysterious than user error. And yet the system hooked up to the "good house" was identical, and we had no such problems over there.

The "bad house" was also plagued with disappearances. Props, tape, and personal articles would be laid down one minute and gone the next. This happened throughout our preparation of the "bad house" for the haunted weekend. Most of the people working in the houses were young—as college students, nearly all of us were between eighteen and twenty-two. It could be said that we were excitable and impressionable. Many people would have doubted our ability to make sound judgments about our experiences purely based on our ages alone. And yet we were there to make a haunted attraction—not ghost-hunt. We had not come seeking an actual haunting, and most of the people present flatly refused to believe in anything supernatural.

Our director at the time was a no-nonsense senior on an ROTC scholarship who had every intention of becoming a decorated military officer. He repeatedly declared that he did not believe any of the stories he'd heard about Whitethorn Woods (stories that he would then fail to elaborate on). Over the days that we were on the property, whenever we would come to him with a strange experience, he would shake his head and berate our silly belief in ghosts. At one point, he even suggested that mice, not ghosts, were responsible for the articles being lost in plain sight. According to him, the rodents were not only dragging off rolls of duct tape and entire flashlights when we weren't looking—they were conveniently putting these things back several hours later in a different spot!

Disturbances or not, we eventually got the "bad house" up to par and went on with the weekend. As our university actually had some difficulty in getting students to volunteer their time out at Whitethorn Woods, I canvassed my contacts at some of the other local colleges, and got volunteers from Case Western Reserve University and Cleveland State to come out to help for the weekend. Most of these other students belonged to a local Pagan organization, and they were thrilled at the thought of spending Samhain, the Pagan holiday celebrated on Halloween, with bonfires and a romp in the woods.

Like the "bad house," a portion of the woods themselves were set up to be part of the haunted attraction. There were paths and trails in the woods that covered the property, and one trail in particular looped around the pond to end at the back door of the "bad house." This trail definitely took the scenic route to get from one house to the other, passing through a section of the forest. For the purpose of the haunted attraction, it was perfect, because it gave a lengthy lead-in where we could build suspense and use the "bad house" as a kind of grand finale.

Since I was working in the "bad house," I was not present with anyone who prepared the woods themselves. I had walked through the woods once or twice, but I was not stationed there, and I never witnessed any of the events in the forest firsthand. However, most of the students who worked that part of the property reported feelings of being watched. Several said they heard unusual sounds. The most frequently reported sound was a kind of moaning noise, and several people reported hearing someone walking through the forest, only to look up and see that no one was there. I discounted some of these reports, chalking most of their "strange sounds" up to the fact that they simply weren't accustomed to being out in the woods. Trees sigh, leaves rustle, and squirrels as well as other small animals can often make noises that seem ominous or inexplicable to those unfamiliar with such things. Several of the trees out on the Whitethorn acreage had also grown very close together, and when the wind kicked up, it would make the trunks of the twined trees rub together, resulting in a pretty eerie groaning sound. As unsettling as that sound could be, it was nevertheless perfectly natural in origin. When a group of students came out of the woods, shaken and white-faced and certain that someone had been following them on the trail, Mr. ROTC made it clear that all they had been hearing were raccoons or squirrels, romping in the leaves. Supposedly, there was quite a lot of wildlife in residence at Whitethorn Woods. Oddly, however, none of us ever saw any evidence of these animals. Not even the ubiquitous squirrels. The only living creatures any of us saw while we were out there was a largely tamed flock of ducks that came up to the dock of the "good house" and begged for handouts.

Even so, for people who are unfamiliar with the woods, a forest can be a very alien and intimidating place, especially once night has fallen. Most of the university students, who had volunteered to lurk in costume in the forest with only a glow stick or flashlight to light their way, were probably having second thoughts about the arrangements once twilight started to fall. For this reason, I had stocked the woods almost entirely with my Pagan friends, because they were not only familiar and at ease in such a setting but also because more than one of them had had experience working professionally in haunted houses in the area. They loved the woods, and they weren't afraid of lurking in dark corners to later jump out at a passing group of people to yell "boo."

While Joe and Jane Average are largely unconscious of their latent psychic perceptions, the vast majority of modern Pagans tend to be very open about their psychic gifts. In my experience, a great number of people who become Pagan or Wiccan do so often because they are sensitive to otherworldly phenomena, and they have had experiences that most other religions might discourage or condemn. A fundamental part of the Pagan religion involves learning how to perceive and interact with the spirit realm, how to recognize and differentiate between its denizens, and how to affect the otherworldly themselves. Although my friend Evan was part of the Pagan group that came along to Whitethorn, he was not a good example of their group. Most of these people struck me as level-headed individuals who were serious about their religion. Evan, on the other hand, was often a touch too excitable about just about everything.

Admittedly, when Evan came to me with tales of some mysterious power walking out in the woods, belief was not my first reaction. However, when the other Pagans who were staffing the woods corroborated some of his experiences and added a few of their own, I began to take notice. For the most part, they simply repeated what the city-bred students from my own college had been saying every time they stepped out into the woods. Something was watching them, and a few of my Pagan friends had the feeling that it did not appreciate our presence.

If that unseen force was preparing to do something that night, most of us missed it. Due to some conflicts among the staff, I opted to drive back to my apartment Friday night with most of my Pagan friends in tow. Though there was room for everyone at the "good house," some of the students from my college clearly resented the presence of outsiders, and this made my Pagan friends rather uncomfortable. I also did not want to stay because Mr. ROTC and a friend of his had gone into town to purchase some beer. Since alcohol was prohibited on the property and most of the students were underage, I wanted no part of the resulting party.

My group returned later the next afternoon. We helped with some cleanup, did repairs to some of the displays in the woods, then worked on costuming and make-up to get everyone ready for their final night at Whitethorn Woods.

There were not as many students the second night of the event as there had been the first. Our student body was notorious, at least among its own, for its general apathy toward just about any university-sponsored function outside of sports events. It really seemed like no one but those of us who were already present wanted to celebrate Halloween at Whitethorn Woods. As a result, the students in the woods spent a good portion of the night sitting at their stations either in pairs or alone with nothing to do. We eventually called it a night early, and I sent one of the guides to go around and collect the actors from the woods. We all gathered round the bonfire to spend the remainder of the night toasting marshmallows and drinking cider and hot cocoa.

Everyone was glad to be out of the woods, but no one so much so as my Pagan friend Cerridwen. She was very pale and unusually quiet as she walked back from her station, and she kept to herself for the first few hours after emerging from the woods. I was a little concerned by her uncharacteristically reticent behavior, and I was afraid that one of the students from my college had said something uncomplimentary to her. Considering the tensions we'd noted the night before, this seemed highly plausible. For her part, Cerridwen sat quietly, staring deeply into the fire. Every once in a while she would look up and stare across the flames and into the woods. Finally, in somber, hollow tones, she called me over to her side.

"I really appreciate the chance to be out here, close to Gaia, for Samhain," she began. "But I don't want you to ever bring me here again."

"If anyone said anything to you about your religion, I'll go have a talk with them," I assured her. "They're just being small-minded and unfair."

But it wasn't that. Cerridwen had been unsettled by something far more frightening than a few bigoted college students.

Apparently, like just about everyone else, she had experienced uneasy feelings all weekend long. She refused to go into the "bad house," even though I had made no mention to her (or to any of the Pagans I'd brought) that we thought that house was actually haunted. Even so, she had developed an immediate aversion to the "bad house." She had volunteered to be stationed in the woods, but even there she felt that something was wrong. Several times when setting her section up in the late evening and twilight, she thought she heard voices and the sound of approaching feet. She automatically assumed it was some of the other volunteers, but eventually it became clear that no one was around. It should be mentioned that her station was the first manned station on the forest path, and since we had a whole lot of forest and only a few actors to stock it, her station was separated by quite a distance from the next manned station. Once or twice, after hearing someone calling in the woods nearby, she ran over to the next station to see who had called, but Colin, the actor closest to her, had been silently occupied in setting up his own station.

Cerridwen probably would have been fine with just the noises and the voices, had she not perceived such an overwhelming feeling of the threat coming from the woods. She felt like there were constantly eyes upon her—not just from one source but from many things, and none of them happy about her presence. Although Cerridwen was one of the few volunteers who had actually grown up in a rural setting, she felt like an interloper in these woods, despite the fact that, when she was younger, she had often roamed similar forests at night without fear. Something about Whitethorn Woods was different.

Although she didn't like the place, Cerridwen stuck it out the entire weekend because she had given her word to help out. She experienced various phenomena both nights that she was out in the woods. She saw lights, very faint and bluish in color, moving through the forest. These were very deep within the trees, located in the opposite direction as the trail used by the students. The lights moved silently, gliding singly or in groups. After witnessing this phenomenon Friday night, she attempted to search the area where she was certain she'd seen the lights. This area proved to be impassable, clogged as it was with the brambles and thorn trees that gave Whitethorn Woods its name. Furthermore, the lights used by the students and their guides were either standard flashlights or those bright green glow sticks often used by children when trick-or-treating. We had bought them in bulk, and there was not a blue one in the box. I'd helped pass them out myself, so I knew this with certainty.

By the second night, Cerridwen had gotten tired of ghost lights and whispering voices that she never seemed able to understand. Before twilight fell on Whitethorn, she took the time to draw a circle of protection around herself. She also performed a few simple rituals of warding that she knew. She was determined not to step out of that circle all night long. She simply did not trust the things that edged upon her perception in the woods out there. The non-human residents of Whitethorn Woods apparently took her circle as a challenge, however. As Cerridwen huddled safely ensconced in her circle, the auditory and visual phenomena grew even more intense. Finally, about an hour before everyone was called back to the "good house" and about thirty minutes after the last group of students had gone through, all the woods around her grew hushed and still. A terrible tension seemed to fill the air. Then there was a noise that she could only describe as a shrieking. She could not tell whether she actually physically heard it or simply felt it tear through her. She thought she saw something darker than everything else move out of the deeper part of the woods. She could not describe its exact shape, only that it seemed to be flying very rapidly straight toward her. She was absolutely certain that it was neither an owl nor a bat nor any natural creature.

Seeing this, Cerridwen buried herself into the dirt in the midst of the circle she had made for herself and covered herself up in her cloak. Then she felt the intimidating intruder pass directly over her. There was a rushing sound, like a very strong wind, which seemed to surround her for a moment and block everything else out. She remained face-down in the dirt and huddled in her cloak for about forty-five minutes, so terrified that she was unable to move or call out. Finally, when I sent the guide to go get everyone, she followed him through the woods to each successive station, not daring to even walk back to the inviting glow of the bonfire by herself.

In her opinion, Whitethorn Woods was not merely haunted. It was infested with what she described as dark fey. She felt that this was their land, somehow sacred to them, and we were intruding. The spirits resented our intrusion and sincerely wanted to scare us off. Most tales of faeries come from Celtic Ireland, but the concept of the fey is fairly universal. They are generally perceived as nature spirits, native to wild places. They often possess a mischievous bent, and they can be resentful of the presence of humans. Nearly every culture around the world has tales of beings like this, and while the names attributed to them certainly differ, their essential nature remains the same.

Most of the other Pagans present agreed with Cerridwen. Significantly, the thorn trees throughout the property are strongly associated with the fey. Halloween, better known to most Pagans as Samhain, was a Celtic holiday when the wall between the worlds was believed to grow thin. Halloween night was a time when the spirits of the dead roamed the land, and it was also one of the traditional times for a phenomenon known as the "hosting of the sidhe" (an event eloquently described by W. B. Yeats in a poem of the same name). In some of the legends, the fey would fly through the air in a massive, rushing group, picking up any nighttime travelers unfortunate enough to be in their way. During this "hosting of the sidhe," the fey would carry their hapless victims along for a wild and terrifying ride, only to deposit them hours later in some remote and desolate location, frequently miles from their original position.

Fortunately for my friend Cerridwen, she ducked—perhaps just in time to avoid being carried away by something large, unfriendly, and entirely otherworldly. She refused to ever return to the property, lest the spirits she sensed there decide to take a second shot. For my part, I could not quell my curiosity about what really walked the woods at Whitethorn. I was not done with this deceptively bucolic plot of land and, as events would later prove, it was also not done with me.

Cleveland's
Angel of Death

When I was first beginning to seriously investigate the nature of hauntings, I attended a lecture by a local paranormal investigator. She presented some views I hadn't encountered before, and she had some especially strong opinions on cemeteries. Essentially, she told the audience that all of the associations between ghosts and grave-yards are nothing but myth. Spirits don't like to hang around the remains of their bodies. She offered the opinion that ghosts were more inclined to haunt the places where they died. She found the notion of a ghost haunting a cemetery about as likely as the spirit of a cow haunting a side of beef.

Since that lecture, I've learned that this is not entirely the case. I suppose if a cemetery were nothing but a heap of disused bones that everyone simply cast aside, spirits would have little reason to linger there. But cemeteries, by their very nature, remind us of the dead. In a Chinese household, one might maintain a family shrine to one's ancestors so that they feel present in one's life. But here in our Western culture, we go to the cemetery to visit our dead. Some people go so far as to treat gravestones almost like one-way telephones, stopping by the cemetery for a visit to tell Grandma or Uncle Bob what's been going on in their lives. It may seem overly simplistic, but because we, the living, see cemeteries as places where we can commune with the dead, our very belief encourages spirits to gather there. We rarely allow the dead any other space in our lives. Why would they not gather in the one space that we do set aside for them?

Of course, at the time that I attended her speech, I was certain that anyone expert enough to present on a topic had to know more about the subject matter than I did. So I took her words to heart, becoming less inclined to investigate any hauntings reportedly occurring in local graveyards. Which is why it took me awhile to look seriously into the reports surrounding the Haserot angel.

The Haserot angel is a striking monument located in Cleveland's Lake View Cemetery. The cemetery itself is the kind of Victorian-era necropolis one would expect to find in some elegant Old World city—certainly not in the heart of a Rust Belt city like Cleveland. And yet all 285 acres of this grand necropolis are nestled in the very heart of Cleveland, just a short walk from University Circle and Little Italy. Established in 1869, the cemetery feels more like an open-air art museum than a graveyard. It stands as a monument to an important era of American history. Captains of industry, pioneers of technology, educators, artists, and statesmen are all buried in this gorgeous city of the dead. The tallest obelisk of its kind was erected as a memorial to philanthropist John D. Rockefeller, who lived for a time on Cleveland's famous "Millionaire's Row" on nearby Euclid Avenue. A chapel with artwork by stained-glass master Louis C. Tiffany stands in honor of Jeptha Homer Wade, a founder of Western Union and the first president of the Lake View Cemetery Association. James A. Garfield, the ill-fated twentieth president of the United States, was laid to rest in scenic Lake View.

Other tombs and gravesites house such historic personages as Newton Diehl Baker, who served as Woodrow Wilson's secretary of war throughout World War I; John Milton Hay, who served as private secretary to Abraham Lincoln and later as secretary of state for President McKinley; and Garrett A. Morgan, renowned black inventor who created the tricolor traffic lights that have become a mainstay in every city across America. Even the ashes of "untouchable" Eliot Ness, the man who toppled Al Capone's Chicago crime syndicate, can be found within Lake View's looming walls.

And, hidden among all this grandeur, a silent bronze angel keeps watch over a family tomb.

The angel was commissioned by Francis Henry Haserot for his beloved wife, Sarah. Francis was a son of German immigrants who went from working a humble paper route at age seven to being tapped by President McKinley for responsibilities in Puerto Rico after the Spanish-American War. Sarah was the daughter of Cleveland judge Henry McKinney, and she died more than twenty years before Francis did. Francis never remarried, and in many ways the statue that guards her grave can be seen as a testament to his grief for the loss of his wife. Constructed of bronze with a polished granite base, the statue depicts an almost life-sized angel with outstretched wings. The angel gazes out over the family plot with eyes that seem to penetrate eternity. Its hands rest on an upended torch, which represents the life recently snuffed out. The statue, crafted by artist Herman N. Matzen in 1923, is titled, appropriately, "The Angel of Death."

Given the stern features and realistic lines of this statue, the Haserot angel would have been intimidating when it was newly constructed in the 1920s. Yet its years of sitting sentry over the Haserot family plot have wrought in the statue a striking transformation. The

Rust Belt city's pollution, combined perhaps with acid rain, have weathered the bronze a rich verdigris. Nowhere is the weathering more apparent than upon the face of this somber statue, where streaks of black oxidation make it appear as if the angel were weeping blackened tears.

Coming upon such a striking monument amidst the tranquil greenery of Lake View would give anyone pause, but starting in the mid-nineties I began to hear rumors that the Haserot angel was haunted.

The first person to tell me about the haunted statue in the graveyard wasn't the most credible of witnesses. The friend of a friend, she was a quintessential wild child, and she was fairly open about her drug use. She had found a way to break into Lake View at night, and she and her friends would frequently use the expansive cemetery grounds as an illicit playground for their indulgences. Given her background, I had to take any encounter she claimed to have had with an entire salt lick, since something as miniscule as a grain of salt would simply not suffice. She claimed to have had extensive conversations with several spirits in the graveyard, all of which I chalked up to elaborate hallucinations. One of her drugs of choice was LSD, and I had watched someone else under the influence of that drug engage in animated conversation with an orange. I knew for certain that the orange was not a willing participant in that conversation, so I doubted the existence of Leela's ghosts. Nevertheless, her description of the Haserot angel made me curious about the monument itself. If nothing else, it seemed like a piece of funerary art I would enjoy photographing.

Eventually, I found time in my busy schedule to visit the cemetery. Leela was undeniably a dubious source when it came to spirit communication, but she had excellent taste in cemeteries. I found myself getting lost in the somber grandeur of Lake View, just amazed by the beauty and diversity of the monuments it held. She had mentioned that the cemetery was large, but I had no idea that it was big enough to house the largest freshwater dam in the county. And unless you stumbled upon this structure, or knew where to look for it, you could still miss it within the lush and wooded acres of Lake View.

I found myself regretting that I had not visited this cemetery sooner. I was glad I'd brought my camera, because I went through roll after roll of film (a fact that nicely dates this story). It took me hours to finally locate the Haserot monument, situated just at the top of a lane that sloped down into a row of mausoleums built into the side of a hill.

Leela had described the monument as a "creepy Gothic angel," and she said it wept black tears. I thought the tears were an exaggeration as well—yet another colorful detail born of one of her late-night trips. But there was no denying it. The eyes of the statue had been stained black through weathering, and rivulets of the same black oxidation ran like the tracks of tears down either side of its face.

I could not shake the impression that the statue was staring at me with its black and empty eyes.

Of course, the statue couldn't really be haunted. The professional paranormal investigator had made that very clear, and I was still laboring under the notion that she must surely know more than me. So I looked for other reasons to explain my impressions. She had explained that we tend to see ghosts in graveyards because we expect them, but those impressions are really just projections of our own fears. I had never been fearful of graveyards, but I could see how it would be easy to project certain expectations onto this statue. The angel was very lifelike, and I decided that this was the only reason that my mind kept insisting that there was an actual presence behind those weather-stained eyes.

I snapped a series of photos of the statue for a magazine I was editing at the time, then packed up and headed home. But I couldn't get the image of that melancholy angel out of my head. Lake View quickly became a favorite haunt of mine, and I returned to the angel again and again, studying its form through the lens of my camera and often feeling compelled to run my hands along the sensuous curve of its great wings. No matter how many times

I tried to tell myself that it was just my imagination, I could never expunge the impression that there was some profound and somber intelligence locked within the sculpted bronze.

By this time, I had begun to doubt the words of the professional investigator just based upon my repeated experience. But I had spent too much time with this particular statue, so I no longer trusted myself to be an impartial judge of its nature. Thus, it became something of a game for me to invite other psychic friends to come along on my photographic forays into the cemetery. I would not tell them about my impressions of the statue. Instead, I would simply talk up the history and artistic significance of Lake View, giving an impromptu tour of the many famous graves. Eventually, I would contrive to lead us to the melancholy angel, and I would carefully watch the reactions of my friends.

Everyone sensed a presence in the statue. Many of them tried to justify the impression based upon the very striking appearance of the angel, just as I had justified it to myself. Some said that they felt a powerful tingling sensation as they approached the monument. Others touched it as I had numerous times, and they reported feeling an unearthly warmth creeping up their hands. This sensation seemed to go far beyond the ambient warmth one might expect to feel from a bronze statue that had been sitting all day in the sun. All felt those eyes fall upon them with the weight of an intelligent and searching gaze.

Eventually, I brought my medium friend, Sarah Valade, to view the statue. We wandered the cemetery on a lovely spring afternoon, startling squirrels from among the beds of ivy that decorate many of the older graves. Finally, we started on the path that led to the Haserot angel. I walked us to the grave from below the hill, and when we rounded the bend, coming over the embankment, Sarah stopped in her tracks and simply stared. Her impression of the spirit was instantaneous.

"He's beautiful!" she cried. "But so sad."

Sarah cautiously stepped forward and gently laid her hand against the statue's cheek.

"This is what you brought me here for, isn't it?" she asked. "I can see why. There's a spirit in here, in the statue. He's a guardian, watching over this place. But he's not a living person. I know this is going to sound strange, but it's like he's a part of the statue, like the statue itself has a soul."

As I grew more confident in the fact that there was a real haunting going on, I began to mention the monument when I spoke at some local paranormal groups. This led even more area psychics and ghost-hunters to visit the monument at Lake View, all of whom agreed that a presence resided in the angel of bronze. Independent of Sarah's impressions, I kept hearing people describe the spirit in the statue as a "guardian" and something that wasn't human. One psychic with a fairly strong background in New Age thought proclaimed that the spirit in the statue was a bona fide angel who had come to keep watch over the slumbering dead of the cemetery. I was pretty sure that real angels had better things to do than baby-sit dead people from inside a statue at a cemetery, but the impression meant a lot to her. At the end of the day, her impression still boiled down to the same thing that I had heard from just about everyone else: what haunted the statue was a guardian spirit, and it wasn't human.

By the time I sat down to write an article on the Haserot angel for *FATE* magazine, I had formulated a theory of my own. This may strike you as sounding just as strange as the idea of a real angel stuck in the statue struck me, but take a few moments to hear me out.

Cemeteries are cities of the dead. They are spaces set apart from the world of the living where we can go to commune with those who are no longer a part of that world. If we assume no other significance beyond their psychological impact, cemeteries are still places where we naturally project our expectations of communication beyond the Veil. We invest them with belief, and belief has a certain power of its own. We naturally approach the monuments that mark individual graves as symbols representing the dead interred beneath. They are our windows or our gates that allow us to communicate—if not to the people themselves, then to their memories.

Every single person who visits a grave imbues it with a modicum of belief.

Extending this backwards, to the very creation of the marker itself, it is not unthinkable that a patient and focused artist might also imbue his or her work with intent and belief. Matzen, the sculptor responsible for the Haserot angel, was well known for his talent, and he produced a number of striking monuments. Each of these demonstrates a level of hands-on care that we simply do not see in modern markers produced artificially with computerized engraving techniques. How many of the masterworks enshrined in museums seem to breathe with a life of their own—or, more appropriately, breathe with the life given them by the artist who created them in the first place?

If Sarah's impressions were correct, how does a statue come to have a soul? I think that it is possible that some essence or energy was imbued in the statue by its creator—perhaps not consciously, but simply as a result of the very process of creating a work of art. This little seed of being was then nurtured over subsequent visits by friends and family members who projected their belief and intents upon it. I don't think they had to project a belief in its essential reality in order to help build what people now sense in that statue. All they had to believe in was its significance. The statue is very obviously a guardian. It was crafted to resemble the very angel of death. After the family, each and every single person, unaffiliated with the Haserot line, who has since come to stop and gaze upon the statue, whose depthless eyes stare unblinkingly back—they all have been touched by that semblance, and each of them has added belief and energy of their own.

There is no denying that the statue, by the very nature of its form, inclines its viewers to perceive it as more than just a work of stone and bronze. And I still believe that the appearance of the statue itself plays into the haunting that people now associate with it. But these days, I think it is more than mere psychology. We are not simply projecting an image or an expectation on a mute yet striking object. For nearly a hundred years, the statue has been invested with such belief that it has grown beyond the life-less bronze. Call it a construct, a residue, or even a memory ghost; something haunts the angel of death in Cleveland, and while it may not be human itself, I have no doubt that it had its origins in humanity.

Mean
Spirited

For over a hundred and fifty years, Columbus was the site of the Ohio Penitentiary, a huge stone edifice established in 1834 to house the state's criminals. In 1983, due to changing prison policies, as well as the opening of the new Lucasville prison, the Ohio Penitentiary closed its doors. The last prisoners were scheduled to be out of the building by December 31, 1983, although complete removal did not occur until later the next year. After 1984 the building stood empty in downtown Columbus. In 1995 the state purchased the derelict property. The original intent was to renovate the building, but these plans were abandoned as the arena district in Columbus grew, demanding more space and more facilities.

In 1998 demolition began on the historic prison that once housed novelist O. Henry (for embezzlement) and Sam Sheppard, the doctor whose wife's murder inspired *The Fugitive*.

Although demolition began in 1998, the crumbling remains of the penitentiary were still visible in a fenced-off lot adjacent to the arena district as recently as the summer of 2005. Bricks, bits of metal, and stone architectural devices lay scattered among the broken walls of the once-imposing edifice, with cranes and other construction machinery closing in on the last few portions of still-standing wall.

It was in this state that my friends Kristen and Amber, like so many Columbus residents, decided that they needed a few souvenirs. Many Ohio residents had sought bricks from the structure in order to hold on to a portion of this historic site. However, Kristen and Amber were more interested in ghosts than they were in history. The penitentiary, like so many old prisons from its day, had a reputation for being haunted. Of course, there's nothing shocking in the notion that a prison may be haunted. Aside from the typical riots, suffering, and abuse that occurred within the prison walls over its hundred-and-fifty-year lifespan, 315 prisoners were put to death at the penitentiary, first being hanged in a gallows located within the prison walls and later coming to an equally grisly end in the electric chair. In addition to the inmates who were sentenced to death, 322 prisoners and workers lost their lives there in a 1930 fire—a blaze that remains the worst prison fire in U.S. history.

Fearless in their ghost-hunting—as well as their disregard for the law—Kristen and Amber spied a gap in the fence and exhorted all of us to sneak through. It was a bright, hot August afternoon, and security guards and even Columbus police officers were gathered nearby, working crowd control on the concert that had brought us to this portion of the city in the first place. Not being one for criminal trespass, no matter how fitting it might be to break the law when pillaging an old prison, I declined the invitation, as did our other companions. Undaunted, Amber and Kristen darted into the construction site in broad daylight. Picking their way among the crumbling bits of masonry, they tried to open themselves up to any lingering impressions still stamped upon the broken, scattered stones. Their goal was not only to bring back a piece of the penitentiary. They wanted a souvenir that had a little spirit left in it.

If I was incredulous that the two just waltzed onto a restricted construction site in broad daylight with police not thirty yards away, I was dumbfounded by their choice in souvenirs. Not content with any mere brick, Kristen and Amber had uncovered several huge urn-shaped carvings that had undoubtedly stood on the roof of the building. They wrestled with one that was simply too big for the both of them to carry, leaving it in favor of a few smaller pieces. Even so, the stone decoration that Kristen ultimately lugged home was a good-sized specimen, at least two feet high and weighing twenty or thirty pounds, if not more.

Very proud of her souvenir, Kristen immediately gave it a place of honor on the bookshelf next to her bed. Once the piece was properly enshrined and in no danger of falling anywhere, Kristen scurried over to her computer, eager to reread online articles about the history of the place. It was unlike her to be so open about her fascination with hauntings, but it had been a long and strange year.

I had been called over to Kristen's apartment several times to investigate poltergeist activity. The apartment itself was in the renovated attic of an old home, and the rest of the house had been parceled up into apartments as well. It was clear from the aged banister on the stairs and scant few other remaining details from the house's prime that, at one time, it was a gorgeous and very expensive home. However, at this point in its life, the house was rundown, a mere shadow of its former glory, standing among other houses similarly fallen in a rough neighborhood just on the edge of campus.

It is important to note that Kristen herself did not originally call me in to investigate the activity. Kristen's roommate, Crystal, who had originally lived in the apartment below this one, had asked me to look into sounds and the sense of a presence that seemed to come from a closet in her bedroom. When the attic apartment became available and she decided to move there, Crystal felt sure that her haunting would be at an end, as everything in her apartment seemed tied to that closet. As far as Crystal's case goes, the best I could do was verify that there was something odd about the closet. I slept over a few times and heard the sounds myself, watching even as the closet door banged open from the inside. Crystal had cats, which I suspected at first, but when I was there myself, I was able to verify that no cats were responsible for the strange sounds and movements within the closet.

Crystal wanted the presence gone, but no matter what I did, it seemed to return. I had called in another friend who was more skilled at spirit removal, but he also had a tough time with the closet. One thing I learned from his investigation was that the closet opened up onto a dead space in the house. Somehow in the course of the renovations, the builders had put this closet in to complete the bedroom, but it did not fit precisely with the original layout of the house. The back of the closet was nothing but a piece of plywood separating the closet proper from a gaping, empty space that was filled with cobwebs and debris. It was pitch black in that small, hidden space, and even a flashlight had trouble illuminating it enough to show just how far back into the bowels of the house it led. My fellow investigator, a stalwart fellow who is not easily disturbed, picked up such a negative feeling from the closet that he abandoned any further searches into the dark null-space. His best advice to Crystal was to move.

And move she did, getting the apartment above with Kristen, a young artist who scoffed at the idea of a real haunting. Kristen loved a good ghost story as much as the next person, but a previous set of friends had soured her on any serious considerations of psychic phenomena. Her old group of friends had been the sort of believers who credulously attributed every little sound and creak of a house to a ghost, seeing the paranormal everywhere. Kristen was levelheaded enough to realize that most of their spooky experiences were ordinary things trumped up by fevered imaginations seeking something magickal in the world.

Because of her friends' delusions, when I met Kristen she was an avowed skeptic. It was only through meeting her and gaining her trust that I learned that she herself had experienced strange phenomena several times in her life. Her disdain for people who made such a big deal of hauntings and the like kept her from talking openly about these experiences with any but her closest friends.

For these reasons, Kristen did not immediately speak to anyone about the things she was experiencing in the new apartment. Most of the incidents were harmless: lights going on and off, her closet door opening and closing itself, the door to her bedroom behaving similarly. Small items frequently disappeared, only to reappear later in improbable spots. Some of this Kristen merely chalked up to her own problems. With an inoperable brain tumor nestled at the base of her skull, Kristen had some issues with her short-term memory. The tumor often interfered with her sense of balance as well, and so Kristen had learned to not always trust her impressions. All of this, combined with her learned skepticism, kept Kristen silent through several unusual occurrences.

Crystal was another matter entirely. A highly emotional, very sensitive young woman, Crystal was also one of those people who desperately wanted to believe. Throughout her life she had dabbled in the occult, and it was often at her urging that Kristen reluctantly participated in Ouija-board sessions, attempting to contact the spirit—or spirits—in their home. Interestingly, most attempts at communicating through the Ouija board yielded no results. Either the planchette stubbornly refused to move, or the responses would be gibberish. The sessions never lasted very long, as both Crystal and Kristen would grow frustrated by the attempt.

The very lack of communication through the Ouija board told me something important about this particular haunting. In my previous experiences, when there is a sensitive believer like Crystal present at a haunting, the desire for proof can be so strong as to cause the person to consciously or unconsciously invent experiences. If either of the young women had been confabulating elements of the haunting, this would have been the perfect time for one or the other of them to use the Ouija board to elaborate the hoax. And yet the spirits were strangely silent.

Meanwhile, events continued to occur. Crystal began having terrible dreams where she was being attacked by a malevolent presence and held down on her bed. Many of these dreams seemed to be night terrors, where she felt as if she were wide awake yet still experiencing the elements of the dream. She never reported seeing her attacker; it was always a presence of force that preyed upon her, horrific and suffocating. When she experienced these attacks, she explained that she had subsequent difficulty in waking up, and she would feel drained. The dreams got so bad, and so consistent, that she consulted a therapist about them. The therapist related them to a hag attack, a classic nightmare experience that is believed to occur in the hypnagogic state between waking and sleep. Given the way Crystal felt drained afterward, especially considering that she was no stranger to energy work and thus was a good judge of the state of her energy, I suspected more was at work than simple night terrors. The type of experience she was describing could also be related to psychic attack.

Kristen was also having similar dreams, although she did not talk about them. She would be confronted with the most horrific images as she slept, struggling but failing to pull herself out of the terrible dreams. Upon waking, she would feel exhausted. Her head pounded and her thoughts felt sluggish. Some of this she attributed to her brain tumor. Migraines were a common experience for her as the slowly growing mass pressed against the inside of her skull. Even so, the pain and exhaustion that followed these night terrors seemed different—different enough for this reluctant skeptic to finally say something when she heard about her roommate's similar experiences.

I came over and set up wards in Crystal's bedroom. I recommended that she get a dreamcatcher, and I also suggested that she try communicating with the spirit. She pointed out that they had tried communicating through Ouija-board sessions, but my advice was far more pedestrian.

"You're going to feel silly, but just talk to it. Talk out loud and tell it that you know it's here and you're willing to let it stay, as long as it plays by certain rules. Ask it to stop sending you those dreams."

I also suggested that she make an offering of energy, like some Eastern cultures make offerings to the spirits of their ancestors. From the way the women were feeling drained after the dreams, I suspected that the spirit was after sustenance. Strong emotion produces potent energy, and I felt the spirit might be using this as fuel for its other activities. Making a controlled, specific offering and coming to mutually beneficial terms with the spirit might get it to stop taking what it wanted and instead respect the women's space. All of this presumed that the spirit itself was not specifically malevolent so much as misunderstood. I had a hard time accepting that the spirit was "out to get" the women. In my experiences, most spirits that people assumed were evil were simply just trying to exist, like anyone else. Given the fact that all attempts at getting this particular spirit to relocate had failed, I thought it would be best for everyone sharing the space to get along—living and dead alike.

Talking to the spirit did seem to appease it. Although incidents where objects were moved or lights blew out continued, Crystal was resting easier at night. But the peace did not last. Once Kristen brought the piece of the Ohio Penitentiary into their home, the haunting took on a new violence that extended beyond just dreams.

One night, when the two women were in the living room watching television, both of them jumped as something slammed against the inside of Kristen's door. Due to the layout of the attic apartment, Kristen's bedroom opened directly onto the living room. The door was plainly visible, and both women watched it rattle and shake as something on the other side clearly attempted to get out. Although startled, neither of them were exceptionally frightened at this point. They both had cats, and it was logical to conclude that one of the felines had been left in the room when Kristen closed the door. Now, as is common with a determined cat, the animal was trying to set itself free.

The problem with this theory arose when all of the cats in the household rushed into the living room, drawn by the sounds of something scratching and banging on Kristen's door. With all the cats accounted for, the two women were left to wonder whether or not a raccoon had somehow gotten into the attic apartment. They were in the city, just blocks from the campus of the largest public university in the country, so a raccoon was unlikely but not impossible. A raccoon might explain the way the cats alternately approached the door inquisitively, then shied away, afraid.

Abruptly, the scratching stopped. Glancing at her wide-eyed roommate, Kristen got up to open the door. At first, the handle seemed stiff and the door was reluctant to budge. But when Kristen finally threw it open, there was nothing there. The two embarked on a full-scale search of Kristen's room, attempting to locate the source of the disturbance. The room was empty. Convinced that an animal of some sort had to be responsible for the violent movements of the door, Kristen started tapping the walls and searching the back of her closet, to see if there was some way a living creature could have gotten in, and then escaped. This was how they learned that Kristen's closet had a dead space behind it, much like the closet in Crystal's previous apartment one floor below. Curious now, Crystal made a search of the house itself, asking the new downstairs neighbor for a chance to explore her old apartment. What she saw confirmed her suspicions: both closets abutted onto the same unaccounted-for, empty space.

Having seen her share of horror movies, Crystal began to wonder whether or not there was something back there. She couldn't help but conjure visions of a dusty, cobwebbed skeleton entombed in the wall. But exploring the space would require that the young women tear down portions of the walls, and neither wanted to risk their security deposit. They asked me to check things out yet again.

Three different people, myself included, attempted to rid the apartment of this noisy ghost. At the time, no one suspected the pieces of the penitentiary to be involved, as numerous spectral events had already occurred in the house prior to the introduction of these items. I used every method I knew for cleansing a home and driving out unwanted spirits. This would work for a little while, only to have the presence return once I had gone.

Things got pretty intense, and the unexplainable incidents grew stranger and stranger. Kristen woke up one morning to find her arm aching, covered with scratches and bruises. Crystal was quick to blame the spirit, but Kristen tried to convince herself that she had merely thrashed excessively in her sleep, banging her arm against something.

Kristen sent me several photos of the injuries, asking my opinion. I have rarely encountered hauntings in which living people were physically harmed by the dead. As a general rule, spirits can influence energy—making a certain area feel strange, dropping the temperature, interfering with electronic equipment, maybe influencing dreams—but it takes a tremendous amount of energy for a spirit to affect the physical world. A very violent and powerful poltergeist may be able to move small items, like jewelry, dishes, or books. Occasionally, something has the power to move a larger, heavier item, but such occasions are rare. This means that instances where people are physically attacked by spirits are few and far between. That's not to say that no such instances have ever been recorded, but it is a rare spirit that has that kind of power, and malevolence.

I told Kristen that I favored her notion that she had simply thrashed too much in her sleep, but I agreed to drop over to study her bedroom. And this was where I started to revise my opinion. Kristen's bed was just a mattress balanced on top of a bunch of milk crates, so there was neither a headboard nor any proper "edge" to her bed against which she could have so thoroughly bludgeoned her arm. The bookcase that stood next to her bed was the only possible structure she could have banged herself on, and given that none of the figurines or other curios on the bookshelf had been knocked over, I felt it was unlikely that she had hit this with the violence necessary to cause the injuries shown. Additionally, no matter what position I imagined her laying in her bed, the angle was all wrong for the bruises that appeared on her arm.

Communicating with the spirit and making offerings of energy no longer seemed to help. The incidents became so frequent, they would have grown commonplace, but they also grew increasingly bizarre. Crystal had a potted chrysanthemum on the entertainment center. The plant was healthy and well-watered, but one night, after feeling a presence in the living room, Crystal discovered that the plant had shriveled up and gone bone-dry in a matter of hours. She alleged that it had just been watered that evening, and it had been fine earlier in the day. She sent me a photo of the plant to see whether or not I had any explanation.

Kristen had a large glass aquarium with two rats in her bedroom. As the cats were especially interested in the rodents, the lid of this aquarium was a heavy wooden affair, covered with chicken wire and weighted so it could not be knocked off by either cats or rats. Once again, as the women sat in the living room watching television, they heard a strange noise coming from Kristen's room. This was followed immediately by a terrified yowl from one of the cats. The door to Kristen's room was open, and the cat continued to make a terrified, throaty noise.

Fearing that one of the animals was hurt, both women rushed into the room. To their amazement, they found the cat *inside* the rat cage. The rats were staring inquisitively at the cat, but the feline was too terrified to respond. Eyes wide, hair standing on end, the cat was pressed up against the glass on the far end, yowling piteously.

"Serves you right!" Kristen scolded, naturally assuming that the cat had gotten into the rats' cage of its own power.

It was only when she went to get the cat out that she realized the cover was intact. All the weights were still in place and none of the wire offered an opening that the thirteen-pound feline could have wriggled through.

"It teleported?" Crystal joked halfheartedly.

After rescuing the terrified cat, Kristen spent some time going over the aquarium and its lid, but she could find no possible explanation for how the cat had gotten in among the rats.

Kristen reached her limit in this embattled household after the following incident:

After another restless night of disturbing dreams, she woke up suddenly and felt compelled to leave her bed. She went to the bathroom, then searched for the television remote in the living room, hoping to lull herself back to sleep by watching a show or two. She heard a strange grating sound followed by a muffled "thump" coming from her bedroom. Certain the cats had knocked something over, she got up to see what kind of mess she would have to clean up.

When she went into her room, she did not immediately notice what was amiss. She searched all the likely places where the cats could have knocked something over, but she didn't even find a cat present in the room. Puzzled, she went to sit on the edge of her bed, considering trying to go back to sleep. That was when she noticed that the thirty-pound piece of carved stone from the Ohio Penitentiary was no longer resting on her bookshelf. Instead, the entire thing had fallen directly onto her pillow. Had it fallen a few moments before, it would have landed on her head.

Frightened, but still trying to be skeptical, she lifted the heavy stone sculpture up and placed it back on the bookshelf. Then she experimented with how much force it took to actually knock the thing off onto her bed. It took quite a bit of effort. She went so far as to consider the extremely remote possibility that her cat had somehow knocked the massive piece of stonework onto her pillow. But that didn't explain how the row of paperbacks set up next to the stone finial was undisturbed; a cat would have had to stand on these in order to push against the piece of stone.

The second problem evidenced itself when she did knock the piece off onto her bed. Due to the placement of her bed and bookshelf, the heavy stone finial fell, again and again, straight down, landing on the edge of her bed. When it fell on its own, it had landed directly in the middle of her pillow. In order for this to happen, it would have had to fall in an arc, not straight down. Just knocking it over, Kristen could not reproduce this arc of movement. She would have suspected her roommate of playing a prank on her, but Kristen was the only one up; due to the layout of the apartment, Crystal would have had to pass Kristen twice on her way to and from the room—assuming Crystal moved the stone finial. For the first time, Kristen was genuinely scared.

There is no neat ending to this ghost story. Incidents continued to occur, seeming to go through periods of intense activity, then hitting a lull for a short while when little to nothing strange would occur. The introduction of the items from the Ohio Penitentiary seemed to bring about a very intense period of violent activity. I felt there was only a slim possibility that the pieces of the prison were, themselves, haunted. Far more likely in my mind was the notion that these stones still held lingering emotional residues from the prison itself, residues that fed into and fueled a spirit that was already active and present in the apartment.

Both roommates occasionally suspected the other of playing tricks and perhaps adding to the ghostly shenanigans. Especially in the early stages of the haunting, I accepted this as a possibility. I often spent time at the house, observing not only the paranormal "resident" but also watching the roommates when unusual things occurred. I do believe that a few incidents attributed to the ghost had other answers. I'm not entirely convinced that the chrysanthemum wasn't more a victim of forgetfulness than some mysterious force that dried it up all at once. Certainly Crystal became so keyed up from the repeated phenomena that she became inclined to blame the ghost for every odd sound or misplaced set of keys.

For a while, I entertained the theory that Kristen was indirectly responsible for the occurrences, as much of the poltergeist activity seemed focused around her. The vast majority of incidents took place in her room. Her brain tumor offered an intriguing and unique variable in the case. Could the tumor be pressing on some portion of the brain responsible for telekinetic activity? I couldn't even begin to conjecture.

Was there something in the closet—something tied to that dead space in the house? Once we realized that Kristen's closet also opened onto this lost corner of the building, this possibility grew more and more plausible. Quite a number of people had gotten a very bad feeling from that dark, musty space. Interestingly, before the women's lease was up, another company bought the building and began renovations. The repairs were extensive, and rather than wait for all the tenants to leave, workmen started many of these repairs while people were still in residence.

The new owners had a different vision for the house and did not like the many little apartments it had been parceled up into. Walls were knocked down and heretofore blocked-off spaces were revealed in many of the apartments. The construction revealed hidden, dusty dead zones, many of which still had items in them left over from some previous time in the building's past. We learned that the building itself had been erected in the early 1900s, and before the women both moved, they found a lost staircase, a fireplace, and a chimney that had been covered over on their level— and a whole lost section of the house beyond and underneath the closet in Kristen's bedroom.

Visions of a
Distant Land

There are faeries in Hinckley Woods. I feel kind of silly using the word *faeries*, and yet I have no better name for the mercurial spirits that seem to inhabit the forests and meadows of my hometown. They're definitely not human spirits, and yet they are clearly sentient and aware of the other beings around them. Furthermore, they behave with that fickle and enigmatic nature so utterly tied to the fey in traditional folklore. Neither good nor evil, they follow their own agenda; and when their world intersects with our own, it seems that their greatest motivators are equal parts curiosity and mischief.

Of course, when I said, "I think there are faeries in the woods out here," my best friend was immediately incredulous. The best friend in question is Jason B. Crutchfield, a Detroit boy that few would take for a psychic on the first glance. Jay is about my height, which places him around six feet tall, although he carries himself with the air of someone even taller. He's worked as a bouncer for many years, and he outweighs me by almost one hundred pounds of solid muscle. Add to this his goatee, long ponytail, fedora, and black leather duster, and he looks like a character who would be at home in some urban fantasy novel. That, or a biker whose Harley must be in the shop. What he does not look like is someone who practices energy work and occasionally talks to dead people.

Although Jay defies most people's stereotypes of what a psychic should be, he is nevertheless a very gifted and powerful energy worker. He shares many of my talents, including the ability to perceive and interact with spirits. Our friendship is based in part on the talents that we share, but we're also tied together by similar attitudes on those talents. Both Jay and I are naturally skeptical individuals. It's not that we don't want to believe in the paranormal. Rather, neither of us wants to fall prey to blind belief. We question and analyze all of our experiences, double-checking our impressions with one another so that we can remain as objective as possible about our abilities and (hopefully) never fall prey to wishful delusions. We've both seen too much of that in others, and it makes us doubly leery of ever allowing it to develop in ourselves.

Which brings us back to the faeries. I had to immediately assure Jay that I did not, in fact, believe that Tinkerbell was going to flutter out of the trees and land on his hand in a shower of pixie dust. I could tell that he was still skeptical at the concept of faeries, however. Now, Jay is what I like to refer to as a blue-collar occultist, which is to say that most of his knowledge comes from direct personal experience. He knows there are books out there on topics that range from astral projection to faerie guides, but he prefers the hands-on approach to learning. In some respects, he avoids reading all the books that are available because he does not want to build false expectations about his experiences. He wants a clean slate from which to judge things for himself.

In contrast, I'm a reader. I have my experiences and I formulate my ideas about them, and then I have to run out and get my hands on every book ever written on the topic, so I can compare and contrast both my experiences and my conclusions with those of everyone who has explored this territory before. As a result, I had read a great deal of faerie lore by that time, and I tried to explain to Jay how the spirits that I had dubbed "faeries" had earned the moniker largely because their behavior was in keeping with ancient traditions about the fey. They weren't human, and yet they were obviously sentient spirits. They seemed tied to nature, and they preferred wild places rarely frequented by people, although they occasionally ventured into parts of the house. They had mischievous natures and, on the rare occasions that I seemed able to perceive them with my physical sight, they appeared mostly as balls of energy, between three to six inches in diameter. These would flit about the trees or high grass in such a way that it was almost impossible *not* to think of them as faeries. I had owned cats and dogs that responded to the presence of these beings, and in one amusing instance I suspect that one of my cats not only chased one of these ephemeral beings, but he also had the misfortune of actually *catching* the thing. The poor cat spent the next three hours running around madly as if pursued by something that only he could see, eyes wild and tail the size and shape of a bottlebrush. Notably, he did not chase after the shimmering gray blobs of energy that occasionally flitted through our home ever again.

In addition to sometimes appearing as misty gray blobs that *almost* looked tangible, the faeries in Hinckley would sometimes also manifest as tiny little lights that danced in the trees. These could easily be mistaken for fireflies, as they were about the same size, and yet they often appeared in colors that no firefly could boast, including red and blue and even pale shades of lavender. For years I thought fireflies simply came in these colors, and then I learned that the bioluminescence of the firefly almost universally glows a pale yellow-green. That, and the incident with my cat, made me think twice about going out firefly-hunting on warm summer nights. I wasn't sure what the consequences might be if I mistakenly caught a faerie in my net. I didn't think that they were literally *physical* beings, and yet, since I could see their lights in a very physical way, the faeries seemed to nimbly dance around that line between spirit and flesh. My cat's experience only seemed to underscore this puzzling ambiguity.

Jay was still pretty sure that it all came down to little more than fireflies, in the end. Admittedly, this had to allow for the fact that Hinckley had somehow developed divergent species of fireflies that glowed purple and red, but stranger things had happened. In a way, it was easier to believe in the existence of mutant fireflies than it was in the existence of literal faeries. The cat could have just been acting like a cat, which is to say, chasing nothing and ultimately being chased in turn by nothing. Cats sometimes do things like that, as any cat owner knows. The grayish blobs could be anything from dust motes to visual defects, like those strings of dead cells drifting through the inner fluids of the eye that occasionally become visible if conditions are just right. The apparent intelligence of their behavior could be nothing more than mere projection on my part.

I had considered such possibilities myself, of course, and it was only after repeated encounters by myself and others that I'd even reluctantly begun referring to these entities as faeries. The more I read about faerie lore, however, the more I became convinced that these odd little spirits were exactly the things that had inspired much of the faerie folklore that existed. Learning that similar stories existed in cultures beyond the British Isles also helped to shore up this opinion, since it suggested that they were a universal rather than a local phenomenon. But the concept of faeries still remained a little too weird for a boy who grew up in the Motor City.

Then Jay had his own experience with the faeries, and this changed his tune.

It was early one summer in the late 1990s, and I'd arranged a get-together between our large and far-flung group of friends. Jay had come down from Detroit, and one of the evenings we all trooped out to Hinckley Lake for a cookout. Hinckley Lake is a local regional park that surrounds what used to be an old stone quarry. The whole area is full of trees and ledges with some wetlands thrown in for good measure, and it's been a local vacation spot for many, many years. The ninety-acre lake is the crowning jewel of over two thousand acres of parkland. I had been coming to Hinckley Lake since I was a toddler, mostly because the park is only a few miles from my childhood home. One of the things that I liked about Hinckley Lake was the fact that, unlike so many public parks that closed at dusk, this park did not close until eleven p.m. I've always been a night person, and this meant that I could walk alone in the woods after the sun had set and enjoy the nocturnal aspect of the forest, when a completely different population of the local wildlife was out and about.

The park's late closing time was one of the main reasons that our little group chose it as a site for our cookout. We all tended to keep late hours, and we intended to hang out in the park till at least nine p.m. Since we were a group of mostly black-clad Goths, we had chosen a remote little corner of the park in which to congregate, mostly so we didn't end up scaring the locals. This was a heavily wooded area set a little ways back from the lake itself. A stream ran along one side of the area, and there were several ranks of swings tucked in a small clearing in the woods. The trees were so tall here that, even though the picnic area was technically in a clearing, it remained overshadowed by the surrounding foliage. The place lay in cool shadows even at high noon, and only patches of gold-green light made their way to the leaf-carpeted ground.

The problem we ran into with this location was one of lighting. At the time, there were no electric lights in this part of the park. There wasn't even a single streetlamp erected near the parking area. I am very comfortable in low lighting and have excellent night vision, so this didn't really bother me. It was, in fact, why I chose this little corner of the park. My friends, however, Goth or not, were not quite so nocturnally adapted. As the sun began to set, it grew very dark in our section of the woods, and several people began to complain about visibility. The glowing embers in the two or three public grills that we had commandeered were not really helping to illuminate anything, and people were having a hard time navigating around the twisted roots of some of the older trees. To add to the growing discomfort, a bloodthirsty horde of mosquitoes had also descended on the scene almost as soon as the sun kissed the horizon. I'd had the foresight to bring along a few bottles of bug repellent, but these were doing very little to keep the voracious insects at bay.

Subsequently, we started to pack up early and began arranging rides for the out-of-town guests. Jay had driven down with another friend, Patrick, and Patrick approached me, looking for Jay. He'd been searching the crowd, but he couldn't seem to locate him. The clearing we were in was not huge, and so it seemed strange that we had lost sight of Jay. As a staunch city boy, I couldn't imagine him venturing very far into the surrounding woods. And yet, as we looked around, our six-foot-tall biker lookalike was nowhere to be found.

Several people were tired and cranky, and I told them to head out while we looked for Jay. My roommate Paul had come in a separate car, so I sent him off ahead of them, so someone would be home to let them in. Then Patrick and I started to look for Jay. We checked the bathrooms and the area by the swingsets (though the idea of Jay solemnly riding the swings was so improbable that I could barely imagine it). We navigated the rocky embankment that leads down to the stream just in case he was meditating by the water there. Then we circled back to the picnic tables near the parking area, calling his name a few times. Still no Jay.

Patrick was worried, and I was getting a little concerned myself. It's not that either of us thought that Jay might not be able to take care of himself. If he ran into trouble of the two-legged variety, there was no question about who would emerge the victor. But the woods could be treacherous in the dark for someone who did not know his way around. And then there was the lake to consider. There was only one portion of the lake deemed fit for swimming, and that was at the bottom of the man-made waterfall. The rest of the lake was treacherous, filled with rocks and sudden drop-offs into lightless, muddy depths. There were persistent local rumors of multiple drownings in the early years of the park, enough to make even the strongest swimmers wary of its dark, chilly waters.

Jay taking a voluntary dip in the lake was about as likely as Jay riding the swings, but there were some rocky embankments that dropped off into the lake, and if he wandered in that direction and lost his footing, there was a small chance that he could get into trouble. After we'd searched the entire picnic area, Patrick and I turned in the direction of the lake. Beyond the parking area, there was about five hundred feet of flat ground that led first into a stand of trees, then into a very shallow portion of the lake. Most of this was swamp, choked with reeds and cattails. One of the partygoers who had been slow to pack up asked who we were looking for. When we said we were looking for Jay, he mentioned that he'd seen him heading in this direction. No one else in our party had been over there, and the area had been empty of people from the moment we'd arrived. I wasn't entirely certain why Jay would venture in that direction, unless he had gotten bored with things and wanted to take a look at the lake.

Full dark had almost fallen by this point, and Patrick was getting a little frustrated with not being able to see. He decided to go check the truck for a flashlight. I wandered to the far edge of the parking area as I waited for him, peering into the gloom. At this point, it was so dark that all the color had leached from the world. Everything I saw was in varying shades of gray. There were the shapes of a few picnic tables standing out against the deeper shadows. I thought I saw a person standing near one, and I got excited until I realized that it was only one of the public grills. The grill stood much closer to me than the table, but the darkness threw my depth perception off, so that it seemed bigger rather than closer. Squinting again, I could see no one standing in that direction.

Patrick came back, lacking a flashlight. He complained that he could barely see more than a few feet around himself, and he seemed just a touch unsettled by the fact that I could still make out shapes in the darkness. I suggested that we walk up to the other section of picnic tables looking for Jay, but he was reluctant to venture into what he perceived as inky blackness. Instead, we resorted to calling for Jay. We'd called his name a couple of times before in the course of our search, but due to the fact that it was a public park, we had been reluctant to bellow at the top of our lungs. Tired, insect-plagued, and irritable, we now did just that, yelling his name in the direction of the shallow end of the lake.

Eventually, we thought we heard an answer. The sound was distorted, though, and seemed to come from a great distance away. It seemed to take approximately forever, but eventually I could see a shape moving through the darkness. His black clothes made Jay appear like a solid shadow moving out of shadows that were only slightly less dense. He blinked in the gloom, and his face held a bewildered expression that I'd rarely seen on his features.

Grumbling, Patrick said, "Dude, where were you? We've been looking this whole time!"

Jay regarded us both with an air of puzzled introspection. It almost seemed as if he wasn't clearly seeing us. His eyes seemed fixed on some other plane.

"I'm not really sure where I just was," he answered enigmatically.

He didn't talk about it right away, but eventually I learned what had happened that night.

As things started winding down at the picnic, Jay walked past the parking area and toward the second section of picnic tables in order to be alone for a bit. He wanted to get an energetic feel for the area, especially since he had heard me tell so many stories about it. As he headed in that direction, he began seeing fireflies dancing in the direction of the lake. He was entranced by the little glowing swarm, particularly because he noticed that some of them were in colors that he had never seen before. He'd heard my stories about oddly colored "fireflies" in the Hinckley area, but seeing them was another matter entirely. He kept walking closer and closer to the little dancing lights, hoping to be able to catch one in his hands and verify that it was in fact a bioluminescent beetle doing a mating dance and not anything so bizarre as a faerie. But for each step he took forward, the fireflies seemed to retreat the exact same distance. Thus, he never got any closer to the glowing swarm. He noticed that these fireflies didn't seem to blink quite the way he remembered fireflies blinking, and that seemed a little strange as well, but again, not so extraordinary that it seemed obviously otherworldly.

As he walked slowly deeper into this area, the last rays of the sun were slipping behind the horizon. The sun was setting in front and to his left, over a distant finger of the lake. Although all the colors of the sunlight had faded, twilight still settled over the land, and he could see everything clearly in shades of silver and gray. That was when he became more interested in what lay beyond the fireflies' light than in the fireflies themselves. Jay saw a rolling meadow stretched before him, just beyond the slim stand of trees. Fascinated, he paused and studied this, for he did not remember this portion of the terrain. He was pretty sure he had been facing the lake, but instead of water beyond the fringe of trees, what he saw was a twilit field, filled with more of the multicolored fireflies.

Somewhere in this journey, he had begun to feel very disconnected from our bustling party, which he knew should only lie a hundred yards or so to the south. And yet when he listened, he realized that the sounds of people and cars had grown unnaturally distant, as if they were drifting to his ears from miles away. Around him, everything was still and silent, glowing with that silver twilight and speckled with the fireflies that he never seemed quite able to catch. He felt an inexorable pull toward that curious field, but he also felt as if he stood upon a threshold between one world and the next. He could feel something calling him to cross over, but he hesitated, uncertain that he would ever be able to find his way back.

He stood for a while, studying what lay before him. He was filled with wonder as he struggled to comprehend it all. At no point did that eerie twilight fade. Then, distantly, very distantly, he thought he heard his name being called.

When he turned away from the field, he realized that he had strayed very far from the picnic area. The shadows that lay between his location and the parking lot were so deep, he couldn't even see the first group of picnic tables. The sound of his name drifted to him again, and he called back. It seemed as if he were trying to yell across an immense distance.

Turning his back on the fascination of the field and its unlikely fireflies, Jay started walking back in the direction of the party. This seemed to take an unaccountably long time, and he found himself walking through deeper and deeper shadows. Again, he was overcome with that sense of crossing some threshold in reality, and eventually he emerged to see me and Patrick standing near the few remaining cars.

Later, when it was light outside, he went back to the place where he had strayed. He went to the stand of trees that he remembered as bordering the very edge of that eldritch, twilit field. What lay beyond them was a swamp. He spent some time trying to resolve the image of this swamp against the image of the field that lingered in his memory. He considered how he might have possibly mistaken one for the other in the dark, but ultimately he couldn't accept that as an explanation. He has never seen fireflies like that before or since, and it's worth noting that neither Patrick nor myself had seen fireflies in that area at all while Jay was out there.

When Jay told me what he remembered of that night, the experience made perfect sense—if you assume that the fireflies were not in fact beetles doing a mating dance. In the various legends that surround the fey, there are numerous accounts of people being pixie-led. Often, a weary traveler making his way through the woods sees a light in the distance. Assuming that this is a lantern or the light from someone's cabin, he follows it, only to find himself hopelessly lost within a mire or some other treacherous portion of the woods. Other travelers report lights that lead them to the very edge of a cliff, only they see a continuance of the road and nearly step off to their deaths.

Jay's experience is entirely in keeping with this tradition. The "fireflies" led him to the edge of a swamp. He felt compelled to venture into the illusory field, and if he had, at the very least he would have ruined his boots in the muck. But Jay still thinks that if he had stepped forward into that faintly glowing meadow, he would have ended up somewhere else entirely, unable to return to the reality he had known. I, for one, am glad that he turned back when he did.

Closer Than You Think

Some of my haunting investigations have come from referrals. In 1998 an interesting case involving a poltergeist found its way to me through the referral of a mutual friend. The friend knew a young man who was being troubled by a haunting. The young man had heard that I worked with such things, but he was very reluctant to approach me himself. Allegedly, every time he had sought help for his problem, the spirit that was plaguing him would seek revenge by destroying pieces of electronic equipment. The spirit would especially attack devices that enabled the young man to communicate with others. I listened to this, as my friend explained how she had witnessed an entire computer network at a cybercafé crash repeatedly as the young man attempted to explain his situation to another friend over Internet chat. Apparently, he was using the public computers because his computer at home had been fried by a power surge while he was attempting the same thing.

Whenever I am approached with alleged spirit activity, I try to take a skeptical approach, at least at first. This is especially true when people approach me with claims that a spirit is somehow victimizing them. Although the poltergeist phenomenon is well-documented, it has been my experience that full-blown poltergeist activity is very rare. Furthermore, it is uncommon for a spirit to take direct and personal interest in harming an individual, especially someone that the spirit did not know in life.

In the case of this young man, whom I'll call Brandon, I wasn't sure what to think. The friend who recommended him to me was a kindhearted soul who had been led astray in the past by others who appeared earnest but whose motives were anything but sincere. Given that she was the initial judge of Brandon's situation, I approached my initial meeting with him with great caution. There were a number of details in his case that set off alarm bells for me. Brandon was quite young and had been homeless recently. At the very least, this told me that he was financially irresponsible. The way the incidents had been related to me, at least those that were connected with attempts at communication, seemed calculated to produce an aura of dark mystery around both Brandon and his ghost. By this point in my career as an investigator of strange phenomena, this kind of paranormal grandstanding made me very suspicious indeed.

Our mutual friend was acting as a go-between, another fact that was beginning to make me suspicious of Brandon. Despite my misgivings, I felt that Brandon deserved at least an hour of my time. He would not contact me by e-mail—allegedly because the spirit had such an influence over computer systems that he was certain that any attempt would fail. He was reluctant even to contact me by phone, but my friend managed to convince him to do so, on the basis that I had a landline and not a cell phone. Apparently, in a previous attempt to communicate about the spirit using a cell phone, the phone itself had malfunctioned and become unusable.

Our mutual friend kept working on him until Brandon finally made the call. I was out when Brandon called. I just missed answering the phone, and walked in about halfway through his answering-machine message. As soon as he hung up, I played the message back to get his number, then picked up my phone to give him a call. There was no dial tone. This did not bother me at first, because I assumed that I had simply picked the phone up too soon after it disconnected, and somehow this prevented it from connecting to another line. I hung the phone back up, waited a few moments, and tried again. Once more, there was no dial tone.

Confused now, I walked over to my neighbor's apartment and knocked on the door. His phone was working just fine, and so I used it to contact Brandon. There was a club we both frequented, and we agreed to meet there. In the meantime, my phone still refused to work. I had said nothing of this to Brandon, refusing to feed into his belief that the spirit haunting him somehow had the power to attack his methods of communication. I still was not convinced.

It took a visit from the phone company to get my phone working again. The repairman was a little baffled by the problem. I did not understand everything he tried to explain to me, but I grasped that something had become detached, and that this particular something was inside a sealed box where it was highly unlikely for it to become detached. The phone repairman said that the piece looked like it had been snapped off, and yet only the phone company had access to the box where these components were stored; the smaller interior box that housed this particular component was even harder to get into.

I spent a little while trying to understand this. Admittedly, my first thoughts were suspicious ones. Our mutual friend had told me that Brandon was good with computers. From her perspective, this made it all the more baffling when computers mysteriously malfunctioned around him. From my perspective, it made me wonder just how adept he was at faking such malfunctions. Although it bordered on the paranoid, when my phone first malfunctioned I wondered how much knowledge a hacker needed to have in order to cut off just one phone line.

If Brandon was really confabulating his story and he really wanted me to believe in the controlling and malevolent nature of this particular spirit, shutting down my phone line immediately after a call was a very dramatic touch. Of course, all of these thoughts came before the repairman explained that the source of my phone woes was a physical one. A small part of me still wondered whether or not someone could have tampered with the phone box. It was not stored in my apartment itself, but on the lower level with the hot water heaters and other things. If someone really knew what they were looking for, I imagined that they could have found it.

Eventually, I brushed off the incident with the phone as nothing more than coincidence. I prepared myself to go to my meeting with Brandon with an open mind—neither too credulous nor too critical. I waited at the club for him for several hours. However, Brandon did not show. I spoke with our mutual friend who was also there, and she explained that he had encountered a problem with his ride at the last minute. She apologized for him, but I was back to wondering just how many of these endless mishaps were a calculated effort on Brandon's part to build a mystery and suspense.

Later the next week, Brandon called me again on my newly repaired phone line. This time, I was around to answer it. We spoke briefly and arranged another meeting for the weekend. I hung up and didn't think about Brandon's alleged ghost until I went to order pizza several hours later. The phone, once more, was dead. This time I just assumed that the repairman had done a shoddy job and the same thing was broken again. I immediately marched over to my neighbor's apartment, asked to borrow the phone, and gave the phone company a piece of my mind. The poor girl on the other end apologized profusely and agreed to have someone out first thing the next day.

A different repairman came out. He fixed the phone, and came inside to explain to me what he had done. He had the work order from the previous repair in hand and was quick to explain to me that the new problem had nothing at all to do with the previous fix. I pointed out to him that this was the second time I had paid for a repairman in as many weeks. I asked for him to guarantee to me that it would not break again, and he just shrugged his shoulders.

"I don't know what to say, ma'am, except that the phone lines here must be getting old, because all it was, was this piece came loose. I put it back. It shouldn't come loose again," he said.

"A piece came loose last time. How are these little pieces coming loose?"

He shrugged again. "There was a lot of wind this week. This box is on the outside of the building. I don't see how, but maybe the wind shook it loose."

"Isn't the box there to protect things from wind and rain and stuff like that?"

"I don't know what else to say except call us if you have any further problems."

And that was that. I showed him out, closing the door behind him and wondering just how much my telephone problems had to do with high winds.

•　　•　　•

I finally got a chance to meet with Brandon that weekend. We found a quiet portion of the club where we could sit down and have our conversation. The mutual friend who had worked so hard to bring us together, Roxanne, sat nearby, listening. Reluctantly, and with many furtive glances toward Roxanne, Brandon began to tell his story. He was small and slight of frame with an angular face and long blond hair. He was so thin that he almost looked emaciated, and his huge blue eyes were ringed with dark circles. Here was someone who had not slept well in many weeks, whose nervousness was evidenced by the twisting of his hands and the shifting of his feet. He made eye contact when he could, but he often looked away to stare at his hands or at the floor. At these times, I did not suspect that he was looking away because he was lying, but because he felt embarrassed by the whole situation. Embarrassed—and afraid.

"I want you to know that I'm only talking about this because Roxie really trusts you," he said, taking a cigarette so he had something to do with his hands. He lit up, drew a shaky breath, and blew a plume of smoke toward the ceiling. "This is, like, the last step before I just decide that I'm insane."

He took another shaky drag from the cigarette, then told me his story.

Brandon claimed to be sensitive. He called himself an empath, explaining that he was often aware of the emotions of others. Furthermore, he told me that he sometimes had a hard time blocking these emotions, so that if he was around someone who was emotionally distraught he would not only sense their emotional state but often become swept up in it himself. Brandon blamed some of his own emotional turmoil on this hypersensitivity to other people's emotional states, and having worked with other empaths, I was inclined to accept this.

Brandon had gotten out of high school and joined the Navy. He did not last long in the military, however, as he was a very independent soul with serious problems with authority. He had known going into things that the military probably wasn't for him, but he really didn't know what else to do with his life at the time. It did not take long for him to run into disciplinary problems and get kicked out. Since that time, he had drifted from job to job and living situation to living situation. More than once, he had found himself without a home. About six months prior to meeting me, he had gone through another period of homelessness. He was hanging out with another friend who had been kicked out of the military, and they were wandering a neighborhood in Garfield Heights, looking for a place to crash. His friend knew of an abandoned house on a residential street that was in relatively good condition. The house had been on the market for several years and now it sat, forgotten.

Brandon and his friend intended to break into this house to crash there for a while. Brandon was fine with this proposal until they approached the house in question. According to Brandon, almost as soon as they started up the driveway, he felt crushed underneath a sense of something *wrong*. The next few moments were very confusing for him, as he was overwhelmed by a storm of conflicting sensations. He fell to his knees, practically writhing in agony.

"This is where it gets weird," Brandon warned me.

When Brandon collapsed on the pavement, it was because he felt overwhelmed by not one, but two distinct and traumatic emotional states. With the first one, he identified with a young woman or a girl. He felt that this person was a victim, abused and very likely murdered. Held in thrall by whatever force extended beyond the walls of the house, Brandon felt as if he were reliving the moments of her abuse and death. At the exact same time, he could feel a male presence, and he simultaneously experienced the emotions of both the victim and victimizer. At the time, he was absolutely certain that these feelings were tied to the house he was about to break into. Eventually, the sensations waned in intensity, and he was able to stand. His buddy helped him up, but from that moment forward Brandon refused to set foot near that house.

A couple of things about the initial experience confused Brandon. First, there was the fact that he felt two radically different sets of emotions, experiencing them both at once. He could understand one or the other, but did not quite grasp how or why he picked up on both. Further, he felt that his experience was tied to more than just emotional echoes. He really perceived a sense of personality in both sets of impressions. This led him to conclude that he was dealing with a haunting, but this only halfway made sense. From his impressions of the girl, he was almost certain that she had been murdered in the house. He was so certain, in fact, that were it not for his own checkered past, and the errand that had brought them to the house in the first place, he would have reported his suspicions to the police. However, that left the question of her attacker, a presence he felt with equal force. Short of suicide, it made no sense to Brandon that the attacker would have died around the same time as his attack on the girl. Brandon felt no sense of self-harm, just the anger and fury of the attack.

At this point, I suggested that what Brandon had experienced was not a ghost, or ghosts, at all. Instead, I offered up the possibility that all he was picking up on were emotional residues. In the vast majority of suspected hauntings, there is no ghost at all. Rather, when a particularly traumatic event occurs, the emotions experienced by the participants can become imprinted upon the space where the event took place. Probably the most famous instances of such emotional impressions occur on battlefields. Gettysburg is a very famous American haunting of this sort, but in the ancient world it was recognized that the field of Marathon also retained echoes of the bloody battle that was fought there.

"That's what I thought at first, too, Michelle," said Roxie, who, as a Pagan priestess, was no stranger to spirit phenomena.

"I don't know," Brandon shrugged, grinding his cigarette out on the concrete floor. "Is it normal for emotional impressions like that to catch a ride with someone who's sensitive? Because that's what they did. It's like they were just waiting for someone who is sensitive enough to pick up on them. When I left the house, they came with me. I've been experiencing them ever since. Now you know why I think I'm crazy."

Brandon went on to explain that since his experience outside the house in Garfield Heights, he had been in the grip of one or both personalities on several occasions. Sometimes, he experienced them as entities outside of himself. But more alarming were the times when he experienced the wave of emotions internally, as if he were the frightened young girl or, sometimes, the terrible man who had murdered her.

According to Brandon, he had been reluctant to talk about these experiences with anyone, keeping the secret of the lingering spirits even from the friend who witnessed his initial reaction. However, the presence of something supernatural soon became difficult to deny. In addition to sometimes feeling as if these entities were overwhelming his own personality, Brandon began to notice that lights flickered or electronic devices malfunctioned in response to his extreme moods.

As the people around him began to notice that something was wrong with Brandon, a few of them took him aside to ask about the nature of the problem. This was when he first learned that the spirits did not like to be talked about. According to Brandon, at the time of the conversation another friend was playing a console game. As Brandon sat on the couch, relating his suspicions about being plagued by ghostly hitchhikers, the screen fuzzed out, then went black. A crackling sound emerged from the machine, followed quickly by smoke and the scent of burning circuitry.

Roxie was not present for this incident, but I was later able to track down the friend who was. The young man who had owned the console game confirmed that its mysterious meltdown had coincided with Brandon's attempt to open up about his problems. The young man, Greg, still held Brandon responsible for the destruction of the game system, despite the fact that Brandon was sitting on a couch several feet away when it went up in smoke.

Brandon had a strong sense that the game console had been destroyed specifically because he was attempting to talk about the spirits. Understandably, he was frightened. However, he was more frightened at the prospect of completely losing himself to the dominating personality of the furious and violent attacker. He kept his problems to himself for a few weeks, but soon he was trying to reach out to knowledgeable people over the Internet.

When Roxie first learned of his troubles, she attempted to rid him of the spirits, with no result. She claimed to be able to sense the darker of the two personalities, and she had witnessed Brandon in the grips of it. She was afraid for her friend, and felt helpless, which was why she had urged him to contact me. She hoped that with my greater expertise in dealing with spirits, I would be able to rid Brandon of the dominating influence of an entity that seemed bent on possessing him.

After his initial interview with me, Brandon apologized ahead of time for any kind of computer or electronic issues I might experience as a result of speaking with him. At the time, I did not tell him that I had already experienced troubles with my phone. I still was not entirely convinced that Brandon was dealing with genuine ghosts. During the time he was speaking to me, I had sensed nothing. I knew that this did not guarantee that there was nothing to sense, for spirits often seem to come and go in mysterious ways. I tried to cling to my skepticism, however, knowing that I could not entirely dismiss the possibility that these other personalities had their source in Brandon himself—either intentionally or unintentionally.

For someone who was in a difficult financial situation, having trouble holding down a job and keeping a roof over his head, it was not inconceivable that secondary personalities would emerge that could more freely express Brandon's anger and rage at the world on one hand and a sense of being a helpless victim on the other. Cases of suspected possession so closely mirror real and serious psychological issues that a ghost-hunter navigates a very slippery slope when trying to separate one from the other. I did some research, but could find no records indicating that the house in Garfield Heights had been the scene of a murder.

This did not entirely invalidate the possibility that two spirits entangled in the roles of victim and victimizer had been lingering in the area. I had learned long before that it was naïve to presume that spirits could not travel. Although, especially in the case of violent deaths, when strong emotions helped tie a spirit to one particular place, that tie was not an iron-clad fetter. Sentient spirits have far more choice about where they roam than most traditional ghost stories give them credit for.

Over several successive interviews, and having witnessed several more instances in which Brandon—or his spirit companions—interfered with electronic equipment, I decided it would be best to take the situation seriously. I had Brandon come over to my apartment where I could take a good, hard look at his energy in an environment that was not quite as distracting as a nightclub, coffee shop, or diner—all places where we had previously met to talk with one another. When I did get down to the business of looking at his energy body, I saw the telltale tendrils of energy that I had come to identify as energetic links.

Living people form these links with one another through strong emotional interactions as well as intensive energy work. Psychic vampires form these links with others in order to connect to their energy. Spirits form these links to effect a similar connection, sometimes feeding like psychic vampires and sometimes using the link to influence the person on the other end of it. Considering the placement of these links on Brandon—at the base of the skull, in the middle of his back—I suspected the latter.

I grabbed the link, feeling along the pathway of energy and trying to find its source. I know that in my interviews with Brandon, I had never once witnessed the manifestation of the dark and angry entity, either from within Brandon himself or lingering in the young man's proximity. The absence of this entity had certainly contributed to my skepticism that Brandon's case was one of attempted spirit possession. Since no spirit was ever present when I observed Brandon, I kept searching for other explanations. Finally getting my hands on the tendril of energy emerging from Brandon's back, I suspected the entity had been hiding from me all along, withdrawing as far as it could from Brandon whenever he sought me out for help.

I worked with Brandon to detach the entities. Only one really needed to be cut away. The girl, small and scared and timid, seemed tied more to her attacker than to the young man they had both accidentally come into contact with. I felt very sorry for the girl, and tried to help her move on. I got the sense that she was able to, much to the fury of the dark presence that had tormented her in death as well as in life. The dark presence was successfully excised from Brandon, and he has remained both a grateful friend and student since.

Brandon and I both thought the story ended with our session of intensive energy work, clearing him of these unwanted spiritual hitchhikers. However, more than a year later I stumbled upon an unexpected and very creepy final chapter to the string of experiences that started in the driveway of an abandoned house in Garfield Heights.

Late one night, working second shift at a gas station and desperate for something to occupy my thoroughly numbed mind, I was paging through the previous day's edition of the *Cleveland Plain Dealer*, left under the desk by one of the day-shift cashiers. Lost in the back pages of the newspaper, in a section I would never had read were it not for overwhelming boredom, was an article that left me shaken for the rest of the night.

The article told the story of a man who had bought a fixer-upper in Garfield Heights. During the course of his repairs, he had knocked down part of one wall, only to find skeletonized human remains secreted in that dark and musty space. The body was identified as that of a young girl, approximately eleven years of age. No other details of how she died or who might possibly have hidden her there were offered in the article. I clipped the article for Brandon. Perhaps understandably, he was too disturbed to read more than a few lines after confirming that the residence in question was in fact the house that he and his friend had unwisely tried to invade.

The Necronomian Vampire:
A Cautionary Tale

Around May of 1996, a classified ad in the back of *FATE* caught my eye. I can't remember the exact wording, but the advertiser, whose address was in Kent, Ohio, was seeking any information on vampires. At the time I published a journal on psychic vampirism entitled *The Midnight Sun*. I was also a frequent visitor to Kent, which is home to the artsy, liberal Kent State University (my mother's alma mater). Curious about someone so close by with a possible shared interest, I wrote a cautious letter to the person whom I'll call Travis.

After the second or third letter, mostly exchanging basic information on interests, Travis confided in me his reason for putting the ad out. From the little he told me in the letter, I arranged to meet with him in person. If he was bullshitting me, it would be easier to verify this face to face; and if he wasn't, then he needed the help of someone who knew how to deal with spirits and malignant attachments.

The story went like this: he and a friend were both beginning to dabble in the occult. The friend had bought the Simon version of the *Necronomicon*. The two of them had attempted one of the gate rituals in the book, but nothing much happened. They were somewhat disappointed and left off their experiments for a while.

Not long after, however, Travis started to have dreams wherein a voice was calling to him. He got the sense that it was something without a body, just a spirit, and it seemed as if it were communicating from a long way away. Sometimes Travis wasn't even sure these were dreams, as he usually was awake in his own room during the dream and it had seemed as if the voice had woken him from his slumbers.

The voice, which was sometimes accompanied by an eerie glow, persistently asked Travis to help it and to bring it across. Travis also became, as he described it, obsessed with the Simon *Necronomicon* at that time. He would sometimes see sigils during these dreams, as if they were traced in that slight glow on the insides of his eyes. He couldn't make them out clearly, just got impressions of lines and circles and patterns.

This lasted a few weeks. Travis couldn't clearly remember how many. But it drove Travis to sneak into his friend's dorm room one night while the other young man was away and to attempt to recreate the ritual alone, using the copy of the *Necronomicon* stored there.

This ritual went very differently from the last one. Travis was a little frightened by himself during it; he said he started saying and doing things that weren't quite in the book, but that *seemed* right. He also said that he spontaneously started calling out in a language he didn't know. But this also just seemed to come to him and since it seemed right, he went with it.

I'm relying on the truth of his reporting here, so bear with me on what followed. I interviewed Travis, who turned out to be seventeen. He had an older friend attending the local college who was never named and whom I never met. When I spoke with him, Travis was visibly disturbed by his experiences. Judging from his mannerisms, body language, and the emotions he was giving off, if nothing else he believed the rest of what he told me.

The candles he had lit for the rite started acting strangely, their flames extending, then taking on a strange greenish-blue glow that reminded him of the dreams. Travis felt something building in the room. It had started as a kind of prickly feeling that ran up and down his skin, and as the rite reach its culmination, it grew in intensity. Travis also said the room started to feel close, or crowded. Then the candles went out.

Shortly after, a strong and sudden wind then gusted through the window (which I'm assuming was already open and could explain the candles going out). Travis was then thrown back by some unseen force. He hit the wall behind him—then slid to the floor, his knees weak. He was, by his own account, scared out of his wits at that point. He dropped the book and turned for the door. He had trouble opening the door at first, as it seemed like a great weight was pushing upon it from the inside. When he did get it open, it was like the room had been vacuum-sealed. There was a sucking sensation, and it seemed as though cooler, less "heavy" air rushed into the room through the open door. Travis bolted for the hall and the door slammed shut behind him, apparently of its own accord.

Travis thought that was the end of it. But as anyone with experience in these things knows, it never is. Over the next few weeks, he started to feel like he was "changing," as he put it. This is where the vampire part came in. He started to be sensitive to bright lights, and he felt that his night vision improved drastically. He also had trouble eating, but felt hungry all the time. At some point, he became very aware of the life force of the people around him. He felt that he could feel their energy, and something in him wanted this very much.

Predatory thoughts that he described as not being like him started to cross his mind. He felt there was another consciousness in his mind. He would experience thoughts and emotions as if they were his own, but there was a sense that they were coming from a secondary source. His mood started to change and a number of his friends became afraid of him. Some of them drifted away without explaining why they were afraid. A few commented that he wasn't himself anymore. His eyes had changed, they said. They saw his face change sometimes, and they would see a face they didn't really recognize, or at least an expression that was very alien to them and very disturbing.

A part of Travis greatly enjoyed these changes. They made him feel powerful. Although he was just beginning to study magick, he was now able to spontaneously do things. The example he gave involved summoning wind, and a storm. He hadn't learned how to do this before, but after the experience in the dorm room, he now "just knew." A part of Travis was rather frightened by all of these developments, and instinctively he connected the changes to his experience in the dorm room. He was afraid that whatever was going on would cause him to lose himself, and he'd become another person entirely.

It was from the owner of the *Necronomicon* that Travis first learned of his nightly excursions. This other young man confronted Travis about draining his energy. Travis had by this point learned he could do that to people from a distance, but had no idea that he was doing it on an astral level. Apparently, he had been visiting the other young man in his sleep. This young man perceived Travis hovering above him in the bed, at which point he could not move, and he would feel the life being sucked out of him. This, of course, is a pretty classic description of an astral vampire attack, and even though I was receiving it secondhand through Travis, it rang true.

Travis pretty much pleaded with me to get rid of "it," whatever "it" was. He felt that he was losing himself to it, and he was afraid that it would gain complete control over him. At this point I took a look at Travis's energy to see whether or not I could detect evidence of an attachment.

What I saw was this: two thick cords extending into Travis's energy body. One was attached at the base of the skull; the other was attached at about the middle of his back, snaking into the solar plexus chakra. (I have since seen this arrangement in a number of cases of "riders" that are attempting to influence or outright possess their hosts.) These cords stretched out behind Travis for quite a ways, and by connecting briefly to the both of them, I perceived a sentience, rather malevolent and exceptionally self-absorbed, hovering at a distance. Even with this brief contact, it seemed to sense my probing, so I withdrew for the moment.

Notably, Travis's demeanor changed shortly after I made energetic contact to check him out. I found this interesting, as I had not told him that I was doing it. He became furtive and fidgety, and he started to make excuses to cut our interaction short. I asked him if he still wanted me to do something, and he said that maybe it wasn't such a good idea. He was probably being paranoid and there really wasn't anything wrong, and so forth. For the time, we parted ways. I gave him my home number and told him to call me if anything further occurred.

I understood that some of Travis's story could be teenage attention-getting. Gods know, I'd seen enough of that among young would-be magicians and occultists. Some of it could easily have been exaggerated (also hardly uncommon among the young), and the rest may have been fabricated based on occult material he had read about to impress others or to just feel important about himself.

Still, it seemed to me that Travis was quite the novice in these matters. I considered it highly unlikely that he would have enough knowledge of the subject to conjecture or outright fabricate some of the more accurate descriptions he had offered, such as the sensations, both physical and energetic, produced by his experimental summoning in his friend's dorm room. His descriptions of how he vampirized energy also were very accurate. This was shortly before

Konstantinos published his book *Vampires: The Occult Truth*, and so this information was exceptionally hard to find.

Finally, Travis's sudden change of heart regarding the whole matter after I'd done a preliminary scan of his energy body cinched it for me: the boy had called something that had decided to attach itself to him. At the very least, it was feeding through him in order to strengthen itself, and at worst it was slowly wearing away the boy's will in preparation for a full possession.

In my work with spirits and the Otherside, I've encountered quite a number of otherworldly beings that are not human and never have been. Many of these entities seem wholly spiritual. That is to say, it seems that they have never physically incarnated but exist wholly on the astral, the near astral (what I typically refer to as the "subtle reality"), or in points even further removed from our reality. Furthermore, a large number of them seem to really *want* to incarnate, but for some reason they cannot.

I personally think their energetic structure is so alien, especially to a human body, that they simply cannot make the incarnation work. However, a number of them seem capable of taking over a body once another spirit has successfully incarnated in it. The naïve inadvertently allow these beings to get a foothold on them; the power-hungry occasionally intentionally invite them in, erroneously assuming that a partnership with such an entity is possible and will enable them to harness that entity's powers. The Temple of the Vampire, one group I'm not too thrilled with, is pretty famous for this.

Anyway, to continue on: I felt I was dealing with a vampiric/parasitic entity with Travis. When I asked him what entity he had attempted to call up, he said "Akharu," a name that is given in the glossary of the Simon *Necronomicon* as meaning "vampire."

Having skimmed through the Simon text, I knew that it drew heavily upon Sumerian or Babylonian sources, so I tried finding the real meaning of the word *Akharu* (call me crazy, but I didn't quite trust the scholarship or legitimacy of the Simon *Necronomicon*). I quickly learned that there were precious few Sumerian, Akkadian, or Babylonian dictionaries to be had anywhere, and the few texts I did track down that had something of a glossary (*Poems of Heaven and Hell*, for example) did not have *Akharu* in them.

Through the coincidental interaction of some research, I did find an ancient Egyptian word *Akhekhu*, which I felt was too similar to *Akharu* to just ignore. A few Egyptian scholars I've read conjecture that Egypt inherited its language from Sumeria (a point I don't precisely agree with—but I will admit that there was a cultural and linguistic *exchange* between the two cultures). This added some weight to the notion that *Akharu* and *Akhekhu* might have the same root, or at least share some basic meaning in common. In the Budge translations (hardly the most reliable, but certainly the most widely accessible source on the ancient Egyptian language), this word is given as meaning "darkness" or an eponymously demonic being that stalks the darkness. It was also listed as a word for night.

At this point, I took time to further study the Simon *Necronomicon*. Knowing the real origin of the *Necronomicon* as a creation of supernatural fiction writer H. P. Lovecraft, I'd always looked upon this text with a certain amount of disdain. It could only be a spurious text, created expressly to cash in on the mystique that surrounded Lovecraft's invented tome. But as I flipped through Simon's work, I saw that whoever had patched it together had drawn upon legitimate Babylonian sources. I recognized some material from Inanna's descent into the underworld and the invocation of the fifty names of Marduk. Obviously some things had been tweaked in order to better fit with the Cthulhu mythos, but I began to realize that someone who *believed* in the validity of the text could probably harness the rituals for an actual working.

Who or what *Akharu* really was became irrelevant. I decided that the Simon *Necronomicon*, in the hands of a naïve, aspiring occultist, worked the same as a Ouija board. Performing any of the rites amounted to lighting up a great big neon sign that flashed "Come mess with me!" Any number of otherworldly entities would have answered that call, happily assuming the guise of Akharu, Hastur, or even Nyarlohotep if that was what the would-be occultist was expecting. Some would do this for energy, others for the attention (which basically equals the same thing), and a few would do it just for shits and grins.

Since Travis was reluctant to arrange a second meeting after his "change of heart," I tried doing the work of removal from a distance. I didn't feel this was successful. While I felt I got a good hold on the entity, it seemed like it reconnected almost as soon as I left off wrestling with it.

Certain that he was headed for a really bad experience, I continued to write to Travis with suggestions and cautions. After a while, I managed to get a second face-to-face meeting with Travis. He looked more haggard and haunted than before, and once more he was pleading with me to rid him of the thing. We sat down in a quiet, wooded area of Kent State's campus, and I got to work. I don't use a whole lot of tools in my work; I work with energy on the subtle (near-astral) level, and so my energy and my Will are normally all the tools I really need (though I do sometimes go in for something a bit more ceremonial).

I got to work severing the attachments—first at the base of the skull, then at the solar plexus. These practically had a life of their own and kept on trying to reattach themselves as soon as I'd cut them. Ultimately, I took to cauterizing the points of contact that had been made on Travis's energy body, then grabbing the attachments and cauterizing their ends. I did a minor banishing, but the entity would just not go away, so I grabbed the tendrils it kept sending Travis's way and went toe to toe with it. I used its own tendrils to connect to its energy and beat the hell out of it energetically, alternately draining its energy and sending nasty spikes down the line. When I was satisfied that I'd beat it into submission, I then flung it as far elsewhere as I could, put some (more) shields up on Travis, and gave him a crash course in shielding and psychic self-defense.

The end of the story is uncertain, and a little disappointing. Travis did well for a while and seemed to get back to normal, but he retained a fascination for working with the Simon book. In spite of my warnings, he was sure there was a "right" way to perform a summoning and had some vague sense that this would do something useful for him. The first attachment seemed to have been dealt with, but I'm almost positive that he ran headlong into work that ultimately earned him another one. Eventually we lost contact with one another.

It's occurred to me to look him up now and again, but since that time I've run across a number of aspiring occultists like Travis, and have learned that they cannot all be saved from themselves. For the amount of work it took to sever the attachment and kick the nasty little astral vamp back to whatever plane of existence it had come from, it was a waste of my time when all Travis did was try valiantly to just attract another with the mistaken assumption that he could ultimately control it.

Counting Crows

After the adventures we had in the fall of 1992, you would think that no one would want to go back to Whitethorn Woods, especially not for Halloween. But as much as ghostly phenomena have the power to frighten, their power to fascinate is even greater still. I went back for more in 1993, and I was determined to document as much phenomena as possible. I became head of the committee for the haunted house that year, directing purchases, set-up, and design for the haunted part of the weekend. I also obtained special permission from the university to spend the entire week leading up to the haunted weekend by myself at Whitethorn Woods. Ostensibly this was to prepare the "bad house" and the woods for the weekend's festivities, but I had my own agenda as well.

That year, the haunted house fell precisely on Halloween weekend. I had already arranged for an even larger group of friends and associates—some Pagan, some not—to be driven out Friday night to stock the woods and haunted house. Only three members of the Pagan group that had attended the event the previous year were willing to return. Evan was one of them. Cerridwen, unsurprisingly, was not.

Undaunted, I got together a different crew of friends from outside of the university. A few of these were local Pagans, but most were just interested in having a fun and unique experience for Halloween. The students from my university had of course heard some stories about the events of the previous year, but I had taken care not to pass any tales on to the friends who were helping out that weekend. I wanted them to have no expectations, so they could not possibly think themselves into experiencing something.

I got the keys to the front gate and the houses, as well as the security codes, and drove out Monday afternoon with supplies for the house and food enough to get me through the week. It was late October, but that entire week was clear and rather warm during the day. The first thing I did upon my arrival at Whitethorn Woods was do a little baking. I had done a great deal of research on faeries since the previous year's experiences, and I had decided to accept Cerridwen's explanation for the phenomenon—at least as a working theory. A traditional way of appeasing faeries was to leave them cakes and cream, though I figured whole milk would suffice in a pinch. I'd bought a special muffin pan that made tiny cupcakes—an ideal size for faeries, as far as I was concerned—and I baked a dozen small cakes spiced with cloves, cinnamon, nutmeg, and honey. If this was their land, and they viewed us as interlopers, perhaps a friendly offering would improve their attitude.

As dusk was falling on my first night out at the acres, I selected a hoary old tree stump some distance away from the houses and left my offering to the fey. I placed the twelve little cakes in a ring on the flat top of the stump and dumped a pint of milk out around the base of the stump. Feeling a little silly, but determined to see if this would work, I politely addressed the woods and asked the fey if they would allow me and my friends to share their woods for Samhain. I told them that I would be staying for the next several days, working in the woods. I asked that they allow me to share their territory without incident, and I asked that they allow my friends, when they arrived, to do the same. I concluded by assuring them that we would be out of their woods by Sunday, and we would try to leave everything just as we had found it.

I have to admit, at that moment I was happy I was alone on the property. There I was, standing in front of the tree stump, dumping perfectly good milk onto the ground and talking to thin air. Anyone observing me would probably just assume I was crazy. But as crazy as the whole thing seemed, I also felt a gathering presence from the woods. I had to remind myself that practically every culture around the world had its version of the myth of the "little people," and there is usually a grain of truth to such pervasive myths. In my readings, it seemed as if *faerie* were simply one name people gave to local nature spirits. I suspected that these beings existed on the same level as ghosts, but unlike ghosts, faeries had never been human. Maybe, as my friend Cerridwen insisted, they were guardians of the wild places, and maybe they were just spirits that had an existence separate from our own—an existence that nevertheless intersected with our world under certain circumstances.

Whatever the case, after I made the offering I breathed a little easier in Whitethorn Woods' deceptively tranquil setting. In fact, the next few days were disappointingly uneventful compared to how frightened people had gotten the year before. I won't pretend that nothing happened whatsoever. There were little things that occurred every day. While I was working, tools and props would go missing, only to turn up in a location I had searched before. At night, there were sounds coming from the woods that seemed out of place. The most unusual of these was a kind of whispering or sighing. Although I tried to convince myself that this was only the wind through the branches, I had been raised in the country. I was no stranger to forest sounds, and this just didn't sound right. There was the sound of movement around the house—stealthy noises of twigs snapping and rustling leaves. It was much easier to convince myself that these sounds were nothing but animals come to investigate my presence. I couldn't quite shake the impression of being watched, especially once the sun went down, but at least the malevolence of the previous year seemed absent. Whatever was watching me, it felt more curious than mean.

None of this really lived up to the reputation of Whitethorn Woods that lingered in my mind from the year before. At the very least, I had expected to encounter some nasty specter while I was working in the woods. I spent a lot of time out there, making the trails safe for the weekend's guests. I worked mostly during the day, taking advantage of the sun, but I would often linger until dusk. The only unusual thing that happened as night settled on the woods involved birds. Around sunset each day, a hush would fall over the forest. All the little sounds you don't really think about in a natural setting—birdsong, the buzzing of insects, the chittering of squirrels—stopped.

The absence of these pervasive but low-level sounds seemed louder than the sounds themselves. In the resulting silence, the air would grow taut, as if the forest itself were holding its breath. Then, deep within Whitethorn Woods, from the direction of the setting sun, an immense flock of birds would burst forth. For a few moments, the air thrummed with the sound of wings, and crows —more than I could count—burst from the woods to fly over the lakes and disappear. Once the flock had passed, it was as if the woods suddenly exhaled, and everything came back to life. It was autumn, so flocks of birds were not unheard of, but this particular flock emerged from the same spot at the same time every day I was there, and the silence that preceded its passing just didn't seem natural.

The only other place I had encountered crows on the Whitethorn Woods was, oddly, the stump where I had made the faerie offering. The day after I made the offering to the fey, I'd risen pretty nearly with the sun. When I went out, the dew dampened my socks through my boots. There was a mist hanging over both the lake and the lochs, and it clung to the stumps of the trees and especially around the stump. As I approached the stump, I made out three black shapes sitting on it. They were crows. I stopped my approach, and they sat regarding me for a moment or two. Then, as one, all three took off silently for the woods. The cakes, of course, were gone. Not even crumbs remained. This all by itself was hardly shocking, as crows are scavengers, eating whatever morsels they find.

And yet, the crow has a long history of folkloric associations. In some cultures, the crow acts as a psychopomp—a guide for the souls of the dead. The mythic connection between crows and the dead is obliquely expressed in our term for a large gathering of crows. By itself, a crow is just a crow, but a group of crows together is known as a murder of crows. In Native American myths, the crow is a trickster. To the Inuit people, Raven, the crow's cousin, is a kind of Prometheus figure—the thief of heavenly fire. And in the British Isles, the rook, another black bird related to crows, has some passing association with the faerie folk.

All of these associations were on my mind as I watched the three dark figures fly away into the mist. Although I only put the offering out once, I always saw the same three crows gathered at the stump each morning. Perhaps the birds were just coming back each morning to see whether or not more cakes awaited them, but it seemed odd that there were only three of them—never more and never fewer—perching on the stump.

Aside from the crows, nothing of any great note occurred while I stayed on the property by myself. Gradually, I got everything prepared for the weekend. Then it was the weekend itself, and the other volunteers from the university began to arrive. That year I had convinced a number of my friends from the university to help out as well. Earlier in the year, I had started a band with Dominic St. Charles and several other students. Dominic and I convinced both the bassist and the other vocalist to come along for the Halloween fun. Along with Dominic were our mutual friends Chris and Evan. Evan, whom you might recognize from "The Thing in the Crawlspace," was returning to the event from the previous year. Chris was new to the university's student-run haunted attraction, but as a huge fan of weird fiction author H. P. Lovecraft, he was delighted to be part of the spooky goings-on.

The afternoon with the inner-city children went without a hitch. The kids had a great time, spending most of it marveling about the cows they had seen on the bus ride to the site. Once the kids were on their buses back to Cleveland, we all cleaned up and starting resetting things for the real fun: the arrival of the college students.

I took a quick break from everything else in order to bake another dozen small cakes, and I quietly sneaked out to the faerie stump and made my peace offering shortly before the crows were going to flock. I knew from last year that the students from my university could be boisterous and, sometimes, a little obnoxious. Still feeling a little silly, I asked the spirits of the forest to tolerate everyone's presence. I asked them specifically not to play tricks on people or cause anyone any kind of harm. Then I promised once more that we would all depart Sunday afternoon.

By the time I returned from my little excursion to the tree stump, it was nearly time to begin. The first bus was going to arrive at seven thirty or eight o'clock. My non-university friends were already en route. I went over to the "good house" to check people's make-up and costumes. Then I took Chris, Dominic, and Evan, my three guides, aside to go over their duties one final time. The three of them had more or less memorized the woodland path as well as a rough script that they would say to introduce at each station. All of the guides had some training in theater, so they could project their voices well. They had also been familiarizing themselves with the woods all day, so they were confident about leading people safely through. All of us were excited. A lot of effort had gone into the haunted house this year, and we couldn't wait to show things off to our peers.

The first few groups went through without any problems whatsoever. I was moving between the "good house" and the "bad house," both coordinating and acting. I overheard a few of the students who had just gone through the whole thing boasting that they hadn't been scared in the least, which I took as a good sign that they had been.

Then something went wrong.

College students in general are notorious for drinking, especially if they are underage. Our university was hardly an exception to the rule. The second busload of students arrived with a good number of very drunk, very rowdy jocks. These guys were giving the guides a hard time and heckling just about everyone in a costume, but they seemed to quiet down when it was their turn to go through the woods to the house. This did not last. Several of them not only continued their heckling, but they also destroyed several of the displays and stole a number of props. This did not sit well with me when I learned about it. We had put entirely too much work into the haunted attraction to have drunk idiots ruin it like that.

We got the groups together and tried to get the stolen items returned. At first, I tried to handle this myself, but I was so upset, my anger was only making things worse. I left Dominic and some others in charge of handling the disruptive students. Then I took a walk as far away from people as I could get, trying to calm myself down. I found myself approaching the faerie stump. Unable to quell my curiosity, I checked to see if the cakes were still there. They weren't. I figured a few of the local raccoons had gotten a treat, and yet a part of me hoped that something else had taken the cakes. For a while, I stood by the stump, looking out into the night. In the distance, I could hear the guides yelling at the students, asking them to come forward with the names of the vandals, or at least to return the items that had been taken. Hearing this did nothing to calm me down. I needed to vent my anger. I had come to this stump and talked to invisible things twice now, so I vented my anger here as well, throwing my head back and addressing the thin air.

"Are you out there?" I called. "Did you see that? I promised that we would respect your woods and they made a liar out of me! Well, I'm sorry. I didn't expect anything like that. Those kids are assholes, and they don't deserve any kind of protection. My people stay safe, but it's open season on them. They disrespected my stuff, and they disrespected yours. So you can do whatever you want to them."

I stood, hands balled into fists, staring out into the woods across the lake.

"You hear me? It's open season on those assholes. Unleash your vengeance. Unleash it all!"

As I finished my invective, a sudden strong wind kicked up, blowing leaves everywhere. Across the lake, I could see the tops of the trees bending with the force of it. The wind continued to spike, and the sound it made through the almost-naked branches made it seem as if the forest itself were roaring. Then, just as suddenly as the wind kicked up, everything fell still. It was about that time when I realized I was no longer alone. Dominic, the guitarist in the band, had apparently followed me when I stormed off from the group. I don't know how long he was standing there or how much he heard, but from the look on his face, he had heard enough. A little fearfully, he asked, "Michelle, what did you just do?"

I had no idea, but we were soon to find out. Shortly after my tantrum at the stump, we got the vandals to come forward and return the stolen articles. With the help of some flashlights, we did some quick repairs to the tableaus out in the woods. Then everything was up and running again. From my brief trip into the woods, I could tell that things had changed. At the time, I still did not realize how great a change had been wrought. The place felt very foreboding again, and along with the malevolence there was an air of angry mischief. I hoped I was only picking this up from the actors, all of whom were nearly as furious as I was about the unexpected vandalism. The actors decided to take revenge on the rowdy students by going to every length possible to scare the living daylights out of them. Very shortly, I learned that it was not just the actors who had decided on this approach.

After I had called for vengeance, Dominic was the first to lead a group through the woods. When he returned, he was terribly pale. I knew something was wrong from the look on his face, and at first I half-feared that some of the students had caused problems again. Imagine my surprise when this very grounded nonbeliever asked, in a tremulous voice, "Michelle? What exactly does a hellhound look like?"

I should say a few things about Dominic. He's a year older than me, and for as long as I've known him, he has been a passionate and talented musician. At the time, he was attending college for psychology and communications. We met in a psych class and bonded over our experiences as lab partners. Dominic's dream at the time was to work with young people in recovery. The adult son of a recovered alcoholic, Dominic himself was staunchly alcohol and drug-free. This held true for all of my close friends, which was one of the reasons the drunken behavior had upset us so much. Dominic was also a devout Catholic. His mother was a white witch, so he was at least tolerant of other people's beliefs. Bemusedly open-minded where people like myself were concerned, he had never had a supernatural experience in his life. He often remarked that he might place more credence in his mother's practices if he had.

Apparently, Dominic had been leading his group through the woods when he became aware of something pacing them. At first it kept to the deep woods, moving through sections of the forest that previous explorations had proved virtually impassable. A few of the people in his group noticed it, but assumed it was part of the tour. Then he caught sight of what was following them. He described it as a big dog, about the size and shape of a wolfhound, with feral eyes that seemed to glow. After glancing nervously back at the thing a few times, he realized that the whole animal seemed to glow faintly with a soft, greenish phosphorescence. He heard the students in his group remark on the animal, speculating as to whether or not it was real. They all seemed to agree that it was a very impressive prop.

With the research I had done on faeries, I was perfectly aware of the stories of faerie hounds. It really sounded like Dominic had just described one, though I knew for certain that he was unfamiliar with the concept. Although his mother was a witch, Dominic had more in common with his working-class father. He preferred a mundane approach to reality, studying as little about the supernatural as possible. I knew that if Dominic was convinced about the extraordinary nature of the dog, then it he had already exhausted all the possibilities of it being a mundane animal. I asked him if the dog had seemed to threaten anyone, and he said no. It just walked along beside them for a while. One or two of the people in his group had complained about being struck by something, and a boy yelled generally into the woods to remind anyone within earshot that the actors were not allowed to touch the students. This was to include, he insisted, throwing things at them.

Of course, this fit the stories of faeries perfectly as well. Our term for a stroke actually comes from the notion of being elf-struck or faerie-struck. It was believed, especially in the Celtic countries, that the faeries protected their sacred woods and other lands by pelting unwanted human guests with enchanted missiles that could strike them blind or deaf. More often, however, being elf-struck just made them confused and forgetful of where they were going. This trick was especially useful in very treacherous terrain, because the intruding human was likely not only to get lost but probably hurt or even drowned in a swamp or unnoticed pond.

It was clear from the look on Dominic's face and from the way he acted the rest of the night that he believed that what he had seen was more than natural. He agreed to still lead people through the woods, so long as he could carry a sturdy walking stick just in case the hound decided to attack. But Dominic's experience with the hound was just the beginning. The rest of the night, as long as students were being taken through the woods, all manner of weirdness happened. The guides were witness to most of these events, though they did not suffer the harshest effects. Numerous students complained about being hit with small pebbles and stones. Invariably, this was in places along the trail where no actor was stationed because the undergrowth and brambles were too thick. On the odd chance that someone was taking out his or her legitimate anger on the students, I asked everyone afterward whether or not they were throwing things. If it was one of the human participants in the festivities, no one admitted to the deed.

In addition to being elf-struck, a number of the students found themselves inexplicably detached from the group and lost in the woods. Our guides were leading groups of five to fifteen people, though the average was about twelve. These pretty regularly stuck close together, primarily because if they lagged too far behind, they couldn't hear what the guide was saying as he took them on the tour through the woods. A few of the students who more or less had to be retrieved were very much aware of how little we liked horsing around. They insisted that they had been in the middle of the group one minute, properly following the guide, then suddenly they were in some other portion of the woods, utterly without light.

On several occasions, the students going through the woods were slapped in the face with branches. This was an interesting trick, as we had made a point of clearing the trail very thoroughly. The guide and several students preceding those with this complaint had run afoul of no branches whatsoever, and yet a few of them sported red welts or thin scratches as testament to their misfortune. Again, it's feasible that some human prankster saw fit to grab a low-hanging branch as he passed by and let it loose in someone's face, but given the other phenomenon, this might not be the case. With everything else going on, it seemed entirely plausible that tree branches were just leaping out and attacking people.

After the incident with the drunks, something of a gulf opened up between the students who came to the haunted house as guests and those who were running it. For this reason, I was not told directly anything that was experienced out in the woods by anyone but our actors. Reports of the other students were all secondhand.

But enough was overheard to prove that it was a very interesting night. After more or less giving the students over to the mischief of the resident fey, the walk through the woods certainly seemed to become a lot scarier. This appeared to be a combination of a change in atmosphere, the overwhelming sense of confusion and disorientation experienced by nearly everyone who (fortunately for them!) was led by one of the guides through the woods, and those apparently impossible but "really cool" special effects we had somehow managed, like the mean-looking dog, the glowing lights that would follow the group, and other strange shapes only half-seen lurking in the deepest shadows of the forest.

And the strange effects were not limited to the woods alone. The "bad house" suddenly became a very uncomfortable place to be with the lights out, even for the actors who had spent all day cooped up there in the dark, rehearsing their parts for the night. It became common practice for the actors to turn on all the lights in between groups of people, mostly because the oppressive darkness and the equally oppressive atmosphere was beginning to stifle them. When the lights were out, unaccountable rustlings were heard, and more than one actor felt someone stand near them or brush up against them when there was no one really there. We can only really speculate on what the students experienced as they passed through this house, though I do know of at least one definite occurrence no one could account for.

I was officially stationed in the "bad house," but as I said, I kept running over to the "good house" to coordinate things. Usually, I had enough time in between groups that I could run out and get back to my station before I was missed. However, for at least one run-through this was not the case. Evan, whom you might remember from the crawlspace story, was leading that particular group. Since he was naturally a little jumpy, he had made a point of knowing where every actor was likely to jump out and try to scare everyone. He knew that I was stationed in the living room, wearing all black and hiding behind a black curtain. Despite the "no touching" rules, I had been reaching out and brushing my hand against the faces of some unlucky passerby. As my hands were generally very cold, this was done to great effect.

As Evan passed through the living room, he felt a chill hand touch him and whispered something to the effect of, "Very funny. Grab someone else." Though he got no response, he assumed I didn't want to give myself away to the others. In fact, I hadn't touched him at all. I had just managed to turn out all the lights in the house before the group came through, and I hadn't time afterward to get to my station without being detected. I was on the other side of the room when Evan and his group passed through, and there was no one anywhere near where Evan was touched. How many other ghostly touches were felt by the students passing through that house?

In one of the rooms of the "bad house," we had two actors playing out a rape and murder scene. About halfway through the night, these two young people approached me, asking to be relieved of their posts. They were both pale and wide-eyed beneath the horror make-up, and the woman was trembling. At first, they were reluctant to explain why they no longer wanted to continue working in the "bad house," but eventually Markie, the one playing the attacker, said he felt as if he were losing himself in the character. He wasn't comfortable playing out the scene anymore. At first, that was all either of them would say, but eventually it came out that they both felt as if they were being possessed by something. Raven, the woman, asked me why I had chosen a violent rape for that particular room. I shrugged.

"It's a bedroom. I wasn't sure what else to do with the bed, really. Isolated cabin, deep in the woods—a rape made sense, really."

Staring down at her shoes, Raven said in a small voice, "Well, I think something really happened here, like a date rape or something. Markie and I keep seeing it, living it, over and over. I think it's burned into the walls of that room, and you just picked up on it. I won't go in there again."

I nodded and we did a few quick changes, turning the scene in that room to anything but a rape. Markie was let loose to wander the woods near the "bad house," which we both hoped would clear his head a little.

Barry, the other vocalist in the band and a gifted math major, approached me at one point, asserting that he had caught one of the fey spirits roaming the woods. He held his hands cupped around something, and there was this kind of static-electricity feeling coming off of them. He wouldn't open his hands to show me what he held, because he said he didn't want to let "it" get out. Barry was a great kidder, so I wasn't sure how serious he really was. Later, he disappeared for a good portion of the night. The rest of us were far too busy with the other events of that evening to do more than casually notice his absence.

Allegedly, Barry went for a walk and became confused, coming to his senses only after he had walked so far into the lake that the water was up to his chest. No one witnessed this; again, Barry often played pranks of his own, so none of those present were really sure how seriously we should take this claim. I will say that after that alleged incident, Barry had a totally different attitude toward Whitethorn Woods. Before, he had been amused by the notion of fey-haunted woods, often going to the edge of the forest and taunting the supposed supernatural residents, daring them to do something to him. All that bravado was gone the next morning. For those of us who knew Barry, this was a sure sign that *something* had occurred.

The strange sights and sounds did not end when we shut the haunted attraction down for the night. All of the college students who were just visiting got back on their buses and headed back to the city. Those of us who had volunteered for the event remained so we could clean up the next day. There were nearly a dozen of us, and the houses were rather small, even though they were almost exclusively made up of bedrooms, some with two bunk beds apiece. It would have made more sense for us to split up, so half slept in the "good house" and half slept in the "bad house." After the events of the night, however, no one was willing to do this. Not even me. Instead, we rummaged through closets and drawers for extra pillows and sheets, making up the couches for those willing to crash on them.

The "good house" had an attic room with a trundle bed in it. I had briefly seen this room during my explorations of the house earlier in the week. I say "briefly," because I had not liked the attic room. For some reason, it just felt too close, too . . . something. As safe as the "good house" felt in comparison to the "bad house," I had still avoided both the attic and the basement. I just did not like the feel of either of these spaces, and now, as we were trying to find room for everyone to sleep, I discovered that I was not alone. No one wanted to go up into the attic, even though there was a nicely made bed up there waiting for anyone who claimed it.

For the most part, all of us clung together, loath to be in an empty room. We stuck to the kitchen and the living room for the next few hours, drinking hot cocoa and watching movies. Barry was missing through all of this, and though he was mentioned once or twice, no one was willing to go look for him. Barry was hardly a small person—six foot four and three hundred pounds. We trusted that he could take care of himself. Never the social butterfly, it also wasn't shocking that he was avoiding the crowd of people. He never really knew what to do around a crowd.

Someone had brought a decent selection of videos, so we were all curled up on various couches in the living room, watching *Bram Stoker's Dracula* when a noise from the attic made us all start. For several long seconds, every set of eyes in the room was fixed upon the stairs leading up to the attic bedroom. Then we heard a second noise, far more disturbing than the first. The first sound had been a scraping and a thump, as if something had fallen over and maybe slid a little over the ubiquitous hardwood floors. It sounded very heavy, so we couldn't begin to imagine it was, but it wasn't a completely improbable noise. No, the second sound we heard was the improbable noise. It sounded like nothing so much as claws scrabbling against wood.

Raven, shaken by her earlier experiences in the "bad house" with Markie, was practically going into hysterics. Everyone else was frozen in place, so Dominic and I decided to go investigate.

The light switch for the attic room was located at the foot of the stairs. We switched this on. The single flight of stairs was nevertheless steep, and the way the room was laid out, we had to ascend to the room above in order to see anything. Dominic and I inched our way up. Neither of us were sure what we were expecting, but after all the wild experiences of that night, we were prepared for just about anything.

"Barry?" Dominic called, remembering our friend's penchant of practical joking. Silently, I promised Barry a sound beating, should it turn out that he was just messing with us.

It was at first anticlimactic when Dominic and I made it to the top of the stairs. The room was empty, although it reeked with this strange, musty smell.

"What is that?"

Dominic did not respond immediately, his eyes fixed on something near his feet. There was a huge old steamer trunk up here. I remembered it from my explorations. I had poked around in it a few days before. It was stupidly heavy and filled with blankets and linens. It had been pressed up against the wall opposite the bed, just at the top of the stairs as one came up. Had been—because now it sat about three feet away from the wall. The wooden floor beneath it showed fresh, raw scratches from the edges of the trunk. I didn't have to spend time wondering how the trunk had been dragged across the floor. A panel from the wall that the trunk had been flush against lay off to one side, askew.

"What am I looking at here?" Dominic asked. "Where does that hole go?"

The panel had been nailed into the wall, sealing up an entrance to a crawlspace. Apparently, only part of the house's attic was finished. The crawlspace, not large enough to be turned into a room, opened onto another section of the eaves of the house. The overhead light revealed bare rafters and pink insulation. This was also where the strange, musty smell was coming from.

Dominic walked over and touched the edges of the square opening. There were fresh splinters in the wood around numerous tiny nail holes. Corresponding nails glinted from the edges of the leaning plank of wood. It looked for all the world as if the piece of board had been torn from the wall.

"Was the trunk against that?" Dominic asked.

I nodded, still trying to grasp exactly what I was looking at.

"Something came out of there," he said. "Didn't it? It had to. The wood, the trunk. Something shoved its way out of that crawl-space."

"Looks that way," I admitted.

"But what?" he asked.

The scrabbling sound came again. Both of our heads turned toward the source of the noise. The bed on the far wall had a comforter that came down almost, but not quite, to the bare wooden floor. In the inch of space that was left, all we could see was an inky blackness. Then something clearly moved under the bed. The comforter billowed with the movement, but the inch of space we could see remained pitch black, revealing nothing.

"Both these houses are equipped with security systems," Dominic said. "How could anything get in?"

"Never mind that the panel there is—or was—nailed shut," I pointed out. "Something wanted out. Badly."

"This is your area of expertise, not mine," he said. "What do we do?"

I stared at the shadowy space beneath the bed, feeling the hairs on the back of my neck stiffen. Whatever it was, I did not like it.

"If it wants out," I said, "We let it out. We open all the doors and we get everyone to go outside until it leaves."

"How will we know if it leaves?" Dominic asked.

"I think we'll know."

With Dominic's help, we ushered everyone out of the house. It took a little persuading, as no one was very eager to leave the warmth and relative safety of the building. When our friends asked us what was upstairs, we told them that a raccoon had gotten into the house. It was scared, but it just wanted back out. A few of them saw the pale, shocked look on our faces and regarded us with undisguised skepticism, but we stuck to the story. So, mugs of cocoa in hand, people grabbed sweaters and jackets and marched out of the house. Dominic and I propped the doors opened and joined the knot of people huddling for both comfort and warmth.

Dominic was just about to ask me whether or not this idea was going to work when all the doors of the house slammed shut at once with the sound of a rifleshot. This was followed by a sound of rushing wind. The breeze that rattled the branches of the trees carried with it that same peculiar, musty smell that had assaulted us in the attic.

Everyone jumped, eyes flying to the house. Dominic and I exchanged uneasy glances.

"Hey, guess what," I managed after a few startled heartbeats. "I just saw our little raccoon friend waddle out. It's safe. We can all go in now."

No one asked why Dominic and I went up into the attic to put the board and trunk back into place. We wouldn't have explained it to them if they did.

The house felt oddly lighter once whatever it was had left, and we settled in to a fun evening of movies, conversation, and, eventually, sleep. When we woke up the next morning, serenaded by robins chirping in the trees, the events of the previous night seemed as distant and improbable as a nightmare. Someone put coffee on, and we had breakfast on the porch, watching the sun burn away the last ribbons of mist that clung to the surface of the lake. It was quiet and perfect and beautiful, and it was easy to pretend that everything we had witnessed—even the strange, smelly intruder—had no place in such a bucolic reality. But Whitethorn Woods was not done with us. In many ways, it had saved the best for last.

Cleanup started promptly after breakfast. We weren't in any particular hurry. We had all day to clean the acreage up, taking down the spooky decorations and storing them for next year. The university only wanted us off the property by dark. This seemed reasonable, as the next day was a school day for all of us. We quickly learned, however, that the schedule of the land itself superseded any schedule imposed by the college that owned it. In this case, Whitethorn Woods wanted us gone that afternoon. In case we had any doubts about its schedule, it offered a message that was very, very clear.

Sometime around four that afternoon, a hush fell over the woods. I had experienced this before in the week that I spent prepping the property. I had asked a few people about it, to see whether or not it was just some sort of natural phenomenon I was unaware of. Even though I'd grown up in the country, I accepted that there were many things about nature that remained mysterious to me.

We all felt it, even those who had scoffed at the bizarre events of the previous nights. The air seemed to grow tighter, and all the animals fell silent. Nothing seemed to stir, not even a breeze. We hadn't cleaned everything up yet, although at this point our labors were confined to the area directly around the "good house." One thing that was giving us trouble was the fire pit. We'd managed to build a bonfire so hot, the ground was still steaming whenever we poured water on it.

I remember looking up suddenly when I heard a strange sound echoing from deep in the woods. It was a heavy pounding noise, and it seemed to reverberate on the very air. I looked at my friend Liz, asking, "What on earth is that?" She shrugged, and worked a little more quickly.

Evan came out of the "good house," peering in the direction of the sound.

"What is that?" he asked.

"I have no idea. But it sounds like it's getting closer."

The sound continued its ponderous rhythm, never speeding up but growing in intensity over the next several minutes. We could not shake the sense that something was approaching. And then it seemed as if we had our explanation, for an immense flock of black birds erupted from the woods, coming from the general direction of the sound. The flutter of wings joined the strange, rhythmic pulse, although there were no other sounds to be heard on the heavy, stifling air.

"Just birds," I breathed.

I bent back down to my work, stuffing paper and other debris into a huge lawn bag. Evan continued to stand next to me, ramrod straight. He stared across the ravine to the "bad house."

"What are they doing?" he asked.

I cannot answer that question to this day. I know what I saw the birds doing, but I still have no explanation for it. This final experience at Whitethorn Woods remains something that unsettles me. If I go too long without thinking about it, I can almost convince myself that it never happened. Both Dominic and myself, years later, had just about managed to believe that this last part of the experience was all in our heads, but then we got to talking about it at a party. All we could say at the end was, "That really happened?"

It happened. I witnessed it. I cannot explain.

A flock of black birds erupted out of the woods—crows, starlings, grackles, other birds I wasn't sure I could name. They burst into the clearing above our heads, but instead of moving over us and passing beyond the lake, they started to drop out of the sky. They landed on the "bad house" first, until the roof was black with them. Crows and starlings of every shape and description. When they landed, they fell silent and sat there, just watching us with their beady little eyes. This wasn't horribly alarming until we realized that there was a pattern to this flock. They were marching toward us, inch by inch, covering the clearing in front of the "bad house" until it was just a sea of sleek feathered heads, sharp beaks, and cold, glinting eyes. There was a ravine that separated the two houses, about ten feet deep with sharply sloping sides. A bridge connected the two houses, and the blackbirds descended upon this wooden structure with its flaking blue paint. And whenever a bird landed, it folded its wings and fell silent, staring, and its fellow would land in the space just before it. On and on this went until blackbirds covered every inch of the yard in front of the "bad house." They filled the ravine. They covered the bridge, and with each new wave that dropped from the sky, they drew inexorably closer to us. Underscoring the eerie silence of the birds was that strange pulsing that still emanated from the woods.

Barry reacted before anyone. He jumped into his purple Geo Tracker and gunned the engines.

"I'm getting the hell out of here!" he cried, glancing with bulging eyes at the oncoming wave of creepy birds.

"But you've got the keys to the gate!" Evan cried.

Whitethorn Woods was gated and had a high fence all around. The only way in—or out—was up a winding one-lane gravel drive that crossed one of the lochs and through the gate. We were expected to lock this behind us when we left, then surrender the keys once we returned to the university.

"Five minutes!" Barry yelled, poking his head out of the sunroof on the Tracker. "I'll wait five minutes. You guys don't come by then, I'm locking this place up and getting far, far away."

Spitting gravel out behind his spinning wheels, Barry careened up the drive, toward the distant gate.

The pounding continued. The air was thick, and birds kept dropping out of the sky, only to land closer and closer, staring silently at us with bright black eyes. The air was stretched tight against the afternoon, and it seemed as if something was just on the verge of crossing into our reality, but there were just birds and more birds, and that sense of something coming . . . coming . . .

If this were a work of fiction, I would tell you that in the next moment, as I stood there gawking, something terrible burst out of the woods. It pushed the trees aside with the very bulk of its being, and yet it was something so grotesque, so immense, that I could barely comprehend it. Some hulking creature, out of space and out of time, glinting in colors that no human eye could see, erupted from the shadows between reality and loosed an ear-splitting scream.

But reality is rarely as neat or predictable as a work of fiction, which always must have a beginning, a middle, and an end. As I stood there, taut anticipation thrumming upon the air, I expected something horrific to explode out of the woods. And yet, all I saw, minute by minute, were more blackbirds. There was that continuing crescendo of sound, but it seemed as if the crescendo had no end. The sense that something was coming continued to build, and yet it, also, had no apparent denouement.

I suppose I could have waited for the blackbirds to get so close that they would cover me—or perhaps go into a frenzy and, like the avian extras in an old Alfred Hitchcock movie, begin to shriek and peck me to death. But despite my curiosity, my friends wouldn't allow me to tempt fate and stay. I really wanted to see—needed to desperately, because there had to be something more to this experience than just some manic flock of birds, descending out of the sky in mind-boggling droves, just sitting, silently, regarding us from the ground.

I never got to see the conclusion. Barry had already beat feet in his Geo tracker, and we could only hope that he remained near the entry gates, keys in hands and engine idling, waiting for the last straggling refugees of Whitethorn Woods to escape.

I got in my car and drove away. Glancing into my rear-view mirror as I navigated the narrow bridge over the lochs, I saw that the birds were still coming, dropping on the sky and filling the spaces along the grass where we so recently stood. I never found out why, and I never got the opportunity to return. And that's what separates this real-life horror story from a work of fiction. There is no satisfactory end, no twist in the final lines that makes a sudden and eerie kind of sense. Why were the birds behaving as they were? Was there meaning behind their silent descent and the way they just stood there, watching, watching? I always think to myself, "If only I'd stayed a few moments more . . . "

But then, would I still be here to tell the tale? I will never know.

A Stitch
in Time

In the early nineties, I was in a band called Sacrosanct, along with several other friends from my university. The driving force behind the band was Dominic St. Charles, a figure who has appeared several times within these pages. Like most people, once I graduated I got busy doing other things, and the band fell by the wayside. I got wrapped up in my writing career, and really didn't give my musical side much thought for many years. That is, not until Dominic contacted me late in 2002, inquiring about the rights to a song.

Since our college days, Dominic had moved to Chicago and was hard at work with another incarnation of the band, this time called URN. Sacrosanct had been a gothic rock band, while URN had a distinctly metal feel. Even so, Dominic felt a couple of the songs from Sacrosanct could be updated for his new line-up, and he wanted my permission to use some of the things we'd written together.

It's always good to hear from an old friend, especially when you feel that you've fallen out of contact for no better reason than sheer inertia. As life goes by and people move away, it's so easy to become too busy to just reach out, even to good friends. As Dominic told me about his new band, the pride and excitement in his voice reminded me how much joy it had brought us to make music together. Before the conversation was over, I had not only agreed to let Dominic use the music I had co-written, I had also offered to come along on the next tour as a guest vocalist.

Traveling with a band is one of the most demanding, exhausting, and exhilarating experiences a person can have. Unless you are in a band that has achieved a national reputation, touring is far less glamorous than most people might suppose. If you're lucky, your band has a van to store both its performers and its gear, and if you're even luckier, you get paid enough after your gigs to actually afford a hotel room for all concerned. More often than not, bands are offered "crash space" as a part of their deal. This is when the promoter arranges some place for the band to sleep. Sometimes, this place is a hotel, but more often than not, it's the house of someone connected with the show or the promoter, or just someone's friend who's into music enough to open their house to a band for a night.

Needless to say, sleeping on the couches of complete strangers makes for an interesting time. Sometimes it's interesting in the Chinese-curse sense of the word. Rock musicians make strange bedfellows to begin with, and the kinds of people who are willing to open their homes up to a random band tend to have residences that are, to put it mildly, *colorful.*

To take some of the stress of unpredictable lodgings away from the already stressful experience of touring, Dominic would make arrangements with his many far-flung relatives and close personal friends in order to provide the band with safe places to stay. Comfort and safety were so important that sometimes we would arrange the tour around these familiar way stations, stopping by an uncle or an aunt's house for a home-cooked meal and a fresh, clean bed in between gigs at smoky nightclubs in forgotten corners of big cities.

It was at one such stopover that I met Vera. Vera was Dominic's grandmother, and she had died several years before.

Dominic knew that his grandmother still haunted her old house in a scenic small town in Maryland, but he did not see fit to warn us about this. As the touring van wound its way along the serpentine country roads that twisted through the foothills of the Appalachians, it was the keyboardist, known by her stage name Sophia, who mentioned the ghost in the first place.

"Michelle's going to sleep in Vera's room, right?" she asked. "Because I won't sleep in there anymore."

"Uh, sure," Dominic responded, glancing up at the rear-view mirror to see what I thought about this proposition.

"As long as there's a bed, I don't really care," I sighed wearily.

"Well, I won't sleep in that room," Sophia declared. "You know she doesn't like me."

Dominic tightened his grip on the steering wheel. Navigating the overloaded van and its trailer through these narrow country roads was getting pretty dodgy, but I could tell that it wasn't just the roads that had Dominic unsettled. Since our days together in college, Dominic has always had a curious relationship with the paranormal. A devout Roman Catholic, Dominic is open to the idea of psychic abilities, but he really doesn't believe in them for himself. Nevertheless, he is repeatedly drawn to people and situations where something strange is afoot—case in point being our very unusual adventures at Whitethorn Woods. Dominic himself professes to have all the psychic sensitivity of a block of cheese, and his inability to perceive the things his sensitive friends experience contributes to his skepticism.

"So what's wrong with the room?" I finally asked.

All but squirming in his seat, Dominic said, "Sophia says my dead grandmother is still at the house."

"And she doesn't like me," the sprightly keyboardist replied. "I'm too wild for her. She wants Dominic to settle down with a nice, normal girl. I'm a rocker and a practicing witch. Vera does not approve."

Dominic sighed, but I couldn't tell if he was just aggravated at the idea of ghosts or at the notion that his grandmother was still trying to run his life from beyond the grave.

"Hank's seen her, too," he admitted. Hank was Dominic's step-grandfather who now lived alone in the house.

For the final fifteen minutes of the drive, Dominic and Sophia recounted Vera's story.

Several years before, Vera had gotten very sick. She went home once it became apparent that there was nothing further doctors could really do. Dominic took time out of his life, moving in with his grandmother to help care for her. Over this time, he grew very close with Hank who, although not related to Dominic, took to the young man as if he were his own grandson. Together, Hank and Dominic did what they could for Vera, who, from the stories, was not always the most gracious of patients.

A stern and old-fashioned lady, Vera was quick to voice her disapproval of people, especially when it came to things like her grandson's love of rock-and-roll. This was ironic, because she herself was one of the sources of Dominic's love for music. She was an organist, and some of Dominic's fondest memories were of her playing the organ that still sat enshrined at Hank's house.

Eventually, Vera succumbed to her illness, dying in her home. Hank was crushed. Although he was surrounded by reminders of the dead woman, he was determined to remain in the home they had shared together during life. He could see her touch everywhere —in the furniture, the family photos, the decorations, and especially the organ still set up in the sunroom. When we asked about Vera, a bittersweet sparkle lit up Hank's tired old eyes, and the first thing he showed us was that organ.

Hank, an old widower and the kind of practical, levelheaded person who others often describe as "salt of the earth," tried to move on with his life. Sharing a meal with him in his spacious home, it was evident that he still missed Vera, but he tried not to let his grief consume him. This was difficult, because he often felt as if Vera was still present in the home. At first, he attributed this to the fact that so many of her things were still there, reminding him of their life together. As the sense of her presence continued, growing even stronger, he began to worry that maybe his grief had unbalanced him. Sometimes he could swear he heard her voice, and on more than one occasion, he heard her at the organ, playing favorite songs.

Hank did not speak openly about these experiences. He was an old-timer who had spent his entire life in that small rural town, and claiming that the ghost of his dead wife was appearing to him was just not something he would do. Although Hank was not the sort of person that one would peg as a believer, he wasn't at all frightened by his experiences. In fact, he would have found them comforting, if not for the fact that they made him question his sanity more than once. When Dominic brought his bandmate Sophia out to spend some time with his beloved step-grandfather, Hank was overcome with relief when she bluntly pointed out that Vera still lingered in the house. Sophia felt Vera's presence in the room where she had died, but her sense of the old woman was most powerful when she sat down at Vera's beloved organ. Vera's connection to the organ was so strong, in fact, Sophia almost felt overwhelmed by the woman.

"When I play her organ, it's like she tries to possess me," Sophia explained as the band settled in for the afternoon. "I can feel her trying to work my hands, so she can play, too."

Sophia felt that her reaction to Vera was heightened by the fact that she was naturally sensitive to spirits.

"As a witch, I work with spirits a lot, so I'm used to seeing and communicating with them."

We gathered round the organ, admiring the old instrument. There was certainly a feeling of nostalgia that seemed worn into the smooth, ivory-colored keys, and as Sophia played around, I almost thought I could smell a sweet, powdery perfume. Later, as I was settling in for the night, the atmosphere of Vera's old room seemed to grow heavy, and I could not shake the impression that there was someone standing over me, looking down with a certain amount of disdain. Vera was hardly a malevolent spirit, but she still clung to her old-fashioned values. It seemed clear from the tightness in the air that she had measured me with my short hair and my Gothic fashion, and she did not approve.

The next day was a day off for the band. Hank's house was situated on a hill overlooking vast, rolling fields. Several of us walked around the property, just enjoying the view. It was autumn, the air was crisp, and we were miles away from any of the distractions or pressures associated with performance. Of course, a musical group of any genre doesn't get very far by resting on its laurels, so by evening, most of us were going over our parts or double-checking our gear. As a vocalist, I was the lightest traveler of the bunch. My instrument was me, so I had no wires or amps that might break during the drive. I did, however, have several stage costumes that I had brought along for our various gigs. Our next show was in New York City, and it was a pretty big one. The folks who came to this club in Gotham tended to dress in high Victorian fashion, so I had packed my favorite ruffled poet's shirt just for the occasion. In going over my gear, though, I noticed that there was a huge, gaping tear at one shoulder. The shirt was several years old, and it looked as if a seam had finally given way.

About the only "girly" thing I can do is cook, so I despaired of being able to fix the seam. I wasn't even certain if anyone had a needle and thread. I went to Sophia, who had enough of a domestic streak in her that I thought she might be able to help. I showed her the torn seam, but she shook her head gravely.

"Do you know if there's a needle and thread around?" I asked.

"My grandmother's sewing kit should still be around here somewhere," Dominic offered. "Hank hasn't thrown any of her things out. Let's go see."

Hank directed us to the sewing kit, which was a rather elaborate affair. I dug through the collection of spools and thimbles and bobbins, finally pulling out a thread that matched the ivory color of the shirt. I had the kit out on the kitchen table, and Dominic, Sophia, and Hank were all sitting around me, each sipping coffee of tea.

"If my wife was here, she'd fix that up in a jiffy," Hank said, gesturing to my torn shirt. "She was always sewing buttons and stuff back on shirts for me."

As I struggled simply to thread the needle, a less-than-conventional thought occurred to me.

"Sophia," I asked. "You said Vera's appeared to you at the organ?"

Sophia nodded.

"Not appeared, exactly. Whenever I play it, I can feel her standing over me, and eventually it feels like she's trying to possess me. I guess I don't play it the way she wants me to, so she moves my hands herself."

"I wonder . . . " I said, and got up, heading for the sun room.

"Where you going?" Sophia asked.

"Light's better here in the kitchen," Hank called after me.

"That's okay," I called back. "Give me a few minutes alone in the sunroom. I want to try something."

The room was chilly, not being insulated as well as the rest of the house. It was full of shadows, for night had fallen nearly an hour before. I flicked on one of the lights, then took a chair near the organ.

"I know you don't like me," I started, talking generally, to the air. "Dominic told me how you were old-fashioned, and how you felt ladies should behave like ladies, that there were just certain things women should know how to do."

The room was silent around me. Distantly, through the closed door, I could hear jovial conversation continuing in the kitchen.

"I was never taught most of those things. I really don't have a talent for any of them. But if you can, I'd like you to show me. I need to fix this seam, and I have no idea how to do it."

I felt Vera's presence gather near me, as if she had been standing on the other side of the room and now she deigned to draw near. I could still sense that stern disapproval, but underscoring it was another emotion. I can't reduce it to simple words. It was something like that annoyance a parent has for a child who just refuses to do something for themselves. There was irritation, but the real foundation of the emotion arose from care and concern.

Feeling as if Vera stood now, over my shoulder, I threaded the needle, not really needing more than the weak light from the one lamp to see. I made a few inept stabs with the needle, trying to draw the seam closed from one end. Then I could almost hear Vera clucking her tongue at me, and the sense of her presence grew even stronger. I felt almost as if hands closed around mine, very gently, guiding me. I could feel her communicating with me—a rapid question-and-answer that happened at a speed greater than conscious thought, so it seemed as if I just knew what to do next.

Fifteen minutes later, the shirt was repaired. I held it up and examined it in the light. It was almost impossible to spot the repair to the seam. Perfect and straight, it held tight. As a seamstress, I usually stick the needle into my fingers more often than I stick it through the cloth. But this work evidenced skill I did not possess.

Did necessity simply inspire me to rise to the occasion and accomplish the admittedly simple task of sewing a seam? Or did Vera actually offer me tailoring advice from beyond the grave?

I wore the shirt in New York City and at several other events during the course of the tour. It's one of my favorite pieces of clothing, and it's taken a lot of punishment over the years. Even now, years later, I continue to wear the shirt on certain special occasions. And, perfect and straight, the seam has held. As for me, I still can't sew on a button to save my life.

Walking the Thin Line

I worked in the hotel industry for a number of years, running the night audit at the front desk on third shift. A lot of people don't like third shift, because it is a lonely shift. Unless you're working a five-star hotel in a big city, you are likely to be the only one behind the front desk, if not the only employee in the entire hotel. All of the guests are asleep, and in the silence the hotel seems to take on a life of its own. Even without the presence of spirits and the lingering echoes of emotion left to build up in the rooms, a hotel at night can be unsettling. Noises from the ice machines and elevators, the faint insect buzz of the fluorescent lights, the hum of the computers behind the front desk—every little noise becomes improbably loud and strange. People who are easily disturbed by the unknown typically do not last in the job.

I really enjoyed working in hotels, especially on third shift. One of the hotels I worked at was widely known to be haunted. Even the local police recognized that the hotel had ghosts in it, and one lady on the local force would often come in while she was on duty, ostensibly to check the safety of the hotel but mostly to discuss ghostly phenomena with me. She was sensitive herself, and was at first baffled as to how I even managed to work third shift at that particular hotel. It took me awhile to convince her that I actually liked it. The ghosts rarely bothered me, and when they got too rambunctious, I just told them to settle down.

I could fill another book just with stories of the employees' experiences at that hotel. Normally, chain hotels like to keep the ghostly phenomena that occur within their walls a secret. Employees are instructed not to speak with the guests about weird experiences. Although some bed and breakfasts have established their reputations based on ghosts, most standard hotels feel that haunted rooms are bad for business. That particular hotel had a kind of "don't ask, don't tell" policy with the guests. Employees were free to talk about their experiences with one another, so long as they were discreet about it and the guests did not overhear. If you worked at that hotel, eventually you had an experience. The only person who refused to believe any of it was the owner, and I still believe that he just didn't spend enough time to get to know the ghosts under his roof.

The hotel had quite a population. We had an old lady in the dining room who smelled of White Diamonds perfume. Sometimes she roamed the halls, but more often than not she lingered near the food. I learned from the psychic police officer that an exceptionally obese woman had died in the hotel. Natural causes had claimed her body, but her love for food seemed to have claimed her soul. There was a businessman who had hanged himself from his bathroom door when his extramarital affair took a bad turn. When housekeeping went to check on the room the next day, they couldn't get the bathroom door open at first because his body was wedged up against the door. Chillingly, this was the most common complaint from people who subsequently stayed in that room—the bathroom door would get stuck, often feeling as if something was leaning heavily against it from the other side. We never explained to the guests that they were struggling to open the bathroom door against the dead weight of a suicide who never checked out.

In addition to the spirits of people we could prove had died on the premises, there were a few spirits that no one could rightly account for. There was a little girl in a white dress who sometimes ran up and down the halls. The front-desk manager saw her a few times. From his descriptions, her clothes seemed a little outdated, so she may be connected to a building that stood on the property before the hotel. The couple dressed in evening wear was as mysterious as the little girl. This couple was encountered by two guests and an employee. All three living people approached the couple to comment on their clothes—but when they got too close, the couple disappeared into thin air. Of all the spirits at the hotel, none of them seemed malevolent, with the exception of something that lurked in the kitchen. Whatever was in there did not feel human, and it often had a habit of rattling the pans. It was a dark presence, and one of the few things I might be tempted to describe as "demonic." It never ventured out of the kitchen, which was just fine with me.

If I told all of the stories connected to that hotel, I could fill another book completely. I worked there for three years, and it was rare that a week went by without a report of some ghostly phenomenon. I witnessed quite a few myself, but one of the most educational cases involved a nervous-looking older woman who checked in for a week. For privacy's sake, I'm going to call her Gertrude.

Gertrude was a small, fine-boned woman who appeared to be in her fifties. She was well-dressed, with carefully coiffed, graying hair. I first saw Gertrude when she came up to the front desk asking for more coffee. At the time she seemed pleasant, if a little tightly wound and exceptionally particular. As she stood at the front desk waiting for me to finish taking a reservation, she busied herself by neatly arranging every stack of paper within her reach, from the hotel chain's flyers to the registration cards left out for guests. She collected all of the pens and put them in a neat row on one end of the counter, and when there was nothing left to fuss with, she picked at the cuticles of her nails. Nothing seemed immediately strange about this. She simply struck me as just another neat freak.

I gave Gertrude her coffee, and after thanking me in warm, if formal, tones, she minced back to her hotel room. A few hours later, I got a call.

"I really don't want to bother you," the person said on the other end. I recognized Gertrude's clipped and formal tones. "But I think there's something in my room."

"Something?" I responded.

The phone indicated what room she was calling from, and I double-checked the number. Gertrude was staying in the business-man's room. We often had people check out of that room with-out explanation. Sometimes they would call down first, asking us to fix the bathroom door—it was sticking, they would say, almost like someone was holding it closed from the other side. Once in a great while, we had a guest brave enough to simply point out that the room was haunted. If I was on shift, I would acknowledge this, even though I wasn't supposed to. I know what it's like to sense something and feel like you're crazy for sensing it. I figured affirm-ing their impressions was the least I could do, considering they got stuck with a haunted room.

"Something," Gertrude said carefully, "or someone. I feel like there's a presence here. Watching me. Do you have someone stay-ing in the next room?"

I looked at my registry.

"No," I assured her. "There's no one on either side of you."

"Are you sure?"

"There's almost no one in that entire hallway."

"What about above me?" she asked.

"Ma'am, the hotel only has two floors. You're on the second story of the building. There's no one above you."

"Well, there's something in the bathroom," she said, dropping her voice to a whisper. "Right now. A man in the bathroom, and he's staring at me."

"Would you like me to move you to another room?" I inquired.

"Are you sure there's no one above me? I hear things in the ceiling!" Gertrude said, continuing in that frightened whisper.

"Should I send someone down to check on you?"

"No!" came the immediate reply. Then Gertrude slammed down the phone.

All of this was a little weird, especially given Gertrude's fear, coupled with her reluctance to leave the room. At the time, I just assumed she was sensitive to ghostly phenomena. She was, after all, in a room that had a ghost in the bathroom, so her impressions of the man staring at her weren't exactly wrong. Short of relocating her to another room, however, there was precious little I could do.

I made a note of the complaint, knowing exactly what my manager would think when he saw the room number. Then I went back to my duties for the night audit, which at that point in the night amounted to a whole lot of nothing. Fortunately, no one objected to me reading on the job. A little while later, the phone rang again. It was Gertrude.

"Does this hotel have rats?" she asked. Her voice was sharp and whispery, like she was trying to keep her voice down but holding her mouth very close to the phone.

"Rats?" I responded. "No, ma'am. There have been no reports of rats in the hotel."

"There are rats here. I can hear them," she insisted. "In the ceiling. If there's no one above me like you said, it must be rats!"

The old woman sounded terrified. At that point, I made a judgment call and decided to bend our ghost policy just a little bit. Clearly, she was hearing and sensing things, so maybe I could put her mind to rest by explaining them.

"Ma'am?" I asked. "I get the impression that you're maybe one of those people who is sensitive to things. Do you sometimes feel things when you walk into a room? Like if people have been arguing, but they're not arguing anymore, can you still feel the conflict, hanging on the air?"

"Yes," she replied. "Yes I do. How did you know?"

"Well, that presence you're sensing in the room. It's not just your imagination. There is something there. I can guarantee that it cannot hurt you. If you want to move, I can switch you to another room, but if you stay there, that presence is not likely to go away. It's just something people sometimes sense in that room. If they're sensitive to certain things."

"Oh, is that all?" Gertrude said, as if I just offered the answer to the most profound riddle in the universe. "Well, thank you. You've been very kind and understanding."

And then she hung up. But that was not the last I heard from Gertrude that night.

For some people, there is a fine line between psychic and psychotic. In our modern culture, most of us with psychic gifts are encouraged to question our sanity. Neither science nor psychology have much use for the paranormal, despite numerous experiments addressing issues like telepathy, telekinesis, and astral projection. Because these gifts are not widely accepted, most people with psychic abilities spend at least some of their time wrestling with the specter of mental illness. Whenever an experience occurs, there is always the fear that, this time, it is nothing more than a delusion. The most difficult part about accepting the legitimacy of psychic abilities is the fact that some people can be both very psychic and very disturbed as well. I was soon to learn that Gertrude walked that dangerous, thin line.

The phone rang again.

"Young lady?" she asked. "I'm sorry to bother you again, but you seem so very knowledgeable. I have another question for you."

"All right," I replied.

"Are the electrical outlets in this hotel grounded?"

That was not the question I had expected.

"Um . . . yes," I said, after a pause.

"Are you certain?" she persisted.

"Everything's fine with the electrical system. Why do you ask? Are you having trouble with an outlet?"

Gertrude did not answer right away.

"Well, I think one of them is leaking," she told me.

And this is where my conversation with Gertrude took a turn for the surreal.

"Leaking?" I asked cautiously.

"Actually, I think someone in one of the other rooms is shocking me. You know, from a distance," she whispered. "I'm getting these tiny little electrical shocks up and down my legs. I think someone is using the outlets here to electrocute me."

"So your legs are tingling?" I inquired. "Like maybe you sat on them wrong and they went to sleep on you? You know, that pins-and-needles sensation?"

"Oh yes," she said. "They're tingling. But it's because someone here is electrocuting me."

For the next several minutes, I attempted to allay Gertrude's fears of long-distance electrical shock. I'm not exactly an electrical engineer, but I knew enough about electricity to understand that it simply could not behave the way she was describing. I was familiar with that electric-shock feeling she was experiencing in her legs, however. I have poor circulation due to an early heart condition, and I will sometimes get an electrical sensation in my legs if I've been sitting for long periods of time. I also knew that pinched nerves can cause a sensation close to what she was describing. I gave Gertrude the benefit of the doubt and assumed that she simply didn't understand what she was feeling in her legs. Instead, she was trying vainly to come up with something that seemed to her to be a logical explanation. And then she started going on about the rats again.

Several phone calls into the night, I could not deny that Gertrude's sensations were the symptoms of mental illness. I had done volunteer work in my teens at a mental hospital with my great-aunt, and I was fairly certain Gertrude was schizophrenic. The worst part about this, for me, was the fact that this particular episode had started with a fairly accurate impression of a known paranormal phenomenon connected with her room. On one hand, Gertrude seemed legitimately sensitive. On the other, she also seemed quite delusional. The more I talked with her, the more it seemed that those two things were wound up together in her mental illness. There were things she knew about the spirits in the hotel that she could only have known had she herself experienced them. Her descriptions of the ghostly occupants, right up to the old lady with her perfume in the dining room, were in line with descriptions I had heard again and again from perfectly sane guests. But then Gertrude would launch into another tirade about the giant rats in the ceiling that were coming to get her, or the man in the other room who was using an unknown device to make electricity jump out of the wires in the walls to electrocute her. It was alarming to hear how completely intertwined the real and the unreal were in her mind. It was especially alarming because I knew that most mental health professionals would insist that *all* of her reports stemmed from the unreal. To most people, even the ghosts were delusions.

Eventually, Gertrude and her delusions became so disruptive that we had to ask her to leave. She claimed that she had nowhere to go, but after some argument she had us call her daughter. We learned from her beleaguered daughter that Gertrude had recently been released from a mental hospital. I asked what Gertrude had been treated for, and the daughter confirmed my suspicions: Gertrude was diagnosed with schizophrenia.

According to her daughter, Gertrude was often in and out of such hospitals, mostly because once she was released, she refused to stay on her medication. The daughter wanted nothing to do with the poor woman, as she was afraid to have her mother stay in her home lest she turn violent. Ultimately, the weary-looking young woman showed up and drove Gertrude to another hotel, putting her up there for another week. My hotel had a pretty good relationship with the other hotels in the area, and eventually we learned that Gertrude started the same exact thing at the new hotel. Like us, the management at that hotel had to ask her to leave. Where she went after that is a mystery.

I called up the night auditor at the other hotel where Gertrude had been staying. I needed to know how many of her impressions were nothing but madness speaking. I asked the front-desk clerk whether or not he remembered Gertrude. He did—she had made quite an impression, just as she had with me. I asked him what she had talked about, and he told me about the rats and the long-distance electrocution.

"Did she say anything else?" I asked. "Maybe about a presence in the room?"

"Nothing like that," he replied. "But man, was the old bat convinced someone was trying to shock her through the walls. How crazy is that?"

"Pretty crazy," I replied.

And yet, as crazy as she obviously was, Gertrude had accurately sensed the spirits in my hotel. How crazy was that?

Hunting the
Shadow People

In paranormal investigations, there are as many different classifications of entities as there are investigators to classify them. Human ghosts are just the beginning—the tip of the otherworldly iceberg. The vast majority of investigators recognize a wide variety of spirits that were never human at all. One of the most ominous classes of nonhuman spirits are beings known as the shadow people.

Shadow people are exactly that: humanoid forms that appear to be made completely of shadow. Their faces are featureless, although some reports describe them as having glowing red eyes. Sometimes three-dimensional, sometimes only two, the vast majority of shadow people are reported as appearing just on the edge of vision.

When the witness looks directly at the shadow person, the being disappears. Sometimes shadow people make their escape by slipping through solid walls, but sometimes they just seem to dissipate, returning to the shadows from whence they came.

Practically all of the ghost-hunters and paranormal investigators out there have their own theories on what various entities really are. Shadow people are no different. Some investigators claim that shadow people are other-dimensional beings, humanoid creatures whose realm of existence sometimes intersects with our own. Others who favor the other-dimensional theory suggest that the shadow people are intentional travelers, scouts, or even invaders whose presence in our reality is no accident. Those who take a more religious approach to otherworldly phenomena interpret shadow people as demonic in nature, their presence a sure sign that evil is afoot. Other investigators equate shadow people with elementals or egregores—spirits that have been created, intentionally or otherwise, out of a focused collection of energy. According to this school of thought, if an area has a violent history, the build-up of trauma, anger, or pain can solidify into an entity that develops its own kind of intelligence and independence. This entity is what others perceive as a shadow person.

In many ways, shadow people are the bogeymen of paranormal phenomena. Once in a great while, someone comes along who claims that these beings are actually guardian angels, but for the most part investigators view these living shadows with shuddering dread. The faceless, fleeting nature of these beings lends itself to horror stories, and for this reason I have always found myself a little skeptical of stories involving shadow people. Not only do shadow people very neatly embody the primal human fear of the unknown, but their habit of appearing just on the edge of vision suggests a more natural explanation for their sightings.

The human brain is wired for pattern recognition, as are our eyes. When we look at random patterns, such as those appearing in clouds, we automatically begin to associate the sequences of shape and texture, shadow and light, with a recognizable pattern, such as a face. Looking at clouds, we do this intentionally, making a game of it. In conditions of low visibility, however, such as a darkened room or a road obscured by rain, we do it completely unconsciously. This can lead to a condition known as pareidolia, in which the brain incorrectly interprets patterns so that we think we see objects or people that aren't really there. When driving, a person might begin to swerve to avoid an object in the road, only to realize at the last minute that the supposed object was actually nothing more than a particularly dense swatch of rain. Walking into a darkened room, a person might suddenly start because there seems to be a figure standing in a corner. With the light on, this figure resolves itself into nothing more threatening than the collected shapes of a chair and a lamp.

In some respects, pareidolia is as much a result of our fear of the unknown as the creatures we sometimes invent to stalk the twilight places. The best way our brains know how to dispel our fears is to give the unknown quantity a shape—something we can recognize and define. And yet pareidolia also demonstrates that we cannot always accurately define the unknown. Sometimes our monsters are nothing but illusions, but there remain those rare occasions when we turn on the light and the ominous figure is still standing there.

My encounter with the shadow people begins in 1996. That was the year I started lecturing to student groups at universities. My first such appearance was at Case Western Reserve University in Cleveland. Case had a pan-spiritual student association called CWRUPA, and in the fall of 1996, members of this group had me come out to lecture on occult history. I had a great time speaking to the group about the occult interests of traditional historical figures, and they ended up inviting me to another function they were having the next month. I got to know several of the student organizers of the group personally, and they started seeking me out for advice on psychic and paranormal phenomena. One of the strangest incidents about which I was asked to offer an opinion involved a student by the name of Paul Trimble.

Paul was in his dorm room with his girlfriend when they both became aware of a presence. Both of them felt very unsettled by this presence. They reported it as seeming invasive. Paul's girlfriend, Beth, perceived the entity as humanoid in form, but made completely of shadow. Paul did not exactly see the entity. Instead, he experienced it in a much more personal manner. Paul reported that he felt as if the entity approached him and reached inside his head. Over the next few moments, he felt as if it were rummaging around through his memories, looking for something. Paul's girlfriend saw the being looming above him, and she was growing more frightened by the moment. Unable to block the thing's invasion of his mind, Paul endured its attention a few moments more. Beth was about to go for help when the shadow being withdrew, leaving just as mysteriously as it had come. Aside from having a terrible headache for several hours afterward, Paul seemed unharmed by this curious attack. He found the experience especially remarkable because he did not ordinarily get impressions of spirits, but his sense of this creature in his mind was quite distinct.

I had no idea what to make of this. At the time I had heard a little about shadow people. Beth's description of the entity—a shadowy, featureless, humanoid shape—seemed in keeping with what I had read about these mysterious beings. And yet I had never encountered anything in the literature that described an attack like Paul's. Even after being violated by this peculiar entity, Paul insisted that he did not get the feeling that the thing was malevolent. Instead, he got the impression that it was merely curious about him. Unable to adequately explain his experience, I instructed Paul in several techniques of psychic self-defense, telling him to contact me immediately if another attack occurred.

It was not long before I heard about another curious shadow person. However, this report did not come from Paul, or even any of the students connected with Case Western Reserve University, as one might expect. Instead, the report came from Dave, a friend who was attending college on the other side of town. I knew Dave through a completely different set of friends. Although I knew he had some passing interest in the paranormal, our main connection at that time was through gaming and the theater. We were both involved in the same production being put on by his college, and after practice much of the cast would go relax at a bar down the street from the school. One night I caught Dave sitting alone at the bar, sketching in his notebook. I glanced over his shoulder and immediately had to ask what he was doing: on the lined paper, he had drawn the image of a shadow person with glowing eyes. It stood in a darkened bedroom.

"What is that?" I asked, ordering another Coke.

At first he was reluctant to explain the image. Most of Dave's social circle was not into the paranormal, and so he tended to be pretty tight-lipped about it himself. More than most, he was always concerned about what others might think of him. Maybe it was the second Long Island iced tea he was working on, but eventually he opened up to me.

"It's something I've been seeing lately," he admitted. "In my room. Does it look familiar to you?"

"I'm not sure," I responded.

"I don't know what to make of it either. It shows up in my room at night and just stands there, watching me. It doesn't have a face, just all shadow, and these big, glowing, cartoon-monster eyes. Sounds crazy, doesn't it?"

"Does it seem like it's threatening you?" I inquired.

"It just watches," he replied.

Once again, I was baffled. Ghosts I could handle—they had become a familiar phenomenon. But shadow people were an unknown quantity. From Paul's report, and now Dave's, they seemed alien. I had no idea where they were coming from, what they wanted, or what they might ultimately do. As with Paul, I described a couple of self-defense techniques to Dave, then asked him to keep me up to date on his experiences. Mostly, I was interested if the entity's behavior suddenly changed.

Thirty-five miles away, another friend was experiencing similar visitations. Mindy was a diminutive blond who I knew through yet another college. Mindy lived in a trailer, sharing it with her boyfriend and several pets. In the fall and winter of that year, Mindy reported seeing a shadowy figure in her home at night. She described the entity as male, very thin and tall. It would stand in the doorway to her bedroom, looking down at her. She did not feel threatened by the creature. Rather, much like Paul and Dave, she sensed curiosity from the thing. Mindy had no contact with either of the groups at the other two colleges, and no one had told her of Paul's or Dave's experiences.

Two more friends, one connected with Dave and one who had no exposure to any of the other experiencers, reported encounters with mysterious, shadowy figures that year. In both of these cases, the entity was described as being humanoid in shape but featureless, as if the entire thing were made completely of shadow. Like Dave's apparition, the shadow people in these cases had glowing eyes, although the color reported in these cases was yellow, while Dave described the eyes of his entity as a distinct shade of reddish-orange. As with all of the reports I had gathered thus far, the entities in these cases were perceived as being curious rather than malevolent, although there was some suspicion in one case that the curiosity might soon give way to threatening behavior. Intriguingly, this particular case occurred in my home at the time, in front of several witnesses. I was not present, but three people reported seeing the entity appear and move toward one specific person. The person in question felt he was being scrutinized by the entity, and he was afraid that if he made any sudden move, the thing would attack. One of the most striking qualities of this incident, beyond the fact that there were multiple witnesses, is that the apparition manifested in a room that had at least one light on. The entity reportedly darted into the shadows that led down to the darkened basement in order to disappear.

For a while I thought that these were the only individuals who experienced visitations from the mysterious shadow people. Yet in retelling this experience a year later, I had another friend practically jump up and down in excitement.

"You mean it wasn't just me?" she asked.

Kate, a spirit medium I was introduced to during my freshman year of college, had apparently seen the shadow people in 1996 as well. She showed me some journal entries to confirm the dates. Kate was someone I fell in and out of contact with. We would lose one another for several years, only to have a chance encounter at a club or a bookstore. Kate had no direct exposure to the other experiencers that I was aware of, although through some twist of fate, it turned out that Mindy's boyfriend had been seeing Kate right before hooking up with her. Mindy and Kate themselves had never met. Kate's description of her experiences matched those of the others. Several times at night, she saw a humanoid figure standing and watching her. The entity stood in darkness and seemed to be made of darkness itself. It had a featureless face, save for a pair of glowing amber eyes, and she felt that it wanted something, but it never communicated what that something was. The being frightened Kate, especially because it refused to respond to any attempts at communication, but it never directly attacked her. This was consistent with practically every other report.

For some of the witnesses, these sightings continued from the fall through the winter of 1996. For others, like Paul, the entity made its appearance only once. These watchers in the shadows never directly interacted with anyone, with the exception of Paul. Their purpose, even in Paul's case, seemed driven by a need to observe and learn. What motivated them and what secrets they were seeking to learn remained mysterious. I never witnessed one of these things myself, so I never felt that I could be a confident judge of their true nature. The timing of the appearances and the descriptions of the entities suggest that the experiences are linked, and yet I have also failed to determine what all of the witnesses had in common—save for a mutual connection to me.

By the spring of 1997 the apparitions had ceased, as mysteriously as they had begun. We learned nothing further from these enigmatic shadows. Some of the people who witnessed them made a concentrated effort to communicate when the things appeared. Several were typically able to communicate with spirits, and they felt that the shadows remained willfully silent. The closest anyone came to communication was Paul, and even then there was no sense of the entity actually trying to communicate with him. Rather, it was searching *through* him for something, completely bypassing any regular channels of communication and going straight into his subconscious mind.

After the first two reports of these shadow people, I started keeping a journal, documenting the events. Every once in a while I still take that journal out, going over the descriptions given by my friends as well as the possible theories I jotted down to explain the events. I have to admit, over a decade later I am still puzzled and confused by the incidents. Not only do I have no real answer for why these things appeared to a number of my friends, but I am also still at a loss as to what the beings even were. I have read descriptions of shadow people online. I have heard supposed experts discuss the phenomenon on shows like *Coast to Coast*. I have heard the theories put forth by professional ghost-hunters like Jason Hawes and Grant Wilson from TAPS as well as well-read experts such as Rosemary Ellen Guiley. Everyone has theories, but no one seems to agree on what these beings are, where they come from, or what motivates them. Nor does anyone have a suggestion for how we might discover these things.

When I look at all of this information, combined with the details I have in my own files, I feel exactly as if I am looking at a collection of shadows and textures that my brain *wants* to put into a pattern—and yet, I wonder if there is a pattern at all? It's so tempting to try to resolve the dates and descriptions, times and locations, into something that makes sense. After all, as human beings we're wired for pattern recognition. But sometimes the shapes in the darkness possess no recognizable pattern. Instead, they coalesce into a form so foreign that the mind simply refuses to grasp it. My run-in with the shadow people made me realize that not all paranormal investigations can be easily explained, nor will they always make some neat kind of sense in the end. Everything may have a reason, but that's no guarantee that the reason will be something we can discern.

Ghost in a Box

When people learn that you can talk to the dead, you get some pretty strange requests. Sometimes, people want to give you things that they believe are haunted, so you can verify that a spirit is actually tied to the object. More often than not, they want their haunted items back, but once in a while they're actually quite spooked by the idea of having a spirit attached to a little statue or antique watch. In these cases I am generally asked to hang on to the item for safekeeping, or at least to make an attempt to detach the spirit. I have dealt with a haunted jewelry box, and my neighbor at one time wanted me to check out the antique bedstead she and her husband had picked up at a flea market. They had been seeing a spirit in their room ever since they started sleeping in the new bed. These items are relatively mundane, and it's easy to imagine how most of them became haunted in the first place. But nothing in my experience prepared me for an item shipped to me via the U.S. Postal Service that had once been the possession of a very unusual friend.

Many years ago, I made the acquaintance of a man who goes by the name of Wraith. Appropriately enough, Wraith does a lot of work with spirits. Like me, he is sensitive to them, but Wraith has taken his sensitivity to lengths that very few are willing to explore. Put very simply, Wraith identifies himself as a necromancer. He can not only perceive spirits, but he claims to be able to summon, compel, and bind them.

I've made no secret in this book that I have a mile-wide streak of skepticism. This skepticism has kept me stumbling around my own talents with spirits for many years. I have always been drawn to learning more about the otherworldly aspect of existence, but sometimes people make claims that challenge my ability to keep an open mind. Wraith's assertions about his necromancy triggered my skepticism in a pretty big way. There's a sense one medium can get about another, at least in my experience, and so I believed that he was sensitive to spirits. But I had a hard time accepting that he had the power to bind them.

Wraith and I do not cross paths too often, so it never became an issue. People have their beliefs. Some are verifiable. Some seem pretty out there, but if someone is convinced about the reality of his or her beliefs, who are we to judge?

In the end, I did not give Wraith's claims about necromancy too much thought. And then he sent me a message. Apparently, he had an item that he felt compelled to give to me. The item was haunted. In fact, Wraith himself had bound the spirit into the item. This particular item came with a fairly involved story, for the ghost was someone who had been very bad in life, and her disposition had not seriously changed after her death. Wraith had noticed that she was earthbound, and deciding that her spirit was an actual danger if left to roam free, he had tied her to the item as a kind of punish-ment. This was all a little odd, but things got a whole lot creepier when Wraith explained that the item to which he had bound this spirit was in fact the cremated remains of the spirit herself. And he needed my address so he could drop this dubious gift in the mail!

I am not in the habit of receiving the mortal remains of spirits either through UPS or parcel post, so I really wasn't sure what I thought about this proposal. I wasn't even certain that it was legal to mail such a thing. But to be frank, I really didn't believe that Wraith owned such an item. I liked the guy, and he was an interest-ing friend, but I simply could not wrap my head around the idea of these haunted cremated remains. In the end, I sent him my post office box information almost as a dare. I truly did not think that anything would arrive in the mail. Excessive skepticism can some-times lead to very strange experiences.

A couple of weeks went by. As Wraith only lived about two hours from me, I began to feel validated in my belief that his haunted cremains were just a tall tale. And then I got a notice in the mail. Apparently, I had a package waiting for me. Since I was checking my post office box after hours, I was going to have to come back the next day in order to sate my curiosity.

Imagine my surprise when I brought my slip into the post office and was handed a plain, square box in brown paper packaging. Wraith's return address appeared in an unruly hand in the upper left corner of what had to be the top of this perfectly square object, with a somewhat more neatly printed label featuring my post office box address dead center. I almost stopped to ask the post office employee about the legalities of shipping dead people through the mail, but decided better of it. I later learned that cremated human remains are one of the only things of their nature that one can legally ship through the mail, strange as it may seem.

I headed out of the post office. I resisted the urge to shake the box. Rather gingerly, I placed it, label up, on the passenger seat of my car and headed home. At this point in time, I lived only a few blocks from the post office, but those few blocks came with a stoplight at every single intersection. I must have been distracted by the very idea of this curious box, because I was too busy staring at it as I approached the first stoplight. I looked up just in time to see brake lights in front of me and to stomp down on my own brake. The car came to a complete, if sudden, halt, and the plain brown box on the seat next to me tumbled unceremoniously to the floor.

This next part requires a little explanation about me. I talk to myself. I do it a lot. I talk to my cats. I talk to my computer. I talk to objects that are utterly inanimate and incapable of answering me at all. I blame the fact that I spend a great deal of my time alone and writing. I do not, at any point, expect responses from the inanimate objects that I endlessly chatter at. Fortunately, my mental health is not in such a state of decline that I have ever heard responses from these objects. So, knowing this, you will understand my surprise at what happened next.

The box had fallen to the floor. I was feeling a little embarrassed for almost missing the light. And so I apologized to the box. More specifically, I apologized to its contents. Wraith had mentioned the spirit's name when he first contacted me about this peculiar gift, and I glibly tried to recall that name.

"Sorry about that, Joan," I said, reaching down to grab the box and place it back on the passenger seat.

In my head, almost immediately, an angry voice snarled, *"Jeanne!"*

I did not hear this with my ears. Spirit communication feels like someone is talking to you, but you are hearing them with an ear that is somehow located inside of your mind. It's difficult to explain to someone who has never experienced it, and it is harder still to explain how a person can tell that the spirit voice is separate and distinct from a natural "inner voice." But generally, when you experience it, it's pretty clear.

I blinked and stared at the box. No further psychic impressions were forthcoming. Clearly, however, I was staring at the thing for too long, because behind me, an irritated motorist laid on his horn. I sped too fast and tried to make it before the next light turned red.

I didn't make it, and given my current rate of speed I once again found myself slamming down on my brakes. I'm really not this bad of a driver under normal circumstances, but playing chauffeur to some poor woman's cremated remains hardly qualified as normal even in my bizarre life.

Of course, when I slammed so suddenly on the brakes in my tiny little car, the box was again sent rolling off the seat. Let me mention now that I am also bad with names. Terribly, abysmally, embarrassingly bad. So my next move was to reach down, grab the box, and place it back on the seat. Patting it affectionately, I said, "Sorry, Jane."

"*Jeanne!*" came that voice once again, and it was not at all happy.

If my two mistakes were not indication enough, I really did not clearly recall the name Wraith had given me for this particular spook. But I managed to pull myself together enough in order to get the both of us home without any further incidents. As soon as I arrived, I rushed to my computer and went back through the commentary with Wraith. Then I looked long and hard at the unwrapped package I held on my lap. My brain scrambled for a "logical" explanation. The unconscious mind is a tricky place. We remember things often without even realizing it. So perhaps I had simply unconsciously remembered her name, even while my conscious mind had gotten it wrong.

The name Wraith had given me, of course, was Jeanne.

"So, you're Jeanne, hunh?" I asked, patting the box.

I did not hear any kind of spiritual commentary, but at that particular moment I perceived a sense of satisfaction coming from the contents of the box.

I sat and went back over the online exchange, committing the details of Jeanne's life to memory. Wraith claimed that she had murdered her family and that she had served several life sentences. She died in prison in the eighties. I was a little unclear on exactly how her remains had fallen into Wraith's possession, and I wasn't certain that I really wanted to know. When I opened up the package, there was a certificate in the box that seemed to make everything legal. It had her name, her birth and death dates, and the time and place of her cremation. Most of this information was echoed on an ugly green label pasted to the top of her box. The box was a nondescript brown not unlike the paper Wraith had wrapped it in. Inside the box was what looked for all the world like a bronze-colored coffee can. Its lid was firmly in place. I did not have the guts to open it and look inside.

I put Jeanne on a bookshelf. Over the next few days I tried to verify her story as it had been recounted by Wraith. Even with her first and last names, birthdate, and death date, I could not uncover any solid information on Jeanne, at least not through the Internet. I remained dubious about the fact that she had been a murderess, and yet I had also failed to believe that she had existed in the first place. It was dumbfounding enough to have Wraith's pet can of ashes sitting on my bookshelf, let alone trying to wrap my brain around the fact that a spirit did indeed seem to be attached to that ash. It defied so many of the things I thought I knew about spirits. How many mediums will assert that the dead do not linger near their bodies or their tombs? Ghosts are supposed to be more inclined to haunt the places they cherished in life, or they linger close to their loved ones.

Yet here was Jeanne, sitting on my bookshelf and making my cat nervous.

That was another thing about the haunting. My cat, Katya, who had already proven herself to be somewhat sensitive to spirits, aggressively did not like Jeanne. There was no logical explanation, except perhaps the possibility that she could smell the ash through the can. But from the moment that Jeanne entered the house, Katya had started acting skittish and strange, especially in the living room where the box sat on an upper shelf.

Finally, I had to test it. I thought I could sense a spirit tied to the ashes, but Wraith had set those expectations up for me. What I needed was a friend who was also sensitive to spirits, someone who knew nothing at all about Jeanne. If I turned her box upside down, it was plain-looking enough that no one would suspect its true nature. If my impressions were correct, and a very angry old dead woman was in fact bound to her own cremated remains, anyone I handed this box to would be in for a rude surprise. But, rude or not, I would know for sure. I decided to chance the experiment.

Sarah Valade is a medium who used to run tours in Wayne County, before her career took her out of Ohio. Wayne County is considered by many to be one of the most haunted counties in Ohio, and Sarah had a particular knack for communicating with spirits. Sarah was due for a visit anyway, so I decided that she would be my psychic guinea pig. I was not at all subtle about it. Sarah came over, and I held out the box. It was upside down, to hide the label.

"Tell me what you get off of this," I asked.

I swear, I tried not to smirk.

Sarah reached out and took the box, a mildly curious expression on her face. She had not held Jeanne's box for more than a few moments before her expression contorted and she practically hurled the box to the ground.

"Eww! What the hell do you have in there!"

Sarah gave a full-body shudder, and then glared at the box as it lay on the floor.

"Oh, fine, bitch at me for dropping you," she said snidely to the box. "Seriously, Michelle. Where did you get her? She's just nasty!"

I tried to look innocent. I don't do innocent very well.

"Ooooh," Sarah said, aggravated and pacing now. She was trying to shake off the impressions, but once you made contact, Jeanne was persistent. Sarah made a face at me. "You knew that would happen, didn't you? You know, you could warn a girl first!"

I bent to retrieve Jeanne's box. I held it, label up, and gave it a little shake. The ashes rattled around audibly in their coffee can-shaped urn. Sarah narrowed her eyes and laughed in a very satisfied way.

"She hates that," she observed. "Serves you right," she added sharply, apparently talking to Jeanne.

"Well, someone sent me these ashes," I said, putting Jeanne back up on her shelf. "And he said he had bound this really nasty spirit into them."

"So you handed them to me?" Sarah demanded, incredulous.

I shrugged. "I needed to know."

For a little while, I wasn't certain that Sarah would ever forgive me for springing Jeanne on her like that. But instead, she seemed content to take her ire out on the spirit herself. From that day forward, whenever Sarah stopped in for a visit, she would make a point of taunting Jeanne and doing things that she felt the spirit did not like.

I have still failed to find any hard evidence of Wraith's story about Jeanne's identity as a murderess. However, I did find a use for this peculiar gift. Jeanne is a pretty lively spirit, and she has a personality that is well-documented among the people who have perceived her. Whether her story is true or not, *she* seems to believe it, so she will eventually recount the circumstances of her murders to anyone with the ability to ask. Given that her story remains consistent, I've taken to using her to teach people how to communicate with spirits. Jeanne's less-than-amicable personality is something of a shock at first, but even this helps to verify people's impressions. When you pick up a nondescript box and hear an angry woman screaming in your head, it's fairly hard to deny that something weird is afoot.

I'm still not sure how Wraith managed to bind Jeanne to her own cremated remains. But I know now that my spirit-wrangling friend didn't really deserve all of that skepticism. I've puzzled over his technique for several years now, and I've just had to accept that there are some things that I have to believe, even though I may never understand. I suppose the world is improved with a little bit of mystery.

A Little Bit of Voodoo

There are certain places where the fabric of reality seems to have grown soft, if indeed it was ever solid to begin with. In places like these, the veil that separates the world of the living from that of the dead is tattered and worn by forces that we can only begin to comprehend. At night, and sometimes even during the day, you can walk the streets and encounter visions from ages past, apparitions that have all the clarity of living and breathing beings. The French Quarter in New Orleans is one of these places. There is something magickal in the air down there. Perhaps it is the commingling of so much history and so many different cultures. Perhaps it's something primal that has seeped into the land from the nearby bayous. Whatever the source of that powerful magick, things are different in the French Quarter, and the rules that many of us are accustomed to working with do not always apply.

My first visit to New Orleans' French Quarter occurred, appropriately enough, on the weekend nearest to Halloween. I was in town for a book signing and a vampire ball. I'd arrived early so I had a few days to kick around the city and sightsee. Usually when I traveled for business, I barely had time to get off the plane and freshen up in the hotel before I had to rush off to my engagement, but this time I had a whole day to myself before things started to get crazy. So, with this in mind, I decided to indulge my inner tourist and simply explore the historic sights the city had to offer.

When I got on the trolley that took me from my hotel to Canal Street, I already felt as if I had stepped into another world. First of all, nothing can prepare a stranger for the heat and the cloying humidity of southern Louisiana. The moisture in the air hits you the minute you step off of the plane, and it wraps itself around you like a wet velvet blanket for the duration of your visit. For the first few days, I got the feeling that I was inhaling water every time I breathed.

But the exotic (for a Northerner) temperature was not the only thing that made Louisiana seem like a totally different world. Born and raised in a quiet little town in Ohio, I was never exposed to a whole lot of cultural diversity. In my town, diversity involved the fact that some of the local families had originally come from Ireland, while others had come from Germany, Poland, and perhaps Italy. I spent the better part of twenty years surrounded only by people whose skin tones ranged from peach to cream with perhaps a dash of olive here and there. In New Orleans, however, I was treated to a completely different palette of color. There was such a range of diversity that I tried not to stare, in case people might get the wrong idea. But the diversity didn't stop just at the glorious range of skin colors. I heard the lilting patter of French, rapid-fire conversations in Spanish, and English spoken with such a rich accent that it sounded like the speakers were making a meal of their words, rolling around every syllable to savor it on their tongues.

I'm something of a sensation junkie, so I was loving this. I became so immersed in the sights and sounds of the people on the trolley that I almost missed my stop. But then I was on Canal Street, diving into the crowd. Canal Street, although easily recognizable as a part of New Orleans, was nevertheless an area that could have been transplanted to just about any other major city in America. It was clogged with pedestrians and traffic, and the buildings that overshadowed the road boasted a fairly common architecture. The shops that populated these buildings were also relatively ubiquitous. I saw one or two chains that must have been unique to the South, but otherwise I spied a Payless, a Walgreens, a Subway, and, of course, a McDonald's.

My sense of direction has never been exemplary, and so I had come armed with a little map from the hotel and a watch that also contained a compass. The French Quarter looked like it would be a piece of cake to navigate. It was mapped out in a very simple grid, with the riverwalk hugging everything at the bottom. I got myself oriented from Canal, picked a side street that boasted the first of many tourist boutiques, and headed in the general direction of the Quarter.

For a couple of blocks, I was surrounded by the same heavy-set buildings that had crouched, brooding, on either side of Canal Street. And then, as I rounded a little bend, it was as if I had stepped directly into the past. I don't know if I have the words to do it justice, for the transformation felt truly magickal that very first time. There I was, stomping along the uneven sidewalk, glad for the relative shade cast by the buildings, and very unhappy about the heat. Then I looked up and saw these gorgeous wrought-iron verandas. They were painted a brilliant white, and somewhere between me and those buildings, the taller structures stopped, so the afternoon sunlight cascaded down onto everything, making it shine, even though I myself stood in pools of shadow. The ironwork was hung all over with some lush green vine that reminded me a little of a philodendron. The word *bougainvillea* sprang to mind, although I had only ever read about this plant in a variety of stories.

I stopped and stared, blinking against the sudden light. The architecture of the buildings that stretched ahead of me was of a completely different type than the other buildings I had thus far encountered in New Orleans. None of these structures were more than two stories tall, and this added to the sense of walking into a living past. Although I had seen such architecture in books before, I had never seen anything like it in the flesh.

The French Quarter, as I would learn later, is one of the oldest remnants of the American past. It has changed very little since the days when Louisiana was a French colony, and some of its original structures still stand. The layout of the streets, those narrow, cobbled little paths that we know as Bourbon and Toulouse and Dumaine, has not changed since the days when people rode horses rather than tooling around the city in automobiles. And the streets still resist change. There are very few cars in the French Quarter. On busy days, motor vehicles are simply not allowed, but even when there's no rule against them, the streets are so narrow and crammed with people that it's simply easier to walk.

I stepped from the shadows of the modern buildings and headed, it seemed, into history. I had a sense that the magickal aura of the city itself settled over me as I did so. As it would turn out, that sense wasn't exactly wrong.

I'm not sure when I first noticed him. Even as I write this, I find myself wondering if he wasn't there on the trolley from the very start. There was that man with the deep, rumbling voice who spoke in rolling, rich French patois. His skin was the color of luscious dark chocolate, and hadn't he been wearing a black topcoat, despite the heat? He caught my eye then, but maybe it wasn't him.

What I do remember is noticing the smell of rum and cigars. Given the ocean of scents that wafted about me the moment I stepped into the French Quarter, I did not originally give this much thought. There were so many restaurants, and the way the two-storied buildings were constructed, most of them had portions that were open onto the street. The scent of food simmering in rich Cajun and Creole spices permeated everything. And then there were the bars, with their racks of shiny beads colored like hard candies, and their novelty drinks, bright with the same candy colors. They added a sultry sweetness to the already heavy air. Scents like lemon and lime and pineapple predominated. Then there were the cafés with their authentic French beignets. They added even more sugary scents, plus maple and cinnamon, praline, molasses, and the warm froth of lattés.

But eventually, even in this sea of mouth-watering scents, I began to notice it, just for its persistence. I would round a corner, and the breeze would bring it to me again: the rich scent of an expensive cigar and the warm, sweet undertone of rum. I don't smoke myself, but unlike many nonsmokers, I do not find the scent of cigars universally offensive. Some cigar smoke is even pleasant, a rich indulgence that speaks of luxury and repose. I began to look around to see who was smoking. I saw people smoking cigarettes, but I never saw anyone with a cigar. This left me vaguely puzzled, but I decided that it had to be wafting out of one of the open-air portions of the bars. I had walked through a good portion of the Quarter by this time, but maybe the smoke kept smelling the same because it was a popular brand. I couldn't think of a better explanation, so I contented myself with this.

I think I had been in the French Quarter for a few hours, intermittently catching the scent of rum and cigars, when I first caught sight of him. I'd turned yet another time to see if there was anyone smoking a cigar nearby, and there he was, standing on the street corner opposite me. Curiously enough, he wasn't holding a cigar, and yet my mind automatically associated him with the scent. He was a big black man, and his skin was a color so dark that it resembled an oil slick. It was black enough that the sun brought out shades of purple here and there on his forehead and on his cheeks. I can't clearly remember his hairstyle, and I'm not sure if he was clean-shaven or if he had some stubble on his face. What I do remember are his mirrorshades. They reminded me immediately of the sunglasses worn by cops, like on that old TV show *CHiPs*. I couldn't see his eyes through the mirrorshades, but when he smiled his teeth were startlingly white against that profoundly dark skin. Those teeth were long and huge, but his smile was not unfriendly.

I didn't see him for long. I returned his smile, but then I was jostled by a knot of raucous gay men, their chests bare and their necks festooned with beads. The sun hadn't even set yet, but they were already well on their way to being thoroughly and gloriously drunk.

When I looked back for the man who had smiled at me, he was gone. It didn't seem eerie then. Of course, Voodoo had never been a subject I spent much time studying, so I had no way of knowing the significance of that particular scent, nor the curious associations tied to a figure wearing mirrorshades.

I continued with my day, marveling at the iron pineapples that topped so many of the fences, staring unabashedly at the performers in the streets. Every corner seemed to boast a living statue, and these people were painted head to toe in silver or white. They stood there on crates, utterly still, until someone dropped a little spare change into the hat or can on the pavement. Then they would come magickally to life—some with more skill than others—and perform some eye-catching feat from atop their crate. As if they were worn clockworks whose springs wound quickly down, their activity lasted only a few moments. Then they returned to that stillness, awaiting the next generous passerby. I suppose if one lived in a city with such performers day in and day out, they would seem as ubiquitous and irritating as the more prosaic beggars I had encountered in other cities. But in the Quarter, they were enchanting, at least to me.

Eventually, my wandering feet led me to Jackson Square. I wanted to visit the Saint Louis Cathedral. Even though I had grown away from my Catholic roots long before, I still retained a deep love for old stained glass and Gothic architecture. But the cathedral was closed for the day, and I remembered that I had an errand on Jackson Square.

Around the central park with its proud, equestrian statue, Jackson Square is crammed with Tarot readers and psychics, seemingly at all hours. Like the living-statue street performers, these people simply show up, day in and day out, stake out a little corner, and set up shop for themselves. They do not officially charge for their services, although most of them have clear lists of prices nevertheless. When I first heard from a friend about the Tarot readers on Jackson Square, I wondered how many of them could possibly be genuine. Since anyone with a deck and the desire to cadge a few dollars from passersby could set up a table, I doubted that there was any kind of quality control. My friend had assured me that the city itself took care of quality control, though I really didn't understand what he meant at the time. Smiling benignly at my confusion, he had insisted that I look up his friend Raven, who often read cards on the square.

Of course, he never gave me a last name or much of a description, beyond the fact that Raven was gay, usually had red hair, and I would know him when I saw him. So I wandered around the Square a few times, peering at the various readers and trying to see if any of them stood out to me. As it turned out, several had red hair, and more than a few were flamboyantly gay. Eventually, I worked up the courage to approach one of them—an adorable young man who looked like he often dressed in drag, and had worn his make-up, if not his wig and other accouterments, to work this day. His cut-off jeans were flirtatiously short, and his long, slender legs were shaved smooth and bronzing in the sun.

"Um, hi," I started, feeling both shy and self-conscious. "I'm looking for a Tarot reader named Raven. Can you help me?"

He looked up from the Dean Koontz novel he was reading and cocked an eyebrow at me.

"Girlfriend, you're gonna have to do better than that," he drawled. "There are at least five Ravens working here today."

"Well, my friend told me this Raven is gay and has red hair," I offered.

The out-of-costume drag queen chuckled.

"Well, that narrows it down to three. Sweetie, you got any more information?"

Helplessly, I looked around the Square. After a few moments, I shrugged.

"I guarantee I read cards just as good as this Raven does. Why don't you have a seat?"

Politely, I declined.

"I'm not looking for a reading. My friend told me to look for his buddy Raven."

Only I didn't say *my friend*. I said his name, a very distinctive nickname that he has had for all the years that I've known him. The Tarot reader perked up at the name. Apparently my friend had not been exaggerating when he said that practically all of the Tarot readers on Jackson Square knew him from the time that he lived in New Orleans.

"You're *his* friend? Well, why didn't you say so? I know the Raven you're talking about, but he's not due in for a couple of hours. Meantime, why don't I introduce you around?"

And very suddenly, with the talisman of a name, I was suddenly no longer just a simple tourist standing on the edges of the little world on Jackson Square. Priscilla got up from her station and ushered me over to a bench where a cluster of other readers were taking a break. I was introduced around and got to hear some interesting reminiscences about the friend who had sent me in search of Raven. When they learned what book I was in town to sign, their enthusiasm for me grew. In the space of about half an hour, I was told all the secret places to hang out in the Quarter—shops to avoid, stores that sold genuine magickal articles, the best restaurants, the cheapest bars. Then they told me about the magick of the city: where to stand when it rained so you could hear the ghostly Requiem; where to experience an echo of the cries and alarms that reverberated down the centuries from a time when the French Quarter nearly burned to the ground; what graves in the cemetery to seek out if I had a hankering to practice Voodoo or its country cousin, Hoodoo. It was like being inducted into a secret world woven throughout the fabric of that already magickal realm.

After an engaging discussion, I offered my thanks and told them to let Raven know I was looking for him. Now that they all knew me on sight, they promised to point me out to him the next time I wandered through Jackson Square. Then I said my goodbyes and started off to explore a few of the interesting places they had recommended to me.

As I was walking away, one of the readers jogged to catch up with me. She was some mix of the various races that populated New Orleans. Her skin was the color of caramel, with a scattering of darker freckles across her high, sculpted cheeks. Her hair, the color of raw honey, was twisted into thin, neat dreadlocks that fell halfway down her back. I remembered admiring that hair while talking with the other readers, but I also remembered that she had been very quiet during our talk, seeming to be preoccupied. Now she fixed her green-flecked eyes on me—although she also kept glancing nervously over my shoulder. The gesture was so persistent that I was tempted to look behind me myself, to see what on earth might be looming over me.

"You hang on a moment," she said. "Please. I gotta tell you something."

"Okay," I said gamely.

But suddenly she was short on words. After a few false starts, she finally started talking about a spirit called Papa Ghede. He was a big black man who often wore mirrorshades, and apparently she'd seen him following me.

"I was starting to wonder about that guy," I said, relieved. "I've been catching him out of the corner of my eye since I got into the Quarter. I don't usually see ghosts like they were living people anymore. He's got to be a pretty strong spirit."

Again, her eyes flicked to that spot over my shoulder. From her anxious expression, I almost thought she was checking to see if I had offended him. Maybe she was, because she wasted little time in explaining to me the difference between Papa Ghede and your garden-variety ghost. You see, Papa Ghede is a *loa*. Loas are particular to Voodoo. They're like ancestor spirits with an attitude. They have human passions and even human weaknesses, but they possess all the power of demigods. The closest thing in a Christian context would be to compare them to the saints, and, appropriately, each loa is associated with a specific Catholic saint. Still, most Catholics would be shocked and amazed if any of their saints deigned to step out of heaven in order to appear and even occasionally possess one of the devoted. With the loas, this was par for the course.

I didn't know anything about this at the time, having had no interest at all in the practice of Voodoo. Like many people in Western culture, I'd been exposed to a little too much Hollywood where Voodoo was concerned. My only real points of reference were bad B-movies that went on about mysterious Voodoo curses and, of course, the 1988 film *The Serpent and the Rainbow*. Although that film had presented itself as being based on a true story, it had been touched by Hollywood to the point that it really challenged my ability to believe.

"So, I'm being followed around by a Voodoo spirit?" I asked, nonplussed.

"You talked shop with Priss and the others, so you better know that's no bullshit. There's a ritual tomorrow night that honors Papa Ghede. You should go. He wants to talk to you."

She told me the time and the place. Unfortunately, the ritual was running at the same time as one of the events I had been contracted to attend. I told her as much. She shook her head and glanced behind me again. For a few seconds, her eyes lost focus, and I had the distinct impression that she was peering into another world.

"If you can't make that ritual, you do this one thing at least. You get some rum and a good cigar. Get down to one of the cemeteries if you can, but be careful if you go at night. Bad people hang around some of those places and you might get yourself mugged. But you try to get yourself to a cemetery and set out that rum and cigar at a headstone. Don't matter which one. Just tell Papa Ghede that you're leaving it for him."

"Rum and cigars," I muttered. Of course, I'd been smelling them all day.

"You just do that, okay?" she said. "Promise me."

And she was staring over my shoulder again, meeting the gaze of someone who, if I turned around, I might or might not see.

I promised and made a mental note to go shopping for the offering before the end of the day. The next day my schedule was going to get crazy.

As I walked away a second time, taking the shortcut through Pirate's Alley, it occurred to me that I had just lived through a moment that could have been a scene in some cliché Voodoo thriller. It also occurred to me that the only things I knew about Voodoo at the time were similarly cliché. Despite my wide and voracious reading through all aspects of the occult and world religions, I had skipped over Voodoo and its related traditions. To be honest, I had found it hard to take Voodoo very seriously specifically because it had been the subject of one too many spooky and over-the-top B-movies. I briefly considered the possibility that the Creole Tarot reader had just been pulling my leg and having a little fun with the ignorant Northerner. But then, for about the fiftieth time that day, I caught a whiff of rum and cigars.

Cliché or not, I was going to find a cemetery before my visit was over and leave some things to Papa Ghede. Falling back on my old attitudes toward all things psychic and otherwise strange, I figured that it certainly wouldn't hurt to make the offering, and it might even help if there was something really going on. Although my head still loved to question everything, my instincts definitely had other things to say.

The rest of my trip was filled with a very different set of adventures (some of which were fictionalized by a friend in a novel entitled *Pedestrian Wolves*). Very quickly, time got away from me. Finally, it was my last night in New Orleans and I still hadn't gotten around to appeasing Papa Ghede. I'd caught sight of him a few times in the interim, so I knew he was still interested in talking with me—or whatever it was a Voodoo loa really wanted from a pale Yankee adventuring in the French Quarter.

When the woman (who gave her name as Carmel) had first talked to me about finding a cemetery, I immediately thought of the tombs at Metairie. I'd wanted to visit that cemetery ever since I'd seen photos of the mausoleums there. Since I lacked a car and was short on time, however, Metairie was out of the question. Apparently there was a cemetery within walking distance of the Quarter, but every native I approached for directions warned me away from it because of the neighborhood it was nestled in. After the third set of dire warnings, I decided it wasn't going to be an option. This left me with my rum and cigar, a few hours of night left, and no cemetery.

I'm that person who never reads instruction manuals. I've always preferred to figure things out for myself. It might take me a little longer to put a bookshelf together, but by the end of the project, I actually understand the process. I learn through trial and error. I don't take much away from the process if I just blindly follow something that's already been laid out for me, step by step. As so many of the tales in this book attest, that quality of mine extends beyond building projects to include all things psychic and magickal as well. Many of my most potent experiences have come about from doing what felt right at the time and exploring the consequences, rather than adhering to some formula that others claimed should bring results.

So I started wondering about the formula Carmel had given to me. I had the rum and a cigar, of course, because their persistent scent really seemed to confirm their necessity in this case. But how essential was a cemetery? It occurred to me, eventually, that a headstone is simply a memorial. Sure, there's usually a body underneath it, but the bones don't always care. It's more the spirit of the thing. Cenotaphs or markers honoring a burial at sea connect to the spirit at a distance, but they still serve as focal points that the living can use to connect with the deceased.

Lacking a cemetery, I decided that any memorial erected to honor the dead would have to do. Fortunately, there were two such memorials prominently displayed in the French Quarter. One was the statue in Jackson Square itself. I went there first, but the little park inside the square is surrounded by an iron fence, and it was locked up tight that night. I'm sure others more adventurous than I have found their way through that fence and into the little park after hours, but police officers tend to call that trespassing. I've never liked to push my luck with the authorities. That left me with the one other memorial I had admired earlier during my stay.

My feet led me easily down to the riverwalk. Earlier I mentioned that I tend to lack any kind of directional sense. This holds true in every city I have ever visited, with the exception of New Orleans' French Quarter. Maybe it's the simple grid pattern of the streets, maybe it's the relative size of the space. And maybe it has something to do with Papa Ghede, guiding my steps as he walked along behind me. I have no idea, but I do know that, for once in my life, I didn't have to worry about getting lost or hopelessly turned around someplace. I found what I was looking for with relative ease, and given the hour, I was additionally graced with relative solitude.

There's a statue near the riverwalk, amidst a promenade of flags. I honestly don't recall what it commemorates, and I haven't been to the French Quarter since before Hurricane Katrina hit, so I haven't checked the statue recently. But it had a plaque to indicate that it honored something, and considering the circumstances, that was good enough for me.

I approached the side of the statue that faced away from the busier part of the riverwalk. Given all of the wild and crazy things I had already witnessed going on in the French Quarter that weekend, I couldn't imagine anyone would stop to question me. But I still didn't relish the notion of having to explain myself. So I crouched down in the pool of relative shadow, opened the tiny bottle of rum (one of those little bottles that get stocked on airplanes or in hotel minibars), and poured it out as a libation upon the ground. Then

I unwrapped the cigar and laid it down at the base of the statue. I called to mind the image of the man in mirrorshades, and I said the name that seemed so strange to me. *Papa Ghede.* I closed my eyes in silence for a few moments, hoping that Papa Ghede shared my view that, in both magick and prayer, it's less about what you do than the intent with which you do it.

The wind kicked up over the water, carrying with it a cool, though moist, breeze. I didn't ascribe the wind to any supernatural agency, though it felt good on that hot and sultry night.

After the wind, nothing else happened. I crouched there for a few moments, mentally leaving myself open to communication from the Otherside. I thought I felt a presence, but it came and went so quickly that I really wasn't sure. Spirit communication is so easy to confuse with one's imagination, especially when you're expecting something to happen. That night, crouched before the memorial near the riverwalk, I wasn't sure what to expect, but given the persistence of my earlier experiences, I expected something.

After a while, I stood up and started the long walk back to my hotel beyond Canal Street. I left the cigar, damp with the spilled rum. After some of the stuff I had seen strewn across the pavement on Bourbon Street, I was fairly certain that one lone cigar would remain unremarkable. No sunglass-clad specter appeared to haunt my steps as I walked back to the hotel through the quiet streets. The only people I encountered on my way were weary travelers like myself, each following the siren song of sleep after the endless parties of Halloween weekend.

The absence of contact, after so many persistent experiences, seemed curious. Carmel had seemed very certain that Papa Ghede wanted to communicate with me. Had I skipped the wrong part of the recipe by opting to use a general memorial rather than a cemetery stone? I allowed that this was possible. But maybe I simply didn't know what to look for or even how to listen. The whole subject of Voodoo was a mystery to me, and perhaps the biggest mystery of the moment was why a Voodoo loa would even want contact with me in the first place.

When I got home I was still wondering about the experience, so I hit the books. I wanted to learn more about this mysterious Papa Ghede and what he might mean to me. I got chills the first time I read an entry about him. You see, Papa Ghede is the Lord of the Dead in Voodoo. He's sometimes also known as Baron Cimetière —the Lord of the Cemetery—or Baron Samedi. If Carmel had mentioned him by that name, I would have recognized him, albeit through the dubious medium of a role-playing game.

In Voodoo, the Baron often appears wearing a black top hat, a black top coat, and mirrorshades. At least one of the sources that I consulted noted that his sunglasses are typically missing one of their lenses, a sign that he peers into the realms of both the living and the dead. Despite his associations with death, he is known to be fun-loving and jolly. He's a real spirit of the crossroads in that respect, because he oversees sex and fertility at the same time that he watches over death and the dead. This is why the Baron of Cemeteries is syncretized with Saint Gerard, the Catholic saint of childbirth. For him, life and death are part of the same revolving door between the world of spirits and that of the flesh.

If any of the loa were to take an interest in me, it only made sense that that loa would be the Baron Samedi.

My travels have taken me back to the French Quarter several times now. Each time, for the first few hours that I walk through the Quarter, I am dogged by that scent of rum and cigars. If I look, I'm likely to catch sight of a smiling man with skin black as an oil slick, still wearing those mirrorshades. He never speaks to me, just lingers on the edge of my vision. I've come to accept that, despite Carmel's impressions, he didn't want to speak with me. He just wanted me to acknowledge his presence. I don't know if we have anything to say to one another beyond recognizing that each of us is aware of the other's presence. Admittedly, I've never had the guts to attend any of the Voodoo ceremonies held in the French Quarter around Halloween. I would feel like a stranger trying to usurp another person's culture. Voodoo just doesn't feel like something that belongs to me. But the Baron himself seems colorblind, so maybe I will explore it one day. In the meantime, whenever my journey finds me in New Orleans around All Hallow's Eve, I make a point of leaving an offering of rum and a cigar as a nod to the presence of Papa Ghede.

Late
Check-Out

The problem with taking a vacation from work is that the to-do pile doesn't just go away because you are gone. The minute you get back, there's always something waiting for you. I remember taking a three-day vacation early in my writing career. I'd gone out of town for some promotion or another. But once the weekend was up, I had to come back to my very mundane job. Since the writing hadn't really gotten to the point of supporting me yet, I still worked nights at a local hotel.

I liked the job because it was relatively stress-free, and that gave me time to concentrate on other things. Since it was such a low-key job, the surprises that typically waited for me after a short vacation were never of such a magnitude as to be unworkable. Usually I just had a list of rooms that were offline for maintenance issues, and maybe I had a note about some last-minute tour group coming through (the tours were the bread and butter of our hotel). But otherwise there was rarely anything pressing.

I loved my job at the hotel, and some days I still miss it. People fascinate me, and a hotel is a perfect place to people-watch. You get to see these little slivers of their lives, often unadorned with the usual masks, since they're travel-weary and intent not on maintaining pretenses but only on getting to bed. I saw moments that were heart-breakingly sweet, like the young couple who were stealing away for the first time to spend some time together. They weren't like your usual teens trying to rent a room. They were both old enough, but just barely, and painfully self-conscious about what they were about to do. The boy was so desperate to make sure that everything was perfect, and you could see in her eyes that even if they had stayed in a hovel, so long as he was there, it would have been like a palace to her.

Not all of the snippets of humanity that I got to see from behind the counter were so flattering to the human race. Just as people often steal away to a hotel in order to have a steamy night of romance far away from nosy family, so, too, do rougher sorts use the relative solitude and privacy of a hotel room for other things. I became acquainted with the local police on my shift, because there was more than one fugitive who had chosen to hole up in our hotel. Conveniently placed right off a major highway, the hotel was a prime location for someone on the run.

This placement led to another problem that sometimes arose at our hotel. Every once in a while, someone would check in with the intent of committing suicide.

A lot of the psychology of suicide is revealed in this often unspoken event at hotels. Believe me when I say that my hotel was not unusual in the fact that people sometimes came there to take their own lives. The exact same placement right off the highway that made the hotel occasionally convenient for a fugitive from the law also made the hotel seem like the perfect place for a fugitive from life. Suicide, after all, is all about escape. It's the ultimate method of running away. Often, a person who is seriously contemplating this very final step gets in their car and goes for a long drive. Partly, they drive to get away from the source of their turmoil, which is almost always some issue at home. Partly, they drive to give themselves time to think about the course of action that lies ahead.

These tear-filled late-night drives sometimes end up with them returning home with a clearer head and a renewed ability to wrestle with life's problems. Sometimes the drive was just not good enough, and they look up to find themselves near a cheap hotel. They pull off the highway and check in, telling themselves that it will be easier to think if they're alone. These sorts check in because they still aren't sure if they want to take that ultimate step in running from their problems. They figure a good night's sleep might help put things in perspective. Others check in because they have already made up their minds, and they do not want to be interrupted. I've heard from one or two who almost went this route, that they ended up at a hotel because they could not imagine putting their loved ones into the difficult position of having to find them when it was all over. They would rather have a stranger clean up than force their children or husband or another relative to wash the blood out of the carpets or rinse it down the tub. Either way, these sorts check into the hotel to get away from the people they know, and sometimes, when morning comes, they check out again and go back to these people. Every once in a while, someone like me would call down to their room to ask if they wanted a late check-out.

Eventually we would find them. And after the coroner and after the police, after the cleanup crews with the really expensive service that exists to handle the kind of mess only death can leave behind, after all of that, we would rent the room out again, and never talk of it. This code of silence is maintained for the privacy of the individual and their family as much as it is maintained for the business of the hotel. If you knew that someone had ended their life in a fit of despair in the very bed you slept in, would you be able to stay in that room? Or step into the tub, knowing that someone's lifeblood had run sluggishly down the drain?

Ignorance is bliss, and the hotel industry banks on that.

There had been three deaths at my hotel. All of these deaths had occurred in the years just before I started working there. One was definitely a suicide. One was due to natural causes, and one was apparently still under investigation, because we were not even allowed to discuss that particular death among ourselves as hotel employees. At least two of the people connected with these deaths lingered at the hotel in spirit. I had come to know them over the years of my employment, and even become fond of them. They were harmless spirits. Most of the ghosts that walked the halls or lingered in the rooms of that place were harmless, and it was easy to grow accustomed to their presence there at night. They rarely got up to mischief, and the one entity that did cause problems always kept to its territory in the kitchen. It would bang the pots and pans on occasion, and it made that room of the hotel bone-chillingly cold, but most of the time it kept to itself.

Truth be told, I had come to view the spirits at the hotel as companions and friends. A few of them would sometimes wander near the front desk in the wee hours of the morning, dropping in as if to say hello. I know other people found this behavior creepy, and it was one of the reasons that the hotel management had a hard time keeping people in my particular position. During the day, it was sometimes possible to forget just how spiritually active the hotel was. On third shift, when all the guests had settled in for the night, it was a lot harder to dismiss the presence of the ghosts.

The sheer familiarity of the spirits at the hotel was one of the reasons why, when I returned from vacation that week, things felt immediately off. I didn't think too much of it at first, assuming that some of my discomfort had more to do with having to leave the glamour of the big city behind and settle back into my relatively ignominious position as a desk clerk. At the time, I lived in two worlds at once, shifting, not always comfortably, between Michelle the mousy and efficient night auditor and Michelle the charismatic author of vampire books. If I'd spent a lot of time in one role, it was sometimes difficult at first to shift gears into the other.

So I didn't really think too much about the odd feeling I got when I walked into the hotel that night. I just chalked it up to an uneasy transition. The second-shift person filled me in on room outages and such, but he was always in a hurry to get home and away from work. He scooted out as quickly as he could, and soon I was left all by myself. It was a Monday night, so the solitude was deep. The hotel's business had declined from 9/11 onward, but even before that decline, Mondays were just not busy nights.

Hardly daunted by the lack of company, I pulled out my laptop and started work on an article for my website. I got a lot of writing done at this hotel, and if you own any of my early works, chances are you own something that was, at least in part, written behind that front desk.

When I write, I get entirely sucked in to the work. Sometimes this meant that a customer could walk up to the front desk, and I wouldn't even notice until they made some kind of noise. The regulars who knew me never got offended by this, and most of the one-time customers just assumed that, since I was obviously hard at work on a computer, I had to be doing hotel business. Still, it's not like I went out of my way to be rude. I just could get easily distracted by my work.

About halfway through the article, my head snapped up. I heard someone clear their throat. It wasn't exactly a patient sound, and so I jumped up to go through the greeting and the rest of the process of checking someone in.

There was nobody there.

Now, one of the other ghosts in the hotel had a habit of coming up to the front desk at night. He, however, announced his presence through a set of actions that was practically a ritual. The ledge of the counter squeaked if you leaned on it, and he would lean forward, making it squeak under his nonexistent weight, and then he would give a rap on the wood with his knuckles. He was almost always invisible throughout, but you would get the distinct impression of his presence as he leaned against the counter. The sound I heard was not in keeping with his usual routine, and the presence I felt on the other side of the counter was certainly not him. Our wayward business traveler could be melancholy at times, but on the whole he was a friendly and passive ghost. The presence I felt on the other side of the counter now was hardly friendly. It seethed with anger and impatience. I stood there, awash in waves of unaccountable fury and accusation, completely baffled by the presence that I felt. This was not one of our usual ghosts. And, whoever it was, they were having a very bad day.

I'm not always 100 percent comfortable with speaking out loud to spirits, at least not with other people around. I'm always afraid that doing so makes me look like one of those crazy people who blithely talk to things that aren't there. But alone at the hotel, with little chance of another person being around, it was easier to speak out loud in order to communicate. I still felt a little funny about it, but it's one of the easiest ways to communicate with spirits.

The spirits themselves don't really need to hear our words. Their method of communication bears more in common with telepathy. But I've found that it is easier to clarify my own intent by speaking and not simply thinking in the general direction of a spirit. I also find that it makes the communication feel a little more normal—albeit, only as long as some random person doesn't walk by and witness me conversing with thin air.

"I don't who you are," I started somewhat cautiously. "And I don't know what you want. But you've got to settle down, okay? I can tell you're pissed about something, but you really need to chill or I won't talk to you."

What followed was a barrage of sensations that took me a little time to sort out. Spirit communication can be hard to describe. The minute I put it into words, it suddenly sounds neater and cleaner than it really is when it happens. I get messages from spirits, and in order to share those messages with others, I have to put words to them. I do my best to maintain the tone and feel that is unique to the spirit, but the words are mostly my own. The communication on the part of the spirit is often this split-second flash of data that has so many roiling layers of meaning and emotion that it takes longer to understand it than it does to receive it. Every once in a great while, I'll encounter a spirit that can communicate in such a way that it almost feels as if I really am hearing someone speak with my mortal ears. But such communication is rare, and I think it depends more on the abilities of the spirit than on the abilities of the receiver. More often than not, spirit communication is just this barrage of images and sensations, and I'm left to sort it out and make it sound more ordered than it really is.

This spirit, with its extremity of emotion, was more disjointed than most. I got the impression that my visitor was a woman. I didn't get the sense that she was old and I didn't get the sense that she was very young. But there was a sense of weariness that made me think that perhaps she was in her late thirties, at a time in her life when she felt that most of the idealism and promise of her youth was gone. I never once perceived her with my physical eyes, but I nevertheless got an impression of her appearance. Short, maybe five foot four, five six at the most. Blond hair, dyed. I got the impression that her skin was either weathered or very tanned. And, strangely, I got the impression of some kind of accent, like she was from West Virginia or somewhere similar in the South.

I knew from experience that these details in her appearance had a lot to do with her image of herself. Ghosts aren't physical. All they have are the memories of their physical body. More often than not, these memories are idealized, sometimes skewed to be more beautiful than they were, sometimes skewed to be uglier. Some spirits are so disconnected from who they once were that the self-image they project is little more than broad, impressionist strokes that vaguely resemble their once-human form. Others are so completely anchored to the life they just led, they seem nearly as solid as a living person. A lot really depends on the emotional state of the spirit and how that spirit feels about his or her previous life. Appearances could even change, depending on the spirit's emotional state, so that something that originally seemed hideous and inhuman could, as it made peace with its life, develop into a shining thing of golden light.

With details like the overly tanned skin and the brittle, peroxide-blond hair, I knew the spirit that I was dealing with was still very anchored to the life she had just led. And she was not seeing herself in the most favorable of lights. Her anger, frustration, and disappointment were so strong that it was hard to sort out the source of them, but all of it resolved into the sense of an urgent question:

Why? Why am I still here?

I didn't hear the words, but after being blasted with that storm of emotions a few times, I finally sensed their meaning. A little logic mixed with a dash of supposition, and I thought I had an idea of what was going on. The woman before me was a suicide. She had come, presumably to my hotel, in order to get away from whatever unresolved emotions had troubled her. She had come seeking escape from the worry and the feelings and the pain, and now, here she was, stuck exactly in those moments and those sensations that had led her to seek oblivion. Nothing had resolved itself. She had found no escape. And now she wanted to know why.

Suicide, when someone considers it with all seriousness, usually hinges upon the idea that this life is all that there is. A suicide is gambling for oblivion. They want escape from their pain, from their responsibilities, from the consequences of poor choices. The last thing they want is more consequences. Unfortunately for the few suicides that I have encountered in spirit, their gamble did not pay off. They worked themselves up to the point where they could take that extreme and terrible step, and most of their courage had come only from the certitude that it would be the end. And then, once the dust settled over their mortal life, they woke up to realize that death did not mean that anything was over. Death just meant that now they had little choice to do anything except brood upon the pain and turmoil that had led them to that step in the first place. It's a perfect kind of hell, really. This woman, especially, felt betrayed by reality. Where was her sweet oblivion? Where was her sense of release? Why did she still feel like the same person with the same burdens weighing upon her?

She stood in the lobby of the hotel and metaphorically screamed these questions at me. To an outside observer, very little was going on, and even to my own senses, there was just the impression of her emotional storm, like a distant echo of screaming and tears. Yet nevertheless it was very real and persistent. And she would not go away.

For my part, I tried to explain things to her. Eventually, I stopped feeling self-conscious, talking to the air, and I simply gave her what she needed: counseling. From the previous few paragraphs, it's obvious that I don't really agree with suicide as a way of escaping one's worldly concerns, but I still understand the impulse behind it, that irresistible urge to run away. So I spoke with her, and I explained that now she was going to have a great deal of time to think about her problems and that she would have to make peace with them if she was going to move on.

She was hearing none of it. Whatever had led her to this place, all of it was too immediate, too raw for her even to consider beginning to let it go. As I tried to calm her down, she only got angrier. At first, I got the impression that she stomped off in a huff. One moment, she was there, and then the presence of her had faded and left this subtly empty spot in the reality. I shrugged and went back to my article, making a mental note to ask my manager about a short, tanned woman with dyed blond hair. It certainly seemed like her suicide had been recent, but the second-shift guy had said nothing about it. If it had happened in our hotel over the weekend, surely there would have been a note in the ledger at least?

I didn't have long to contemplate this, for she returned to the lobby with the force and fury of a hurricane. She was angry at everything, and now much of that anger was focused on me, apparently because I had told her things she didn't really want to hear. She started lashing out at things, trying to break stuff. Her energy was too chaotic for her to really direct at first, so aside from the *sense* of motion, she didn't manage to knock anything over or blow any of the pictures off the walls. She didn't succeed in moving so much as a pen, and this, I think, only made her angrier.

The lights flickered, and one of them, directly over the spot where she "stood," blew out. She was a fast learner. Spirits are comprised almost entirely of energy. Working up the kinetic force to move physical objects is an immense effort for them. But energetic shifts—temperature changes, electrical interference—seem to be much simpler to accomplish. I got to observe as she realized this.

And went straight for the hotel computer.

The surge protector whined an alarm as its red light flashed once and went out. At the same time, the images on both monitors in front of me collapsed down to pinpricks of light and then disappeared entirely.

There is nothing quite like battling something that is there and yet not there, that you can see and yet not see. As I fought to get the hotel computers back up and running, another one of the lights in the lobby popped and went out. I felt sorry for her, but this was getting annoying.

"Look, lady!" I yelled out into the lobby. "I'm sorry that you think you got the shitty end of the stick, but that is no reason to take things out on me. Calm the hell down already!"

Should I have been scared? A decade before that time, I probably would have been swinging wildly between excitement and fear. But there was something in the very human quality of her anger that made me react to her more as a living being having a tantrum than some scary poltergeist—which, if she didn't calm down, she was well on her way to becoming. Despite what she'd managed to do to the computers, I wasn't scared. But I was getting pissed off.

That night was especially frustrating for the both of us. I would get the hotel computers back up and running, sweet-talking the archaic system into loading and working right again. She would fume some more, wander off (presumably back to her room), and then come back all riled up again. There would be another power surge, and the front-desk computers would go down once more. This really pissed me off when she did it in the middle of the night audit, a process that rolls the system over from one night to the next. If the process is interrupted, you have to start the whole thing over from the beginning, and it ties up the computer so that you have to check people in or out by hand if they arrive in the intervening time.

She knocked out the computers three times in the middle of the night audit. By that point, I was ready to kill her, if she hadn't already done the deed herself. We fought back and forth for most of the night. Somewhere around five in the morning, she finally gave up and wandered off for good. I was rushing to get the night audit done as most of the hotel's guests were checking out, a fact that did not leave me in the best of moods.

Now, I can be a little bit of a poltergeist myself. It's a combination of my natural psychic abilities and all the training I've had in energy work. On a bad day, this means that a migraine might just knock out the computers in precisely the way she had done —which is partly why I wasn't even shocked that she had managed it. At the very least, it means that when I am upset, I project that emotion in much the same way the ghost had been projecting all night. The end result is that anyone who is sensitive will walk into the room and get a faceful of how I'm feeling. I've been told by roommates and others over the years that it's not exactly pleasant, which is why I make a concerted effort not to lose my temper. I don't always succeed, but at least I try.

Unfortunately, after my night-long struggle with the angry ghost, I was seething with anger and frustration, not unlike the ghost herself. My manager, an adorable little gay man in his fifties who did not so much flame as he bubbled with exuberance every time I saw him, wandered behind the front desk for the start of his shift. He walked up to greet me with his usual early-morning flounce, but the words died in his throat when he locked eyes with me. For a moment he just faltered, then he shot me this look. That look told me that he didn't really want to know, nor did he want to be around to find out. Rather hastily, he retreated to his office, turning up Cher as loud as he could. (I know it's stereotypical, but he listened to Cher every single morning that he worked there.)

He hid in his office for a little while, not even wanting to ask what was wrong. I took a couple of deep breaths and tried to rein in some of the angry energy that I could feel buzzing around me. I felt a little less homicidal, but still annoyed. I wanted answers.

Poor little Jeff about jumped out of his skin when I opened the door to his office. He looked up somewhat sheepishly and tried to put his professional face on.

"Michelle," he said. "What can I do for you? Was there some kind of trouble last night?"

I rolled my eyes.

"I'll say," I responded, dropping my reports onto his desk. As nonchalantly as I could manage considering the circumstances, I added, "So when were you going to tell me about the chick who killed herself?"

This time Jeff's eyes did register fear. Not fear of me, exactly, but that guilty, furtive fear that an employee gets when they think their butts are on the line. He glanced quickly at all the papers on his desk, apparently checking to see if any incriminating documents had been left out.

"Who told you?" he asked. "Dammit! Everyone was told they could not talk about that. Jesse's gonna have my head!"

"Nobody told me," I responded. "That's the problem. The crazy bitch spent half the night up here making my life miserable. She knocked the computers out three times during the audit."

No stranger to the hauntings at the hotel, nor my ability to sense them, Jeff immediately paled.

"She was here? You saw her?"

"If she's short and blond and has a West Virginia accent, yeah," I said.

Hands shaking, Jeff dug through one of the drawers of his desk and produced a registration card. It held a woman's name and a West Virginia address. I picked up the card and looked it over. The most puzzling thing to me was the fact that the person in question had checked in for two nights. The other suicides I had heard about usually checked in and checked out on the same night.

"She gave herself some time to think about it?" I wondered out loud.

Jeff shrugged.

"All we know is she called down Saturday asking for a late check-out. Nobody thought anything of it. The guys remember seeing her in the bar Friday night. Seems she was a real spitfire."

"Tell me about it," I grumbled.

"Nancy found her. She'd done it on the bed. It was a real mess. Jesse didn't want anyone to talk about it. Things like that are bad for business," Jeff explained.

"What's bad for business is her messing with the computers so I can't even do the night audit," I complained. "I was nice last night, Jeff. I've cleaned spooks like her out of people's houses before, but it was obvious she was upset. But if she comes back and gives me trouble again tonight, I swear I will use every energetic trick I know to kick her butt clear across the Otherside. I don't usually advocate forcing spirits to move on, but she is a royal pain in the neck."

Solemnly, Jeff nodded. Slipping the registration card back into his desk, he added, "I'd appreciate it if you kept this to yourself. And if she's causing other trouble in the hotel, by all means take care of it. I'm just glad we've got you around for things like this."

Silence passed between us for a few moments, and Jeff looked up fondly at me. We had an odd relationship, since I was one of the few people at the hotel that he was completely out to—not just about his sexual orientation, but also about his psychic gifts.

"You know, sometimes I feel like I'm crazy," I admitted. "I just spent half the night having an argument with an invisible woman in the lobby. But she was really short and blond with a southern accent?"

Jeff nodded.

"Why is it," I wondered, "that I always feel crazier when I find out that it's true?"

I left Jeff to his early-morning work, and then finished out the last thirty minutes of my shift. I actually packed my ghost-chasing gear the next night, bringing along a bell and some Tibetan tools that I'd found to be really useful for amplifying my style of energy work. As it turned out, I had no need for these things. She never made an appearance again, at least not to me. I don't know if my threats ultimately scared her off or if I actually managed to get through to her. I never got any reports from guests who stayed in her room, either, so I can only hope that after throwing such a grand temper tantrum, she managed to get some perspective on things and actually move on.

Casting Shadows

My days in college weren't wild, but they were filled with the social growing pains that come of trying to cope with psychic abilities. Psychic phenomena aren't widely accepted (especially not at a Jesuit-run Catholic college), and regular experiences can leave a person feeling like an outsider with a secret they can only share with a select few—or risk getting laughed at for being a freak. My personal process of coming to terms with my talents was not an easy one, and there was collateral damage along the way. Most of that collateral damage came in the form of close personal relationships. When you aren't sure what you believe about yourself, how can you open up to let others in? My answer was, you don't. Consequently, I have only a very small handful of friends left over from those awk-ward and experimental times. As several of the tales in this book indicate, Dominic St. Charles is one of them. He has stuck with me through good times and bad, no matter what kind of crazy turns my life has taken over the years.

Dominic himself is a curious sort of character. I first encoun-tered him when I got involved in my college's gaming group, men-tioned back in "The Thing in the Crawlspace." Consequently, I've known Dominic since my second day of college. At the time, he was a study in contrasts. He was a gamer, but he was also some-thing of a jock (this was remarkable in a world where gamers and jocks were generally diametrically opposed entities). He admitted that his mother was a white witch, but he himself was a devout Catholic, though he was certainly tolerant of other faiths. He was a Pittsburgh Penguins hockey fan, was thoroughly nonviolent, but he loved some of the hardest metal I'd heard at the time. And at over six feet tall, with long blond hair and a generally sunny disposition, he nevertheless liked to hang out with black-clad freaks like me who have come to be widely known as Goths.

In all the years that I've known him, this study in contrasts has only grown more profound. You see, Dominic doesn't really believe in ghosts or the supernatural. He accepts that others might be able to sense and see these things, but he maintains his own ignorance to the world of the unseen. He's never felt compelled to be a believer. Despite this, a great number of my most astounding haunting expe-riences have occurred while in his company. Dominic was there at Whitethorn Woods, and he still recounts the experience at dinner parties now and again. He won't deny that he saw things in the haunted wilds of northeastern Ohio, but what he saw were mainly *physical* things. Even with all the craziness at Whitethorn, Dominic has never directly experienced what he could identify as a psychic impression. As a result, he remains cautiously skeptical about the true nature of the otherworldly.

Given Dominic's history of staunch ambivalence toward ghosts and hauntings, it seemed only fitting that he resided in one of the most spiritually active houses I had ever encountered. Located in a relatively quiet neighborhood near Chicago's historic Bronzeville district, barely a stone's throw away from the old cattle yards, the house was a three-story walk-up located on a corner of South Union Avenue. By the time that Dominic moved in, the house had been divided into several apartments. The first floor was occupied by a beauty salon, and each floor after that was split into two separate living spaces. The building was old, but none of us knew its exact date of original construction, although Sophia, Dominic's roommate at the time, had learned from someone that the beauty salon had been a bar in the sixties and seventies.

As seems to be par for the course in Dominic's life, he himself remained oblivious to the ghostly tenants of his new residence, although Sophia picked up on the spirits right away. All of them seemed harmless, with the exception of one. Three floors worth of stairs gave access to the apartments, and these stairs were uncommonly steep. I had no doubt that one of the ways that Dominic and Sophia stayed fit involved navigating those stairs day in and day out. The spirit in question seemed to linger at the very top of this long flight of stairs, waiting with malignant glee for the chance to push somebody down—or, at least, to watch them fall. The spirit itself didn't seem strong enough to be able to offer a solid physical push. Instead, it was like it put the idea in your head that it *wanted* you to fall.

Starting down a long flight of steep and dimly lit stairs with the unshakable impression that some wizened old something (we could never tell if it was male or female) was standing right behind you with every intent of giving you a push is not easy on the nerves. The first few times, it's possible to assume that the circumstances of the stairs themselves are responsible for inspiring a fear of falling. The carpeting has given them rounded and treacherous lips in places, and the steps themselves are fairly narrow in addition to being unusually steep. Anyone with a jot of common sense would have been a little nervous about descending those stairs. But the impression of a malevolent other was persistent. Every single time I stood at the top of those stairs, I would get a flash in my mind of a figure behind me, followed by a long and painful fall. Maybe it was just the echo of a past event, but there was a pervasive meanness to it that seemed both deliberate and self-aware. Comparing notes with others, I found that I was not alone in my impressions, which lent credence to the notion that this was an actual haunting and not simply natural anxiety about the stairs.

True to form, Dominic never sensed this spirit, although he accepted the assertions of others who swore to its existence. Eventually, Sophia brought in a friend of hers who was a talented spirit medium. He went through the apartment and picked up on no less than six individual ghosts. The most benign of these appeared to be a dead hippie who had some connection with the bar once housed on the ground floor. Now, he lingered mostly in the spare bedroom, where Dominic stored all of his musical gear. Allegedly, he was drawn to the profusion of guitars. He also seemed utterly unaware that he was dead. Having spent so many of his days in a mellow, drug-induced haze, the shadowy limbo that he now lingered in simply did not seem strange. I have no idea how one can be dead and still stoned, but this guy seemed to manage it somehow.

When I visited Dominic and Sophia, I often slept in this spare bedroom-turned-guitar storage. I really wished they had warned me about the wandering hippie. It was deeply unsettling to wake up one night and see a shadowy figure in the door staring at me. Since he had long hair, I initially mistook him for Dominic, but then, as the fog of sleep cleared, I registered his straggly, unkempt beard and round, John Lennon sunglasses. Only after jerking completely awake with my heart in my throat did I subsequently realize that I could see right through this nighttime visitor, and most of my impressions of his physical form weren't being registered with my flesh-and-blood eyes. He seemed just as surprised to find me sleeping in there as I had been surprised by his very existence. But, in true stoner fashion, he just drifted quietly away, no doubt aimlessly wandering other portions of the apartments.

Given the lively nature of the place, such encounters were part of the ordinary routine, and I simply learned to expect them whenever I came out for a visit. Since I did guest vocals for Dominic's band and we sometimes collaborated on songs, my travels took me out to this haunted apartment with its ominous staircase on a fairly regular basis. After a while, I even got accustomed to the angry soul who haunted the top of the stairs, quietly assuring it that it had no business pushing me down whenever I had to descend to the street below. It never seemed entirely mollified, but it grudgingly came to accept that I was going to resist it, whatever it tried.

One of the things I've learned over the years, especially when it comes to haunted houses, is that familiarity breeds not contempt but apathy. When the haunting isn't violent, or if, like the thing on the stairs, it contains a threat that is never aggressively realized, even the most extraordinary occurrences can become commonplace. When you live day in and day out with the cupboards opening themselves and banging shut at a certain hour and if, day in and day out, nothing more unsettling than this happens, it is possible to learn to accept that the cupboards banging is just the way of things. I think it can be likened to living in an apartment situated very close to a railroad. The very first time that the train rolls by, rattling all the windows and dishes, the new residents are going to find the experience unsettling, if not outright alarming. After the fiftieth time, however, they might have grown so used to the racket that they barely wake up in the night as the whistle blares through their neighborhood.

The ghosts in Dominic's Bronzeville apartment were just like that train. Once you knew that they were simply a part of everyday existence, there was very little they could do to shock and amaze. That is, unless you were totally new to the apartment and no one had properly warned you about the proverbial midnight express.

And this is what led to the experience of my friend Pete. It was March 2006, and I had to head up to Chicago to work with Dominic as well as do a photo shoot with my favorite Milwaukee-based photographer. Dominic and Sophia were also hosting a combined birthday party, since their birthdays were both around the end of March. I mentioned the road trip to my friend Pete, and asked if he'd like to tag along. Pete was totally game for a road trip. It should be noted that Pete was one of my more-or-less normal friends. He was a gamer, like a lot of my friends, but aside from that, his life was fairly mundane. He worked a nine-to-five job for a big corporation doing something with computers that was mystical to me. A mutual friend had introduced us about a year before, mostly because Pete had some questions about empathy. He had slowly come to realize that he had an unusual ability to connect with other people's emotions. Since Pete had zero background in any aspect of the occult, he wasn't really sure where to start looking for reliable sources that might help him understand and control this ability. Our friend had recommended me.

Despite Pete's knack for empathy, he really didn't believe in a great deal of the paranormal. Sensing the emotions of other people was about his limit at the time. Given Pete's background, he would not have even entertained the notion that there was something paranormal to his empathy, if not for the fact that he'd examined and exhausted all of the more mundane and rational explanations for his ability.

As a result, Pete generally looked upon the rest of my beliefs and personal experiences with a kind of bemused tolerance. Our relationship was founded on that, and on the mutual understanding that he wouldn't try to force me to accept his skeptical worldview, while I, for my part, wouldn't try to force him into any of my weird beliefs. Ironically, my relationship with Pete was a little like the relationship that I'd had with Dominic all these years, which was the main reason that I thought the two of them would enjoy meeting one another. That, and since Pete was a huge fan of Jim Butcher's *Dresden Files*, it didn't hurt that he'd get to see in person some of the Windy City locations that Butcher had used as a backdrop to his fiction series.

Little did Pete know that he was going to be visiting a part of Chicago that bore more in common with the fictional world of the

Dresden Files than it did with his more familiar world of big business and computer code.

I don't cram my beliefs down other people's throats, but I don't make any attempt to hide them, either. So, one night during our visit, Pete inevitably overheard me talking with Sophia about the ghosts that haunted the apartment. He was instantly skeptical, and he spocked an eyebrow at Dominic to see what the big guitarist thought of all this ghost nonsense. For his part, Dominic took the same stance that he always did. He admitted that he himself had experienced nothing strange or unusual in the apartment building, even during those times when Sophia and several of her friends were very certain that something was going on. However, he was also quick to point out that he accepted Sophia's beliefs (and, by extension, mine). It was clear to him that she was definitely sensing something and, just because he couldn't pick up on it, who was he to judge its veracity?

It didn't take an empath to be able to tell that Pete found this answer to be terribly wishy-washy. He made it clear that he had never experienced anything that he would call a ghost. Furthermore, he was strongly suspicious of other people's so-called experiences. He acknowledged that people *wanted* to believe, and left it at that. I finished up my discussion with Sophia, and Dominic introduced Pete to the wonders of his latest Xbox game. Nothing more would have come of it, except Pete's phone started to ring.

Dominic's apartment, even though it was on the third floor, had terrible cell-phone reception. In a few areas, you could maintain a bar or two with a wing and a prayer, but then you would take a step and unaccountably slip into a dead space that just swallowed the signal whole. I could never determine whether this was a fault of the apartment or the ghosts or maybe even some effect Dominic has on his living space (he's moved since, and the new place has the same problems). Or it could just be that wide swaths of the city of Chicago simply have a crappy cell-phone signal. Whatever the case, the solution, as Dominic had discovered, was to go out on the porch and sit in this one spot overlooking the street. After Pete had dropped his call once or twice, Dominic revealed his secret haven of cell-phone reception and suggested that Pete take advantage of it, especially since it was an unusually balmy night for Chicago in March.

Pete went out, and Sophia and I watched as Dominic continued to play on his Xbox. We chatted idly in the meantime, and eventually we almost forgot about Pete completely.

That was when Pete burst in through the door to the back porch looking like—well, like he'd seen a ghost.

He was so agitated that he wasn't willing to talk about it right away. At least, not coherently. And then, in the way that some people have when an experience has really shaken them, he started to over-explain. He reiterated the story several times to the three of us, as if sheer repetition would make it easier to believe. It was obvious that he was trying to convince himself that he wasn't crazy, so we let him prattle on. An interesting story unfolded, one that seemed to reverse Pete's stance on ghosts one hundred and eighty degrees.

Pete had been out on the back porch, sitting on the picnic table there, just as Dominic had suggested. It was fairly late in the night, but even in this residential neighborhood, there were still cars and pedestrians out on the street. For a while, as he talked, Pete had looked idly down at the street three stories below, just people-watching. And then, as if Chicago was living up to its reputation as the Windy City, a gust kicked up and it started blowing Pete's hair into his eyes. Pete turned his back to the wind, which meant he was facing the blank wall of the apartment. Eventually he noticed what he thought was Dominic's shadow on the wall, pacing back and forth. Something about the shadow gave Pete a peculiar sensation that niggled at the back of his brain. Since he was fairly intent on his telephone conversation, he didn't pay much attention to it at first. But as he kept talking, the shadow kept pacing the wall, and something about it began to bother him.

The bottom dropped out of his stomach once Pete realized that, for Dominic to have cast this shadow, he would have had to cast it *through* the wall of his apartment. Pete glanced over at the door leading from the porch to the apartment. It had a window, but it was covered with venetian blinds. These were closed, and they were still covered over on the inside with the extra layer of plastic insulation Dominic had applied to stave off the chill of Chicago's harsh winters. No one could have moved the blinds had they wanted to, without first removing that layer of plastic.

Besides, Pete's brain finally informed him, there was no way that Dominic or anyone else in the apartment could have been casting a shadow through the window on the door—at least, not a shadow that would subsequently land on the same wall that held the door. The impossibility of his initial, off-handed assumption slammed home even as Pete continued to watch the shadow pace in front of him.

Maybe it was coming from behind him. Pete turned and looked. Behind him, down on the street, was a little gas station. The station was closed, so the sign itself had long ago gone dark, but there were still lights down by the pavement. Clearly, someone was down there, on the street or near the gas station lot, moving back and forth in front of these lights and thus casting the shadow up to the wall in front of him.

Pete finished up his phone conversation and went to the railing, peering down. No one was in the lot of the gas station. No one was walking in the little alley between the gas station and the apartment building. And on closer inspection of the lights down there, Pete realized that there was no way, short of walking nearly three stories up in mid-air, that someone standing between him and the lights could cast a shadow at just the right angle to produce what he was seeing. Even so, this mysterious wind-walker would have had to cast a shadow through the railing, through the picnic table, and even through Pete himself in order to land on the wall in exactly the same place.

Nevertheless, the shadow remained. Only now, Pete realized with mounting panic, it seemed aware of him. When he glanced back at it, didn't it hesitate for just a moment, no longer pacing?

Pete waved his arms about, making absolutely certain that he was not accidentally casting the shadow himself. But it had paced while he sat on the picnic table, and now, as he waved his arms about, it paused to stand there, as if looking at him. Its arms did not wave. Pete turned this way and that, struggling to be sure. No matter how he tried to silhouette himself against the gas station lights, his shadow spilled away in a totally different direction, angling to his left. The shadow on the wall was not his.

Pete judged it to be the shadow of a man, broad-shouldered, approximately six feet in height. It was easy to see why Pete's brain had initially registered it as Dominic. Of course, during this time, Dominic was on the couch, shooting aliens or engaged in some other epic battle for the safety of the earth.

Pete stared. The shadow stood on a blank wall, three stories up in an area where there were no other buildings of a similar height for nearly a block on every side. He wasn't casting it. No one on the street could be casting it. And now, it no longer paced. In fact, Pete could not shake the sense that the shadow itself was a sentient entity. And it was watching him.

That was when he practically launched himself at the back door and burst into the apartment.

Pete eventually talked himself out and calmed down enough so everyone could sleep. At least, the rest of us slept, since we were used to a certain measure of weirdness in that apartment. It's not like the mysterious shadow was really doing anything to bother anybody. In all likelihood, it had just been curious about the new guy.

Pete did his best to sleep, but it was like he was desperate to block out the sound of that proverbial train. He just couldn't get comfortable with the prospect that something was out there. He was suddenly very wary of every little sound in Dominic's apartment. Sophia's cat startled him at least once, and he offered the cat a very colorful opinion of its ancestry.

Ever since that night, Pete has been a good deal less vocal in his skepticism. He has never come right out to say that he is a believer, but he was never able to develop a rational explanation for what he saw. Of course, since that night, Pete has also never asked to go on a road trip with me again. I swear, I lose more "normal" friends that way!

Ghosts and Gadgets

Several years ago I was invited by Nick Reiter of the Avalon Foundation to accompany him on a Cleveland ghost tour. I remember being surprised to learn that Cleveland even had a ghost tour. Although I knew of several haunted locations throughout the city, none of them struck me as the sort of place that would allow a camera-toting tour group to shuffle through, seeking to snap pictures of the resident ghosts. When Nick mentioned that the historic Franklin Castle was one of the stops along the tour, I was simply flabbergasted. The Franklin Castle is one of the most notoriously haunted houses in the Cleveland area. It had been closed to the public for years, and gaining access to it had become something akin to discovering the Holy Grail, at least among local ghost-hunters. The minute I heard about the Franklin Castle, I was in. As it would turn out, the ghost tour did not exactly live up to its advertising, but something fascinating occurred nevertheless.

In order to fully appreciate the significance of the incident that happened on the ghost tour, I need to give you a little background on Nick. Nick Reiter is self-proclaimed mad scientist. He works full-time for an alternative energy company in northwestern Ohio, and he investigates the paranormal on the side. The mad scientist part comes in because he often constructs many of the gadgets that he uses to measure paranormal phenomena. He started off with an interest in UFOs, but since his earliest explorations he has also brought his vast knowledge of energy, electronics, and the scientific method to bear on the issue of haunted places and other ghostly encounters.

I had met Nick through the local paranormal lecture circuit. At first, I think he only knew me as the vampire lady, since vampires were the topic I lectured on most frequently. I liked Nick as soon as I met him. He was a smart, funny, educated family man who was not afraid to laugh at the failings of the field he nevertheless remained passionate about. Even so, I remained hesitant to come out to Nick about everything else I was involved in. In my experience, there was a definite gulf between the people who approached the issue of the paranormal from an objective scientific angle and those who experienced paranormal events in a psychic and therefore subjective manner. The psychics and the scientists were divided into two opposing camps, and there were often bitter recriminations from one to the other.

Those who took the scientific or skeptical approach, seeking measurable and repeatable proof, tended to find the psychics overly credulous. At best, they viewed psychics as posers and flakes. At worst, some of the skeptically minded paranormalists I had encountered were actively frightened by psychics, fearing that their abilities may have an unwholesome source. It was hard enough worrying whether or not someone might think that you're crazy because you claim to be able to perceive spirits. Having them subsequently decide that you are in league with Satan was even worse.

I knew that Nick had worked with psychics before, so I really shouldn't have worried. But at the time, most of the paranormal community knew me more as a researcher than as anything else. I didn't even widely advertise my involvement in haunting resolution. Nearly all of my referrals came through close friends. I was more open within the Pagan community than I was around the paranormalists, largely because of that rift between skeptics and experiencers. Admittedly, I had developed a bias of my own: I was skeptical of the technology.

Chasing ghosts with a camera and a tape recorder seemed tantamount to chasing a sandstorm with a vacuum cleaner. Sure, you might eventually suck up something, but you certainly were not using the right tools for the job. From what I had learned through my own experiences with the paranormal, I didn't think that anyone had yet invented the right tool for the job. When I "heard" a spirit's voice speaking with me, it was not with any capacity of my physical ears. There were no sound waves that I could discern. Instead, it seemed as if sound were the closest sense into which my brain could translate the experience. The same went for spirit mediums, such as my friend Sarah who could visibly perceive ghosts. Although the image of certain spirits would manifest to her with as much clarity and detail as a living person, she understood that this was merely how the otherworldly presence of the spirit manifested to her. To assume that a camera, which was only built to snap pictures in the visible spectrum, could somehow capture the image that Sarah perceived, seemed to misunderstand the nature of spirit perception on a deep and fundamental level. Yet some investigators insisted upon approaching technological evidence as some kind of Holy Grail, seeking orbs as absolute proof of the existence of ghosts.

Despite my personal opinions on ghosts and technology, I nevertheless wanted to see Nick in action. While orbs and drained batteries left me nonplussed, Nick had some items that went well beyond my limited technological expertise. I wasn't sure if I believed that a super-low-frequency electromagnetic field detector would react in the presence of spirits, but I certainly wanted to hear from Nick why he thought such a thing should be possible.

The tour had us gather at a small café in the city. As things turned out, I had two friends in from out of town the day of the tour, and I brought them along as well. They were both Pagans, and while they weren't your average paranormal investigator types, they found the idea of the tour intriguing. Most of my Pagan friends didn't find ghost-hunting nearly as exciting as the paranormalists that I knew did. Since Pagans accept the existence of spirits as a matter of faith, there's often no point in trying to obtain scientific proof, photographic or otherwise. In contrast, most of the paranormal investigators that I had met seemed more fascinated by the very *possibility* of spirits. Hunting them was therefore especially exciting, since they didn't deal with spirits through their religious rituals on a regular basis.

Nick had come armed to the teeth with his mad-scientist gear, including the low-frequency EMF detector that looked for all the world like the PKE meter toted about by the character Egon Spengler in *Ghostbusters*. Nick played up this resemblance, jokingly referring to the device as his PKE meter and quipping that he'd have to check his copy of *Tobin's Spirit Guide* for an accurate identification should we successfully locate any ghosts. In reality, the device was something he described as a Gauss meter which he, through his mystical command of electronic equipment, had souped up in such a fashion that it now took readings on a very tight and refined frequency more attuned with natural geomagnetic energies rather than the frequencies given off by man-made electronics. Due to the refined nature of the device, Nick typically had to go around a location first looking for wires and other devices hidden within walls so that he could rule out interference from these sources. Sweeping a room like that, he really did look like an extra from *Ghostbusters*, and we joked about getting him a backpack for his gear to complete the image.

After kicking back at the café and indulging in some good-natured geekery, our tour guide finally let us know that it was time to load ourselves into the bus. The game was afoot!

At that time I had never been on a ghost tour, local or otherwise, so I really wasn't certain what to expect. But when the first thirty minutes of the tour involved nothing more than driving past a few locations in Cleveland, while the tour guide rattled off one or two of the classic details of the hauntings there, I was disappointed. My two Pagan friends felt out of place among all the New Agers and paranormalists who had come on the tour, and Nick held his souped-up Gauss meter rather despondently in his lap. We were all getting restless. I was going to chalk up the entire afternoon as an expensive waste of time when we finally got to stop and get off the bus in order to explore the haunted armory of the Cleveland Grays.

The Cleveland Grays were a private militia founded in 1837 for the protection of the city of Cleveland. At the time, private militias were common, and nearly every major city boasted its own militia with its own uniforms, flag, and weapons. The Cleveland Grays were the first company of uniformed troops west of the Alleghenies, and they were so named because of their gray uniforms. By 1893, they were housed in an imposing stone structure known as the Grays Armory, on Cleveland's Bolivar Road. The Armory, a five-story fortress of weathered sandstone that boasts a ten-thousand-square-foot ballroom, a wood-paneled library, and even its own basement shooting range, is located downtown near the Erie Street Cemetery, another well-known Cleveland haunt.

Grays is known for a number of ghostly phenomena, most of which seem to be tied to Civil War-era apparitions. Visitors and staff alike have reported the presence. Some have heard footsteps when no living person was present. Others have experienced cold spots, visual apparitions, and strange smells. The spirit seems particularly tied to a set of stairs leading to the second level of the building. Some poltergeist activity has been reported in connection with the haunting, and we were shown a room upstairs with a number of glass displays where the spirit reportedly has moved items in displays, broken lights, and even rearranged heavy boxes overnight.

The tour started off in the main office. This spacious room, nestled in the first floor of one of the round turrets that give the building its castle-like appearance, featured a huge, ponderous desk and an elaborate chandelier. There was just enough room for all the members of the tour group to gather in this room comfortably. We stood before the imposing desk, and a worker connected with the armory took over our tour guide's job of recounting the ghostly events. Nick, eager for the chance to start playing with his gadgets, had his Gauss meter out and ready. He first started going around the room, establishing a baseline and determining where there might be wires or other fixtures in the walls that could throw off his readings. He was as discreet and unobtrusive as possible, quietly moving through the crowd as they listened raptly to the armory employee.

As I stood with my Pagan friends in the office, watching the other folks from the tour restlessly clutching their cameras and murmuring about whether or not they were likely to catch orbs in the room, I began to seriously question the point and effectiveness of hunting ghosts on this type of a tour. Given the eager banter I had overheard at the café and later on the bus itself, I had gathered that many of the people here actually expected the hauntings to be perceptible 24/7. Even Nick, as levelheaded as he was, seemed prey to the notion that, once a place was declared haunted, a ghost-hunter could just waltz in at any time of the day or night and expect to obtain some kind of evidence. Orbs were the most frequently discussed, but a few people had little hand-held recorders, intent on capturing ghostly voices in the form of electronic voice phenomena, or EVP.

I got the feeling that they would all be sorely disappointed if the resident ghosts of at least one of the locations didn't show up on some manner of recording device. But from my own experiences of the paranormal, I seriously doubted that the spirits would be interested in playing along with such games. It's rare to have ongoing and consistent spirit phenomena occur in a haunted location on a daily basis, let alone at the whim of a tour guide. A ghost isn't like an ugly old lamp that just stands in the corner of a room and is consistently present each and every time you enter that room. Spirits move around, and I suspect that even more mysterious forces than their own willful movement often influence whether or not ghostly phenomena are perceptible from our side of things.

But so many of the people had come on this tour desperate to experience *something*. I kind of felt bad, standing there and thinking how futile those desires probably were. And then I started to focus on the chandelier.

At the very start of this book, I wrote about the house where I grew up. Around the summer of my twelfth year, a spike of paranormal activity occurred there, and it kept up for a couple of years. One of the most striking things that occurred with regularity was the movement of our chandelier. I'd since come to terms with the fact that some of the disturbances that led the chandelier to describe lazy circles over the dining room table were tied not to ghosts, but to me. And I'd spent a large portion of my adult life learning to harness my ability to influence the unseen energies around me. I didn't usually try to consciously move whole chandeliers, but as I stood there, bored to tears and frustrated by the mediocre ghost tour, I got an idea in my head.

If people had come for proof of the otherworldly, why not try to swing the chandelier?

The chandelier that hung in the office of the Grays Armory was an elaborate and heavy affair, much larger than the little crystal chandelier that had hung suspended above our humble dining room table. I had no idea whether or not I would actually be able to move it, but I was certainly willing to give it a try. I had long ago stopped paying attention to the extensive rambling of the tour guide, and I could think of nothing better to do.

When I work with energy, I focus a great deal with my hands. I typically visualize tendrils of energy extending from my hands to my target, and while that target is typically a person, this was exactly what I did with the chandelier. I was trying to be discreet, so I kept my upturned palm close to my side where people were less likely to notice. I made a gentle rotating gesture over and over again with my fingers, concentrating all the while on making the chandelier swing.

The effort proved worthwhile. After a few minutes, I managed to get the chandelier moving just enough for people to begin to notice. First one, and then another, of the ghost-hunters looked up, quickly pointing out the slight quivering of the crystals to their friends. Encouraged by their reactions, I tried to get the chandelier really going, but it was taking all of my concentration just to achieve that tiny tremor, considering the weight of the thing. I was so engrossed in my work that I never noticed Nick Reiter getting closer and closer to me as he sought out electromagnetic disturbances in the room.

I'll be honest. The movement of the chandelier was so slight that I was not entirely convinced that it tied back to me. I knew I was putting some serious effort into trying to move the thing, but the trembling that was visible might also have been the result of a passing truck or even a low-flying plane. Which was why I was really pushing to get a stronger reaction from the chandelier, so I would know for certain whether or not the motion actually stemmed from me.

My concentration was shattered when Nick Reiter, eyes glued to the readout on his meter, practically bumped into me.

"Michelle!" he declared. "You're radioactive!"

He indicated the digital numbers on his reader, which although they clearly held his interest, were utterly meaningless to me. I was still engaged in that discreet motion with my fingers, however, and Nick's gaze flicked from the readout, to my hand, to the chandelier, and back to me again. He obviously noticed the motion of the chandelier, for he shook a finger in a mock gesture of scolding me.

"The ghosts are supposed to do that," he quipped.

I was so shocked that Nick had apparently gotten a reading off of me that I kept my energy to myself for the remainder of the tour.

On the drive back to the starting point, I sat staring out the window of the bus, playing the scene over and over again in my head. Had he really gotten a legitimate reading? That, of course, presumed that I was honestly responsible for moving the chandelier in the first place. I knew that I *believed* that I was. I went through the motions, I felt the effort. The chandelier did move. I hadn't been obvious about it, but based on what he saw on his little gadget, Nick seemed to connect the chandelier's motion directly to me. Maybe I had to rethink my notions on the limitations of technology.

I never did work up the guts to ask Nick exactly what his gadget had picked up from me. However, years later, I was asked to demonstrate some of my energy work in front of another paranormal investigator. This was part of a television series, and we were trying to see whether or not any of his gadgets would be able to record evidence of my ability to work with energy. We tried voltmeters and radiowave detectors to no effect. Because of the budget of the television series, we even got to play with an FLIR camera —the thermographic device made famous by Sci Fi's *Ghost Hunters*. Although the evidence obtained by the FLIR camera was visually interesting, we deemed it inconclusive given the limits of our tests. However, the investigator had packed a TriField Natural EM Meter, tuned to pick up the lowest fluctuations in electromagnetic frequencies. This gadget, which had not reacted to human activity in the five years that the investigator had been working with it, nevertheless responded in needle-jumping excitement to me.

I still don't like technology, and not merely because it stubbornly refuses to work correctly around me. I think that many investigators who exclusively use technology in their quest for proof of the otherworldly put entirely too much faith in their gadgets' infallibility. Furthermore, I believe that, even when we manage to get a compelling and consistent reading, we are only seeing a very small portion of what is really going on. I don't think they've yet invented a gadget capable of reading the full spectrum of energy that psychic and ghostly phenomena both operate on. But after my experience with Nick and with the later experiments, I am willing to admit that technology may be getting a little closer. Certainly it offers one route to understanding our otherworldly experiences. If we take technology hand in hand with our more organic methods of perception, while accepting that both methods have their strengths as well as their limitations, perhaps we'll be that much closer to understanding the strange and shifting world that seems to exist just beyond the Veil.

In the Shadow
of the Towers

Despite the overall theme and purpose of this collection, what follows here is not a ghost story. It is, in part, a requiem, but it is also a story about a place where I thought there should have been a ghost —many ghosts, in fact. And yet, instead of finding a location that crawled with the restless dead, or even with an echo of their pain, I found a place blanketed with this indescribable commingling of solemnity, introspection, and calm. That unexpected quietude both surprised and enlightened me. I suspect that it will do the same for you.

The month was February and the year was 2002. I had been asked to travel to New York City for the dedication of the Court of Lazarus. This was to be a new gathering—part social circle, part spiritual event, for one of the communities that I wrote for at the time.

I was hesitant to go. It was so soon after the attacks of 9/11, and everything that I had heard told me the city was still in a shambles. Everything around Ground Zero was in ruins, and I heard that in some places, fires were still burning in the rubble-filled wreckage beneath the street. It was a tense and unsettled time in our country, and the whole process of travel had been changed. Did I really want to fly out to New York? Could I bear to see a city still racked with such pain?

My publisher at the time was insistent. Admittedly, I wanted to see my friends who still lived in the city. Very few of them had been anywhere near the towers when they went down, but there were a few who had experienced a near-miss. Everybody knows stories like this now. One friend of a friend worked in one of the towers but called in sick that day and was never so happy to have come down with the flu. Another found himself delayed en route, and the delay lasted just long enough to prevent him from being in harm's way. Then there was the friend who was part of the New York City police force. She had horror stories of what the streets looked like that day, with deadly slivers of glass sheeting from the sky. She assured me that the images of people jumping tens of stories down were some of the tamest sights from that fateful incident. She told me that the news agencies left out the images of people cut to ribbons by the glass on their way down, and no one even dared to talk about the grim reality of her job, which ultimately came down to identifying the pieces of the bodies. These were sometimes reduced to tiny, charred morsels of flesh. But everything had to be gathered and mourned and handled with respect.

Nearly five months had passed since that fateful day, but much of the horror and anxiety still lingered fresh in the nation's collective memory. For those of us who live outside of the city, it lingered in part because of the media circus surrounding the event—all of the political posturing and saber-rattling that started up even before the dust had settled from the towers themselves. For New Yorkers, it was fresh because the disaster was not over. Only a small portion of the debris had been taken away, and efforts were still ongoing to recover some of the victims' remains. The wreck of the towers stood in the city like an open wound, and everyone was waiting to see if it would become septic, and poison even the flesh that had remained unscathed.

And with all of these issues weighing heavily on so many minds, I was still curious. I dreaded seeing New York in such a devastated state, but I felt a certain compulsion to go and put my fingers in the wounds, as it were. No matter how many times they played the destruction of the towers on television, it never looked real. I'd been glutted on too much CGI and too many Hollywood special effects. I needed to see the wreckage up close and personal in order to accept that it had really, truly happened. That this was a part of our world now.

I had been to New York before, and to a certain extent the city was something of an icon to me. When I was a teen, I had religiously watched the television series *Beauty and the Beast*, and I think my romance with the city of New York started there. That I had a glamorous aunt who had gone off to New York to become a successful model certainly helped to shape the city's image in my eyes. For me, New York was the quintessential Big City. It was a scion of the arts and culture, wealth and success. The home of so many of the publishing companies for which I yearned to write, New York was to me a grand symbol of worldly accomplishment. The fact that even the smallest piece of business had called me there told me that I was taking part in some of that accomplishment. When I walked its streets, I walked in a city of possibilities, where the gates of my small-town existence were thrown wide to the reality of a much larger, more diverse world than any I had imagined as a child.

I decided to drive, and to take a group of friends with me. Jason Crutchfield and Paul Trimble were two people who had stood with me through thick and thin, and no matter the type of situation I might find myself in, I always felt safer with either of them around. Crutchfield also had a vested interest in the Court of Lazarus, as he, too, was a significant voice in the same community it was intended to serve. We made hotel arrangements at a place just outside of the city, and then we piled into Paul's trusty car and headed on our way.

We didn't have long to settle into the hotel before we had to meet up with people in the city. We were there for several days, but dinners and meetings had been scheduled for nearly all of them. Accordingly, as soon as we had a chance to wash up and stretch our legs, we were right back on the road again, aiming for a point in Lower Manhattan. As we hit the tunnel into the city, I started to feel a little queasy. At first, I chalked it up to having been crammed in the back of the car too long. But the sensation persisted, and I also began to experience cresting waves of dizziness, as though the world kept going out from under me. Once we emerged onto the streets of New York, an even stronger sensation washed over me. It was familiar and entirely unpleasant, and it made me very happy that Jay had come along.

There are downsides to being as sensitive to energy as I am. One of the big ones involves travel. More specifically, it involves the energy of place. I don't think I would have this problem if I were just a spirit medium, tuned in only to the ghosts and spirits that lingered on the Otherside. But my talents seem to involve a whole range of energies. I am most finely tuned in to the energy of people, but people leave their energy everywhere. The emotional impressions left upon a favorite piece of jewelry that a psychometrist can read are nothing more than residues of energy from the original owner. The "vibes" many psychics can pick up when first entering a home are also little more than residual energy. We are practically living in a sea of energy, and we breathe it in and give it off constantly, every day, leaving currents and eddies and imprints of our passing in every home, every office, and every street.

For one reason or another, I can pick up on all of this. I'm not unique in this ability. There's a whole community of people like me. We don't always talk about it, except among ourselves, but it is an integral part of how we experience the world. Even so, it can be hard to explain to those who haven't experienced it firsthand.

Most of the time, my perception of all of this energy is nothing more than background music playing quietly in my head. When I am used to the sense and feel of a place, I am familiar enough to be able to tune out all but the essentials. In new places, however, the rhythm and the pulse of the song changes significantly. This is especially true of big cities, since they have many more people adding to the layers of this otherworldly music. When I was much younger, my sudden exposure to a big, unfamiliar city was almost debilitating. It was a matter of sensory overload. Given a few days to adjust, I could learn to tune out the nonessentials, but it wasn't always easy. When I had only the dimmest understanding of why I felt spacey and unable to concentrate, new cities were rarely any fun for me. Consequently, I almost never traveled outside of my native Ohio. But my career kept leading me into travel, so I had to learn to master this oversensitivity, or have some difficult explaining to do. It was only through a great deal of study and self-reflection that I got a handle on what was really going on. After that, I learned the methods I needed to cope.

The main method was to shield, which is a very simple exercise that involves blocking out energy and the psychic impressions that it carries. Essentially, you imagine yourself surrounded by a bubble of energy that keeps you in and everything else out. Once it's in place, you have to maintain this bubble in the back of your mind or else it will fade. Of course, I had learned the hard way that if I let myself get overwhelmed too quickly, it was almost impossible for me to summon the mental clarity needed to shield in the first place. Furthermore, when the energies I was shielding against were massive and persistent, they could eventually wear down my defenses. Shielding depends heavily upon mental discipline, and it takes both concentration and a little bit of personal energy to shore up those psychic walls.

When we emerged out of the tunnel and into New York City, I realized belatedly that I should have been more prepared for what I was feeling. I went into this knowing that the city was in turmoil. It had suffered a heinous blow, and the emotional echoes of that blow still reverberated through every street, perpetuated by the minds of nearly all of its residents as they fretted and mourned and worried about the future. In my previous visits to New York, I had found the city's energy to be overwhelming, even without the anxiety brought about by the felling of the towers. I really should have known better, but I had blithely walked into all of this without paying much attention at all to my shields.

And this is where my best friend Jay comes in. I mentioned that I feel safe around him, and this is not just because he is physically intimidating. The big, burly bouncer who could be mistaken for a Hells Angel is also a talented energy worker. He could pick up on the same energies as me, but he also has an inborn capacity to shield. I have never seen him overwhelmed. You can drop him into some of the craziest energetic environments and he is still a rock. Additionally, he is very skilled in helping others to shield and in lending some of that rock-solid groundedness that he enjoys. He's helped me keep my head together in more than one overwhelming situation, so I knew I could count on him to help me here.

As soon as we got out of the car, I let Jay know that I was having problems. We stepped discreetly to one side, away from the curious eyes of others. Then he laid one hand on my shoulder and concentrated on my energy. When he's helping an oversensitive person like me to block out overwhelming sensations, he usually verbally walks the person through a visualization to help the process feel more real. He spoke quietly to me, and I could feel the apparent din of the city growing quieter. When he was finished I no longer felt dizzy, and I could concentrate again. But the tumultuous energy of New York City was still there, roiling on the edge of my perception. I knew it would eventually wear me down. We would do this several more times before the weekend was out.

It was a difficult time to be psychically aware in New York. Whenever I let my focus slip, even just a little bit, the cacophony of energy started pouring in through the cracks.

As I said, I should have known better, but with Jay along, I was able to get by without too much difficulty. Before realizing the immensity of emotion that roiled in the city at the time, we had planned on visiting the World Trade Center site. Now we were a little uncertain. If I was already having trouble concentrating in other parts of the city, what kind of psychic overload could I possibly encounter at Ground Zero?

I'll admit: I wasn't sure that I wanted an answer to that question, but at the same time I felt an obligation to visit the site. Like the assassination of President Kennedy for an earlier generation, the destruction of the Twin Towers was one of those flashpoints in American history that remains galvanized in our collective imagination. I suspect that every person reading these words right now remembers where they were when the planes hit the towers. We remember what we were doing that day and what we thought the moment we first heard the news, because we quickly became aware that we were living through history. Given the impact that incident had upon my country and my world, I needed to go and see.

Accordingly, we all piled into the car on a Sunday afternoon and headed toward the gap in the New York skyline. Only a few months previously, I had been giving a presentation on ghosts and spirits at a paranormal roundtable in Ohio. One of the ladies in the audience had asked whether or not I thought the site of the Twin Towers would be haunted. I had responded emphatically in the affirmative. Even if the spirits of the dead themselves did not linger in that space, I suspected that the echo of the event itself would remain stamped upon the streets for many years. Given what I knew about haunted battlefields like Gettysburg, this only seemed logical. The soldiers who seem to struggle endlessly on that Pennsylvania field are merely residues, echoes of an emotionally traumatic series of moments stamped upon the fabric of reality through their very intensity. The Twin Towers were not technically a battlefield, but given the trauma and terror that descended upon Manhattan in the early hours of that business day, I could only imagine that a similar effect had been in place. And as we worked our way through the ever-crowded streets of New York City, I believed that echoes of that very recent historic event were waiting to overwhelm me as soon as I stepped into the killing zone.

Traffic thinned out as we neared the wreckage of the disaster. We started to look for a parking spot, so we could continue on foot. A sizable area around Ground Zero had been cordoned off, and cars were simply not allowed past those boundaries. It was an unseasonably warm February, and the sun that slanted in from the west glinted off the glass of the surrounding skyscrapers. Then that self-same sun began to expose whole sections of buildings where the reflective glass of windows had been put out. First, there were only a few gaps visible in buildings, and then, in the distance, we saw the first of several buildings that had lost most of their glass. Some kind of protective netting had been hung from the roofs, and it stretched as far down as we could see from our vantage point. As we circled the debris-littered area for some kind of parking, we realized that this netting was in place to prevent further slivers of deadly glass from shaking loose and raining down upon the streets.

Eventually we got to an area where the streets were uncharacteristically empty. The only people who had ventured this far seemed to be visitors like ourselves. I would use the word *tourists*, but that would imply a sense of lackadaisical fun. The people who had ventured to this site were not so much tourists as they were pilgrims. They were not dressed for an afternoon at Disneyland.

The tall buildings that still stood around the site of the attack cast thick shadows upon the sidewalks and streets. It was chilly in those shadows, yet the pavement beneath my feet seemed unnaturally warm. The wind that gusted up now and again carried an acrid scent of burning, and I remembered hearing that some fires still smoldered several levels beneath the street. There was debris of every sort still choking the gutters, and the upper branches of the naked trees had caught streamers of office detritus—including, in one case, the twisted yet unmistakable slat of a shattered venetian blind.

The footprint of the Twin Towers themselves was closed to the public, and cleaning crews had already sealed off a good portion of that area with makeshift walls. But at that time, we could still easily see the field of twisted metal and structural supports, including that now-famous steel girder that jutted out above everything else in one section and had been cut or torn into the shape of a cross. As if in testament to the fires that still smoldered below ground, thick, cloying smoke curled up from the gutters and vents at street level. I saw a few thin wisps at first, growing more persistent the closer we got to the site of the actual impact.

And then we were on the sidewalk outside of a little stone church, and we could go no farther. Everything else was either too unsafe or was still being sifted through for human remains. In addition to the acrid stench of burning plastic, there was a specific scent to the smoke that reminded me strongly of burnt hair and fingernails. I knew what it meant. If anyone else took note of this aspect of the scent, no one spoke of it.

Throughout all of this I had taken in all of my surroundings with my five physical senses, but I had kept my other perceptions on lock-down. It took a lot of effort, but I had entered this place prepared. Now, however, curiosity got the better of me. Especially because I had been asked about whether or not this site would be haunted, I had to open myself and find out. I knew what I thought I should feel, and so I let Jay know what I was going to do. If the experience proved to be too much for me, he could handle it for both of us.

Given how overwhelmed I had been feeling this entire visit, I knew this probably wasn't the best idea, but I trusted that Jay would be there, to catch me should I fall. And so I dropped my shields, expecting every echo and replay of that terrible event to come flooding in. Instead, there was silence. Silence, and this deep, abiding sense of calm. I stood blinking in the slant of the afternoon sun, hardly able to believe it. I whispered to Jay, "Do you feel that, too?"

Solemnly, he nodded. It didn't seem proper to speak above a whisper in this place. It didn't feel proper to really speak at all. I realized, belatedly, that a hush had fallen upon the entire crowd gathered here. Even the sounds of the traffic, an ever-present nuisance in New York, were far away and dim.

There were no Gothic arches curving overhead, and yet I had a strong sense that I was walking in the hushed depths of a great cathedral. The burnt scent that lingered on the air was a funereal incense, mourning the dead. The little stone church near the heart of it all stood as a mute testament to the innocence that everyone had lost, and to the past that we could never return to. Its little churchyard was filled with sloping tombstones, worn heavily by age. That was where we had come from. The tiny little church and its postage-stamp-sized churchyard were from a time when New York was barely a city. This humble, holy place had remained virtually untouched as all the titanic office buildings had thrust their shoulders proudly against the sky around it. The stones sagged like loose teeth in the gaping mouth of an octogenarian, someone who knows that his time is about to end. But then, on the fence that surrounded this somber little churchyard, people had hung the future.

There were photos, mementos, and strings of paper cranes. I remember trying to count how many thousands of paper cranes patient fingers had fashioned, and giving up after the first ten strings. There were hand-drawn pictures of the deceased and banners shipped in from countries all over the world. In English, Spanish, French, Chinese, German, Japanese—and in scripts and characters I did not even immediately recognize—were scribed words of compassion and condolence. The languages were as diverse as the faces, and perhaps more diverse, because even those not directly touched by the deaths that occurred in this place still felt touched by the event itself.

Here and there I saw a favorite T-shirt that had apparently belonged to one of the deceased, and family members, friends, and even complete strangers had signed their hopes as well as their names in Sharpie marker or fabric ink. All of these things were definitely mementos. In one respect, this entire, humble cemetery gate had become a shrine to the deceased, but it really seemed more than that. The sentiments expressed in all of these items were certainly bittersweet, but they spoke more to life than to death. This was a shrine devoted to hope, not despair. A space dedicated to the belief that we could endure, and recover.

And in all of this outpouring of positive emotion, I could not feel the echo of the dead. That is not to say that the effluence of emotion drowned out the voices of the spirits. Those voices simply were not there. Or, more specifically, I could not feel the echo of that terrible day. I knew how many people had lost their lives. I had read eyewitness accounts and had heard similar accounts from friends who lived in the city. But instead of lingering like a gaping wound on the psychic landscape of New York, I felt the somber sanctity of this little church instead.

It had nothing at all to do with denomination. I think it could just as easily have been a Jewish synagogue. Had there been a little park in this space where local Pagans preferred to gather, I think the same phenomenon could have developed. People had recognized the universal appeal of sacred space, and they had erected their own shrine, separate and distinct from any specific faith. Like a pearl, this concentrated section of calm in the bustle of wounded New York had formed around the kernel of the very idea of faith. And somehow all the photos and teddy bears and strings of paper cranes had cleansed the energy of fear and suffering. I dropped my shields expecting to feel horror, but what washed over me in that moment was hope.

Ground Zero ended up being the only portion of New York during that entire trip where I felt not only calm but comfortable. I could have basked in those soothing emotions for the rest of the day. I do not think that this in any way diminishes the significance of the loss of life for those who suffered and died that fateful day. Instead, what it clearly demonstrated, at least to me, is that we, the living, have a greater impact upon the psychic landscape of our world than we often give ourselves credit for. Ghosts may linger upon the site of tragedy, and echoes of terrible events may burn themselves onto the very fabric of the land, but we do not affect our world only through the act of dying. We touch the realm of spirits in every act of *living* as well.

Afterword, or How I Learned to Love the Dead

In a journey of constant discovery, every step takes you to some place you've never been before. In the process of writing this book, I have learned to see some of my experiences in a new light. I have certainly learned a great deal about myself. The foremost lesson has been one of trust. My grandmother left her mark upon me, bequeathing me with a legacy of suspicion, doubt, and shame. Until working on this book, I had not realized that I still labored under her shadow, if only obliquely. Since 2004 I have been publishing books on my perceptions and experiences of psychic energy. Most of these books have been extremely self-revelatory, detailing highly personal beliefs on past lives and the very nature of my reality.

And in writing these books, I had believed, perhaps prematurely, that I had gotten over my issues of trust. In the books I was revealing aspects of myself to the world, risking judgment and censorship and worse.

But I was still compartmentalizing my life, telling one set of experiences to one audience while holding back on others. The main thing I hesitated to write about openly, again and again, was my direct perception of spirits. Certainly I had no trouble telling people how to reach out and communicate with beings on the Otherside; but when it came to my own personal experiences, I balked. I tended to evade the subject entirely, bog it down with qualifiers, or pick only those incidents that I knew were safe to recount.

And yet my dealings with spirits have been as much a part of my learning experience as any of my experiments with dreams or psychic energy. Still, I hesitated. Even when I was first putting the manuscript for this book together, I sorted through my old notes and journals, setting aside events that sounded too implausible. I believed them because I had experienced them, but I thought that others might think they sounded crazy. I was still laboring under that tireless invective, *What would people think?*

As this book came together, I had to confront these issues of trust. I kept asking myself, "Why can you talk about energy work without fear, yet you hesitate to completely reveal your experiences with ghosts?" In the end, it came down to external verification.

This was actually one of the good things my grandmother taught me. Every once in a while, when I was little, I would have a dream that foreshadowed later events. Most of these were perfectly mundane events, like dreaming that our school art project one week was going to involve making a totem pole. On a few rare occasions, I dreamed about something that later made the news. However, my grandmother refused to accept my statement of "I dreamed about that last week!" She told me that anyone could claim to be psychic after the fact. All it proved was a desire to feel special. Also, she pointed out that it was easy to look back on the details of a dream after a big event and try to fit those details to the event. So she encouraged me to write down those dreams that I felt foretold something. They were to be dated and written in ink, so I couldn't go back and change things. This gave me a piece of evidence for outside verification whenever one of those dreams turned out to be accurate.

This taught me that outside verification establishes a credible dividing line between real psychic experience and possible delusions. Certainly, having that piece of verification keeps you from sounding too crazy if you happen to share the experience with a friend. I harp on the importance of objective verification throughout all my other works, and now you know why. In many ways, the ability to verify an experience in a reliable and external fashion became my answer to *What would people think?* If I could present evidence to indicate that something unusual was going on, then I didn't feel quite so crazy talking about that unusual thing.

When it comes to energy work, ESP, and even psychic dreams, methods of external verification are fairly easy. Most of these phenomena involve other people, and it's a simple matter to ask those other people whether or not they shared in the experience. If I am sitting next to my best friend and I suddenly hear a song playing in my mind, I can check with my friend to see whether or not he or she was just thinking about that same song. If my friend wasn't, the song was just something in my own head. If my friend was, and we both happen to realize that we were even singing along silently at the same point in the lyrics, then the experience moves beyond the realm of sheer imagination and into the realm of the paranormal.

With ghosts and spirits, however, things are a little different. If I ask my invisible friend whether or not he just whispered his name in my head, the only way he can possibly respond is through the same uncertain method of communication. Short of having fellow psychic mediums like my friends Sarah or Jackie on hand to double-check each and every individual perception, there is little possibility for outside verification. And this is where my hang-up with ghostly encounters becomes clear. Even when a medium perceives spirits as vividly as Sarah can, the real process of perception is frustratingly subjective. It is, essentially, all in one's head. We see spirits with an internal eye and we hear their voices with an internal ear, all the while painfully aware that sight and sound are just the closest approximation of the actual experience. Given the shifting realm of the human psyche, it can be hard to believe the experience yourself, let alone asking anyone else to believe it.

After collecting so many of my personal encounters in this volume, I have come to realize that I am not exactly worried about belief. When it comes to belief, most people have made up their minds anyway, and it's as hard to convince a believer that ghosts might not exist as it is to convince a skeptic that they do. So why did I hesitate as I put these tales on paper? Why did I struggle against the instinct to place qualifiers at the start of every chapter and to apologize for the extraordinary aspects of my claims?

I'm still afraid of sounding crazy. I've lived through these experiences and I believe them. I've had so many things happen to me again and again that I no longer doubt my own sanity. But I know how crazy some of the stories sound, and I don't want others to think that I'm a nut. I blame my grandmother: *What would people think?*

At the time of this writing, my grandmother is still alive. Nevertheless, she haunts me more than any other person who has touched my life. I see her specter casting its long shadow over everything that I do. I will probably never fully escape her, but I can at least try to live by my words, rather than my silence, and to embrace the truth, rather than fear. For this reason, I am going to end this book with a tale that I had cut out of the original manuscript. It covers concepts that were a little too risky, subjects that were a little too dear. This tale is my way of saying, "I don't care if you think I'm crazy. It is true, and the world is much bigger than any of us can imagine."

There is a group of people closer to my heart than any of my blood family. We call ourselves House Kheperu, and we believe that we have memories of shared past lives. In the fall of 2000, we held our first formal gathering, partly to honor those shared ties from our past. At the end of this mini-convention, we held a ritual reaching out to those members of our extended family who were between lives. We knew that they must exist, because spirits do not remain incarnate all the time, and we believed that they remembered us, because we remembered them. We invited them to join in what we were building together.

I shouldn't have been surprised when they answered.

It started simply enough. That November, after the gather, the atmosphere of my house seemed to change. The air in my living room felt heavier somehow. Even when the room was empty, it felt like it was crowded with people. This was a little thing, really, and it was easy to discount. I had half a billion other things on my mind at the time, and so I chose to ignore it. I simply went about my business.

By December the sense of a presence—multiple presences—in my home was hard to deny. Visitors would remark on it whenever they came to call. The presences seemed especially thick in the living room, but they were perceptible in other areas of the house as well. It should be noted that my living room was where House Kheperu held its weekly meetings, and so these invisible presences became a topic of discussion. A few members suspected that the spirits, whatever they were, wanted to communicate. I had gotten that feeling as well, like a persistent itch in the back of my mind. But I didn't want to be bothered with it. Prior to this point in my life, I only dealt with spirits if they were causing problems for me or for other people. I didn't generally sit down with an intent to just have a friendly chat with a ghost. That was for teenagers with Ouija boards, I thought. So, still, I chose to ignore it.

That was when they decided to really get my attention.

Some years before, I had picked up matching prints of Greek vases. They were matted in these big, faux-gilded frames. The one that I had hanging downstairs in the living room suddenly decided that it no longer needed to be attached to the wall. I only caught its motion out of the corner of my eye, but it seemed as if the paint-ing just leapt off of its hanger and then slid in slow motion to the floor. Thankfully, the floor was thickly carpeted, so instead of being greeted with the shattering of glass as I rushed into the room, the painting only made a dull thump as it landed on the floor. I wanted to blame the cat, but he was behind me, acting skittish. I presumed he was freaked out by the sudden noise. Cornelius has never been the bravest of felines.

I went to check the painting, assuming that the wire had come loose and instigated the fall. However, when I picked it up and examined it, the wire was intact. I stood, checking the hanger nailed to the wall. This also was intact. The heavy feeling that lingered on the air in the living room seemed weightier than usual, but I was reluctant to ascribe a supernatural cause to the fallen painting. I hung it back up on the wall, tapping it a couple of times with my hand to see how firmly the wire and hanging apparatus held. It didn't budge.

"You start knocking things around," I threatened to the trembling air, "and we're going to have words."

Of course, that was exactly what they wanted.

Eventually I was able to convince myself that the painting had probably succumbed to nothing more mysterious than gravity. I hadn't directly seen it fall—I had only caught its motion out of the corner of my eye and arrived in time for the painting hit the carpet. The cat remained a suspect as well, though he would have had to scoot invisibly past me through a relatively tight space in order to knock the painting down and then sit cowering behind me as I heard the thump. But all cats, no matter how timid their personalities, are secretly ninjas, so I didn't rule him out. I went about my business, studiously ignoring the presences in the living room. Then, a few weeks later, they sent me another message. This one was a little harder to discount than the first.

The second painting of this pair had found a home on the wall in my upstairs bathroom. I had lit some tealights as well as some incense and was trying to relax in the bath when this painting also decided to detach itself from the wall. From my vantage point of the bathtub, it was impossible not to see the whole thing. I was staring directly at the painting when it twitched a little, then seemed to move about an inch away from the wall. It hung, suspended in the air, for a few heartbeats, and then it slid very gently to the tiled floor. The motion was slow and deliberate, and I got the impression that the painting was falling so slowly in part so that it would not be damaged when it hit the tile. But also it was being guided so obviously by unseen hands so I could not easily deny what I was witnessing. As I watched, the heavy painting arrived safely onto the tile. That tremulous sensation hung upon the air again, and I finally gave in.

"You really want to talk with me," I observed, resigned.

I always felt slightly silly talking out loud to spirits, but the alternative was to speak with them in my head. When I did that, I often got impressions of answers, and to be frank, that bothered me. It's that whole "voices in the head" thing, mainly. It's one thing to investigate a haunting and to get a hunch about what spirits are present and maybe even what they want. Feeling the energy of a place was easy, and it never made me doubt my sanity. Spirits were just energy, and so as long as my impressions of them remained in that realm of energy work, I was comfortable. But hearing voices in my head not only verged into the territory of potential madness, it was also disturbingly intimate. In many ways, it was easier to question my sanity than to accept that such contact was legitimate—that there are forces out there that remain invisible to us that nevertheless can touch us in places that we ourselves often cannot reach.

But after the slow-motion fall of the second painting, I resigned myself to the fact that the spirits that were undeniably present in my home were going to continue to escalate their activity until they got a chance to say their piece. The easiest and most obvious method of communication would be to talk to them directly. I already suspected that they had been whispering urgently in my mind this whole time, but I was studiously blocking them out. So I turned to a device that I had left behind in childhood, and had often scoffed at since: the Ouija board.

One of my biggest issues with Ouija boards is how very easy they are to push—either consciously or unconsciously. I had serious doubts about the legitimacy of any spirit communication gained through such tools, and yet the Ouija board seemed preferable to admitting both to myself and to others that I thought I heard spirits talking directly in my mind. So I devised a method of using the board that I felt ruled out most of the potential problems with Ouija boards.

First, I had three sitters. They were members of House Kheperu, and I trusted them not to intentionally influence the motion of the pointer. I determined that the person who was asking the questions should not be actively engaged in using the board, just on the off chance that he or she might unconsciously influence the motion of the pointer toward answers. In fact, no one with any expectations about the answers and no personal involvement in the potential content of the messages should be sitting on the board, just to be sure. A fifth person would write down all the answers impartially, recording the letters exactly as they were spelled out on the board. Finally, to rule out the influence of negative, unwanted, or just plain mischievous spirits, we cast a circle around the board. This is a magickal barrier used extensively in Pagan practice, and it is commonly used to keep unwanted spirits and energies out of a given space. A Christian can set up a similar barrier through prayer, asking that no unwanted spirits be allowed to pass through the consecrated space.

Content with this arrangement, we did sittings in my living room over the course of several weeks. I learned a great deal during these sittings, both about the spirits as well as about myself. The foremost thing this experience taught me is the fact that I can hear the voices of the dead. One of the reasons I had been so suspicious of the use of Ouija boards tied back to this capacity. When I used boards at sleepovers as a teen, I often suspected that I was unconsciously pushing the pointer, as I typically "heard" the answers to the questions in my mind a few seconds before the pointer started spelling those answers out on the board. While it had occurred to me that perhaps I was hearing the spirits themselves, it was easier to believe that it was just all in my head.

Having taken myself out of the equation on the board, I still "heard" the messages before they were spelled out. I would also get the impression that the spirits were grumbling about having to work the pointer. That took a lot of effort and energy on their part, and it seemed a waste when they could much more easily speak directly into my mind. But it was still too intimate a contact. At the time, I needed the distance afforded by the Ouija board for my own sake. The verification provided by the board was very helpful. I started learning to trust those whispered impressions of voices, and by the end of the series of sessions held in my living room that year, I had grown much more comfortable with the idea of having spirits speak directly into my mind.

The spirits themselves really didn't have any earth-shattering messages. It was all very simple and generally very personal. I would have been very doubtful if dire messages of impending doom had come through on the board. Instead, the spirits just wanted their voices to be heard, and they were somewhat annoyed at me for ignoring them. They had a right to be annoyed, especially considering that I had led the ritual to invite them in the first place.

As it turned out, these were not random ghosts, but spirits that had known me or others in my group through other incarnations. Unburdened by the limits of the flesh, they recognized us easily. From this side of the Veil, our perceptions were dimmer. It was often as if there was interference from this side to the next. We had to make a conscious effort to open ourselves up in order to communicate effectively. But once we did, we recognized them as well.

A great deal happened in those weeks, and if I were to tell it all, it would likely grow into a book all its own. The main thing was that these spirits were old friends, siblings, and even lovers who simply wanted us to know that they remembered our lives together. They wanted us not to forget them, and they wanted to take us up on our offer to have them present in our lives as we established our group. Since then, they have become friends and companions on the Otherside, often working with me in a haunting resolution to clear residues or chase off unwanted spirits. Two of them stand habitually at the head of my bed, guarding me as I dream. I didn't ask them to perform this function. They seem to consider such work one of the few services they can provide the living from their side of things.

My experience in first making contact with these disembodied members of House Kheperu changed me. I still often struggle with feeling a little crazy, especially when I hear a spirit talking in my head and I choose to engage that spirit in conversation (even though I hear spirits directly in my head, I still often respond to them by speaking out loud, which I'm sure helps me look the part of a crazy person!). Given the influence of my grandmother, I don't think I'll ever completely shake that self-conscious feeling. But the spirits who showed up in my living room on the cusp of the new millennium made it abundantly clear that, self-conscious or not, I needed to acknowledge my gift and actively make use of it. They provided me with enough consistent experiences so I could learn to trust in my accuracy, and more than that, they demonstrated a distinctly *human* side that allowed me to approach them—not as some strange spooky phenomenon, but as companions and friends.

These days, when I sense that subtle thickening of the air around me and feel that telltale itch in the back of my mind, I know to take notice—and to trust that, crazy or not, there is truth to what comes next.